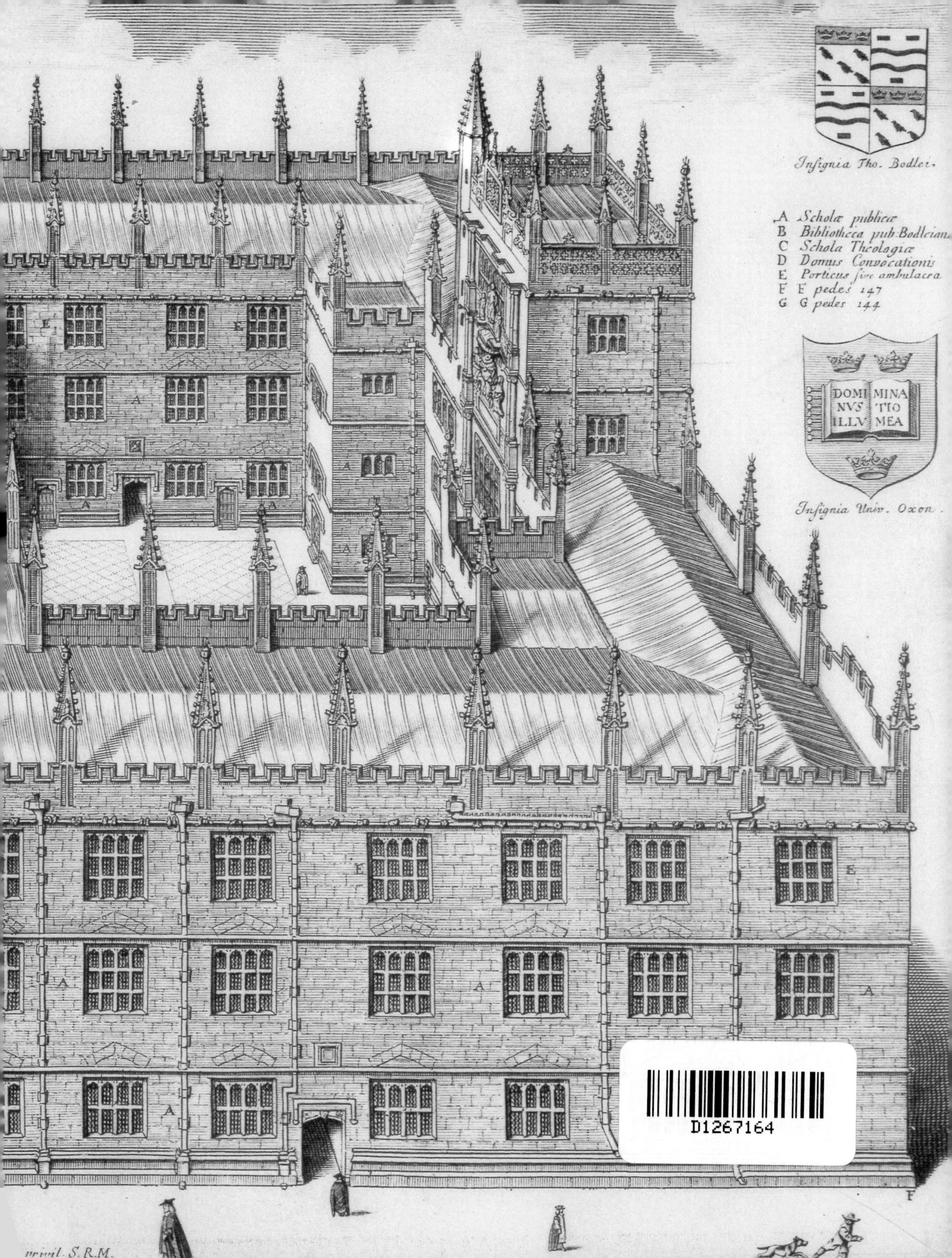

Insignia Tho. Bodlei.
A Scholæ publicæ
B Bibliotheca pub: Bodleiana
C Schola Theologiæ
D Domus Convocationis
E Porticus sive ambulacra
F F pedes 147
G G pedes 144
DOMI NVS ILLV
MINA TIO MEA
Insignia Univ. Oxon.
privil. S.R.M.

THE BODLEIAN LIBRARY AND ITS TREASURES

1320–1700

Posteris, et Æternitati
Sacrvm.
Thomæ Bodlæi qvicqvid mortale
Tabella,
Ingentemqve animam Bibliotheca
refert.
Domi mina
nvs tio
illv mea
Hospes rogatvs siste,
Bodlævmqve loci genivm et Mvsarvm
Mecænatem vltra Cæsares Avgvstvm
Qvi Bibliotecam molemqve hanc stvpendam
Condidit, Intvere.
Hoc volebam nescivs ne esses. Vale.

THE BODLEIAN LIBRARY AND ITS TREASURES 1320 – 1700

David Rogers

AIDAN ELLIS

DEDICATED

TO ALL THOSE PAST AND PRESENT

WHO

CONTRIBUTED TO THE MAKING

OF THIS BOOK

First published in the United Kingdom by
Aidan Ellis Publishing Limited,
Cobb House, Nuffield, Henley-on-Thames,
Oxon RG9 5RT.

A CIP catalogue record for
this book is available from
the British Library

ISBN 0—85628—128—X

Set in Palatino
Typeset by AKM Associates (UK) Ltd
Printed and bound in Italy

DESIGN BY CRAIG DODD

Contents
and List of illustrations

IV Survivals and Arrivals 1640–1665

V Two Great Catalogues 1665–1700

Picture acknowledgements
Chris Cormack – Plate 6: Giraudon, Paris – Plate 3: Robert Potter, FRIBA – Plate 10: Thomas-Photos, Oxford – Plates 2, 8, 9, 14, 38, 42, 48, 49, 71: Woodmansterne – Plate 51

CHAPTER I

The University Library from its Beginnings

1320–1598

When Sir Thomas Bodley planned the great Library which bears his name, and whose treasures are the subject of this volume, he was conscious of bringing to the task a unique combination of gifts and experience. But he was aware, too, that he was building on earlier foundations, and drew inspiration not only from the sight of the noble room left desolate (Plate 8) by the dispersal of Duke Humfrey's Library, but also from what he believed to be the strengths and failings of the two university libraries which preceded his own.

The University began as a federation of colleges, whose members from an early date needed a central place for the transaction of business of common, or 'public', interest. For many years this place was St Mary's Church, in Oxford's High Street, and it was here that the first central collection of books began. Books already deposited were given a new housing when Thomas Cobham, Bishop of Worcester (Plate 1), added an upper chamber to the Convocation House which he began to build at the north-east corner of the church in 1320. At his death in 1327 Cobham left his own manuscripts to the University, but they were taken in settlement of his debts and kept in the Hall of the Blessed Mary (now Oriel College) until 1337 when the University authorities forcibly transferred them to their intended home.

This was the first University Library (Plate 2), confirmed by ordinances of 1412, and in it were deposited the manuscripts given to the University between 1435 and 1444 by Humfrey, Duke of Gloucester (Plate 3). This magnificent benefaction brought to Oxford a collection representative of the new learning of the Renaissance of which Humfrey was so notable a patron: besides the authors of classical antiquity, many in specially commissioned copies (Plate 4), it included a wealth of scientific, medical and theological treatises and works by writers of the Italian Renaissance such as Petrarch and Boccaccio. Such was the scale and importance of Humfrey's benefactions that Bishop Cobham's library could not accommodate them, so the University decided to build a new and much larger library as a worthy setting for them.

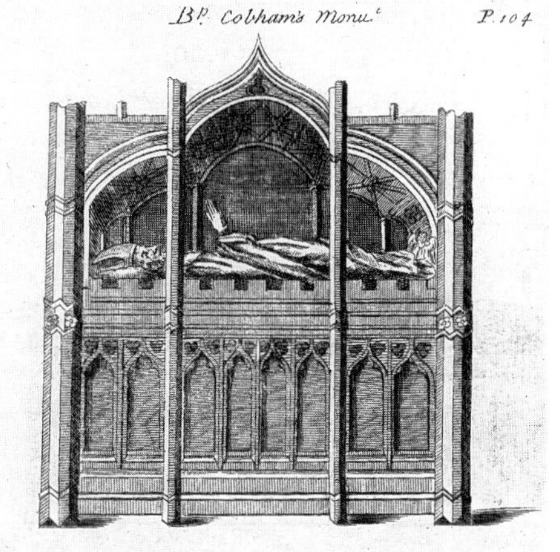

1. The tomb of Bishop Cobham
Thomas Cobham was Bishop of Worcester from 1317 till his death in 1327. This engraving of his tomb was made by James Mynde for William Thomas's *A Survey of the Cathedral Church of Worcester*, published in London in 1737.

Among the schools being constructed in the early fifteenth century for the University's public teaching, the most splendid was the Divinity School (Plates 5, 7) where the decorative effect of fluted columns between huge windows is further embellished by carved bosses on the vaulting, which commemorate by monogram or blason many who subscribed for its construction and other notable contemporaries (Plate 6). It was decided in 1444 that the most suitable way to house Duke Humfrey's books would be to construct an additional room over the School. It was not, however, until Thomas Kempe, Bishop of London (Plate 6), had donated 1,000 marks that sufficient funds were available both for its completion and for the construction

2. **The first University Library**
The room above the Convocation House which was built at the expense of an Oxford man, Thomas Cobham Bishop of Worcester (Plate 1) at the north-east corner of the University Church of St Mary, is the first University building erected for library purposes. It was begun about 1320 and was still uncompleted at the Bishop's death in 1327. He intended also to leave his own manuscripts to the University, but his executors were forced to settle his debts by selling his books to Adam de Brome, the founder of Oriel College. The room has been much restored and is now used as a Parish Room but it is still possible to discern its original layout; it is the earliest example still existing in England of a mediaeval library of the upstairs gallery type having originally three bays down each side (Duke Humfrey's Library, which was built to replace it, has eight bays) and was furnished with lecterns and benches between each lateral window. Its total shelf capacity was probably reckoned only as some hundreds of volumes. Over a hundred years after Bishop Cobham's death, the University, faced with the problem of housing Duke Humfrey's great gifts of manuscripts, wrote to the Duke claiming that already while a reader in Cobham's library was using one book there was not room enough for other readers to consult the three or four volumes chained next to it.

It was at a meeting held in this room in 1942 that the then Vicar of St Mary's and a small group of his friends began Oxfam, which was to grow steadily into the great international relief organization it has now become.

of the vaulted ceiling beneath. The new room, which was finally opened to readers in 1488 (Plate 8), was shelved on a system already in use in college libraries: on either side of a central aisle, rows of double-sided lecterns projected from the walls between the windows. The manuscripts were kept flat on shelves underneath the sloping reading surfaces to which they were chained (Plates 9, 10).

This splendid library was in existence for fewer than sixty-five years. Several reasons account for its decline. In the first place, no endowment was made for its increase, although at that very time printed books were transforming the nature and scale of libraries, so that it remained a monument to princely collecting, while scholars' working libraries were growing up in colleges. Secondly, an inefficient administration permitted the unsupervised borrowing of manuscripts, so that many became permanently alienated. Finally, there seems little reason to doubt the oral tradition, credibly reported by Anthony Wood, the seventeenth-century Oxford historian, that the remainder of the library was removed in 1550, the year of the Act against Superstitious Books and Images, by the King's Commissioners, implementing that policy which since Henry VIII's dissolution of the monasteries had progressively dispersed and very largely destroyed the manuscript heritage of learning in the libraries of the religious communities. Certainly the entire collection had disappeared by 1556 (Plate 11), when Congregation passed a decree permitting the sale of the now empty desks; and so for the next forty-two years the University was without a public library (Plate 12), until the return to Oxford of the greatest of its benefactors, Sir Thomas Bodley.

3. Portrait of Humfrey, Duke of Gloucester

Humfrey, the youngest son of King Henry IV, was born in 1390 and was created Duke of Gloucester in 1414 by his brother King Henry V. With his tempestuous life in war, politics and love this book is not concerned; it was his patronage of poets and humanists that earned him the popular title of 'Good Duke Humfrey'. Though there is no evidence for the claim that he was himself educated at Oxford University he constituted himself its protector and became a most generous benefactor; he gave money towards the building of the Divinity School (Plates 5, 7) and it was the truly princely gift of his own personal collection of manuscripts (more than 281 in number; see Plate 4), which caused the University in 1444 to decide on adding another storey on top of the Divinity School to house them worthily. The resulting noble gallery (Plate 8) has since the nineteenth century been called 'Duke Humfrey's Library'. The Duke promised further funds to aid the building, but because of his death in political disgrace in 1447 these were never paid.

Though he is portrayed in several existing illuminations as a patron in the act of receiving manuscripts dedicated to him, none of these miniatures attempts any formal likeness. For his real appearance there exists only this striking crayon portrait, part of a two-volume collection of French and Flemish royal portrait drawings formerly preserved in the great abbey of St Vedast at Arras and now in the municipal library there. It is probably the work of Jacques Le Boucq, a well-known portraitist who was a herald-painter to the Emperor Charles V and was appointed by Philip II King-at-arms to the Order of the Golden Fleece. Le Boucq, who died in 1573, would certainly have had access to contemporary likenesses of the royal personages he depicts.

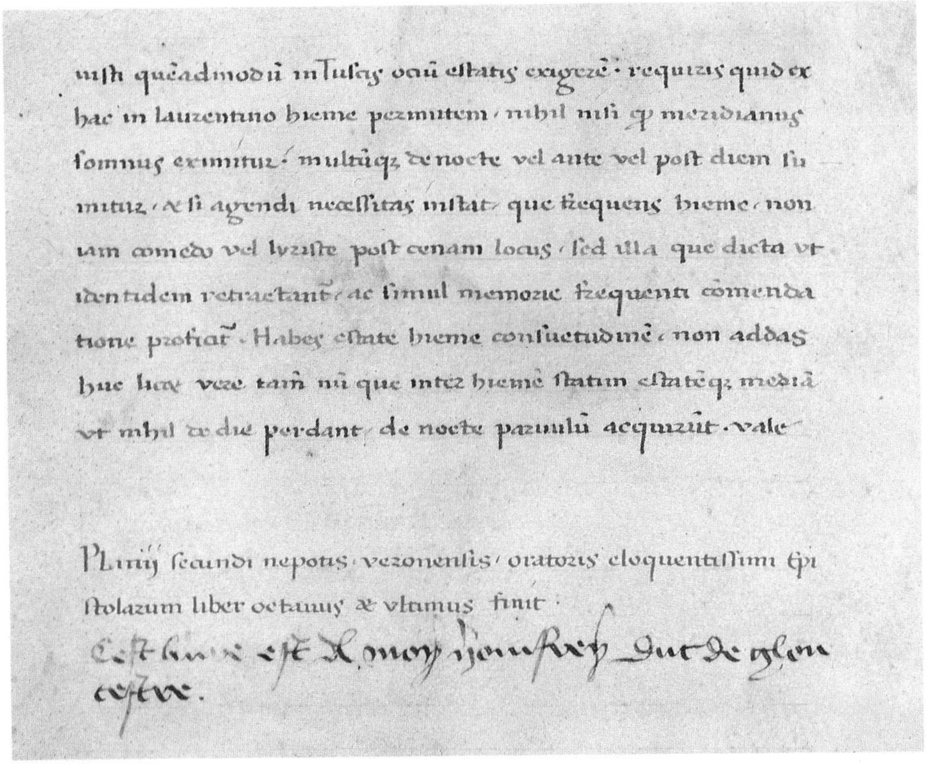

4. Duke Humfrey's Pliny

This manuscript of the *Letters* of Pliny the Younger was written in Italy at the Duke's request by the Milanese humanist Piercandido Decembrio, in formal humanistic script with initials of Milanese style. In the late 1430s Decembrio had made Duke Humfrey the dedicatee of his translation of Plato's *Republic*. In the next few years Duke Humfrey persuaded Decembrio to send from Italy a systematic selection of Latin classical texts (it is not clear exactly how many arrived). In return, Decembrio was offered an annual stipend of 100 ducats, though in fact he really wanted Duke Humfrey to buy him a villa which had formerly belonged to Petrarch; the Duke it seems, politely ignored this request.

Duke Humfrey wrote his standard *ex libris* in French into the Pliny on the final page, here reproduced: '*Cest livre est a moy Homfrey duc de Gloucestre*'. But soon afterwards he gave it to the University of Oxford: it is identifiable in a list of 135 manuscripts which the Duke gave to the University on 25 February 1443/4; this was the last in a series of his donations, which totalled over 281 items.

Only a handful of Duke Humfrey's gifts, later so tragically dispersed, have returned to the Bodleian – not one remained *in situ*. The Pliny was piously restored in 1620 by Dr Robert Master, a former Principal of St Alban Hall, on the strength of Duke Humfrey's *ex libris*.

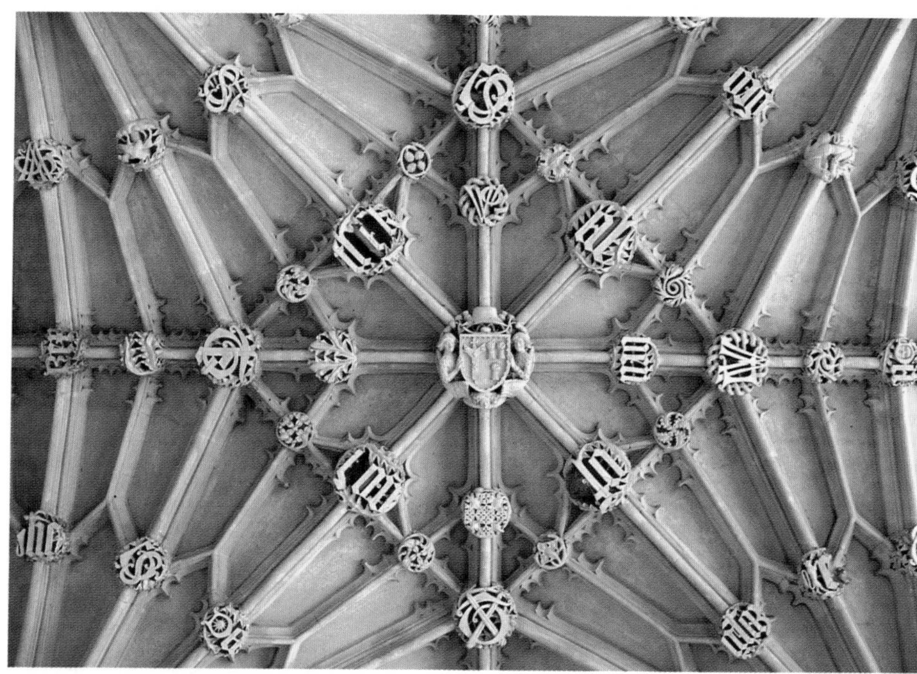

Previous pages:
5. **The Divinity School in 1813**
A view of the interior engraved in 1813 by F. C. Lewis from a watercolour by Frederick Mackenzie for the celebrated *History of the University of Oxford, its Colleges, Halls, and Public Buildings*, published in two volumes in London by Rudolph Ackermann in 1814. It shows a divinity degree 'exercise' in progress with the 'moderator' presiding in the central pulpit (since then removed) and candidates engaged in formal 'disputation', from the two side pulpits. This method of examination by public 'responsions' in syllogistic form still lingered on from the Middle Ages until it was eventually replaced by written examinations. The scene calls to mind the intention which moved the University to build the Divinity School in the fifteenth century and shows this magnificent hall still in use for its original purpose after nearly 400 years.

6. **Arms and monograms from the roof of the Divinity School**
As the last principal benefactor to the University's appeal for funds for building the Divinity School, whose gift in 1479 of 1,000 marks (£666 13s 4d) enabled its vaulting to be completed most sumptuously, Thomas Kempe, Bishop of London from 1450 to 1489, was repeatedly and fittingly honoured in the elaborate network of ornamental ribs which overhangs this masterpiece of Perpendicular architecture. Among the 455 sculptured bosses in this astonishing ceiling, the arms of Thomas Kempe and those of his uncle Cardinal John Kempe, with their badges, mottoes and initials, are found upwards of eighty times. In this plate Cardinal Kempe's arms are at the centre, and Bishop Thomas Kempe's monogram 'T K' occupies the second boss to the left of it. Besides the arms of other notables who probably were mostly also contributors, further bosses present a variety of highly finished figures of saints, religious emblems, monograms, mottoes, leaves, birds and so on: the present arms of the University are here portrayed for the first time, and the initials 'W O' allude to the mason William Orchard, lately the architect of Magdalen College and then of this great ceiling. The whole design thus included a 'Register of Benefactors', publicly displayed, as was to be the great volume (Plates 18, 19) which Bodley caused to be written and chained near the entrance of his restored Library to encourage visitors to emulate their generosity.

7. **The Divinity School, drawn by Loggan**

David Loggan's *Oxonia illustrata*, published at Oxford in 1675, is the first great Oxford topography and portrays with great accuracy and detail the city and its buildings as they were in the reign of Charles II. His book was dedicated to the King, who, visiting Oxford in 1681, 'went incognito to the Schools in the Lord Chamberlaine's Coach . . . going straightaway to the Divinity Schoole, spent some time in viewing the roofe thereof, so much admired by forreigners for its great variety of exquisit sculpture'.

8. **Duke Humfrey's Library-room**
This modern photograph preserves a unique and unrepeatable view of Duke Humfrey's Library. It was taken when Bodley's book presses had been temporarily removed (Plate 9) and it allows the magnificent proportions of this mediaeval gallery to be fully appreciated. The window seen at the far (east) end belongs to 'Arts End', the wing added in 1610–12.

9. **The outline of the mediaeval lecterns**
When Sir Thomas Bodley's three-decker book presses were temporarily moved in 1960 to allow the original floor of Duke Humfrey's Library to be made safe, the outline of the ends of the mediaeval presses were revealed on the walls between the windows. This proved that the fifteenth-century Library had been furnished with tall, narrow double-sided lecterns at which readers stood to study, as is shown in the artist's impression in Plate 10.

10. **Duke Humfrey's Library as it first appeared: an artist's impression**
An artist's impression of how Duke Humfrey's Library might have looked after its completion in 1488. Users stood at the lecterns to read the volumes, which were probably chained to a bar running along the front of the shelves which formed the lower part of each structure. On these shelves most of the books would be kept when not in use. The large window at the far (east) end is conjectural; the window here pictured was replaced by the present great east window when Arts End was built in 1610–12.

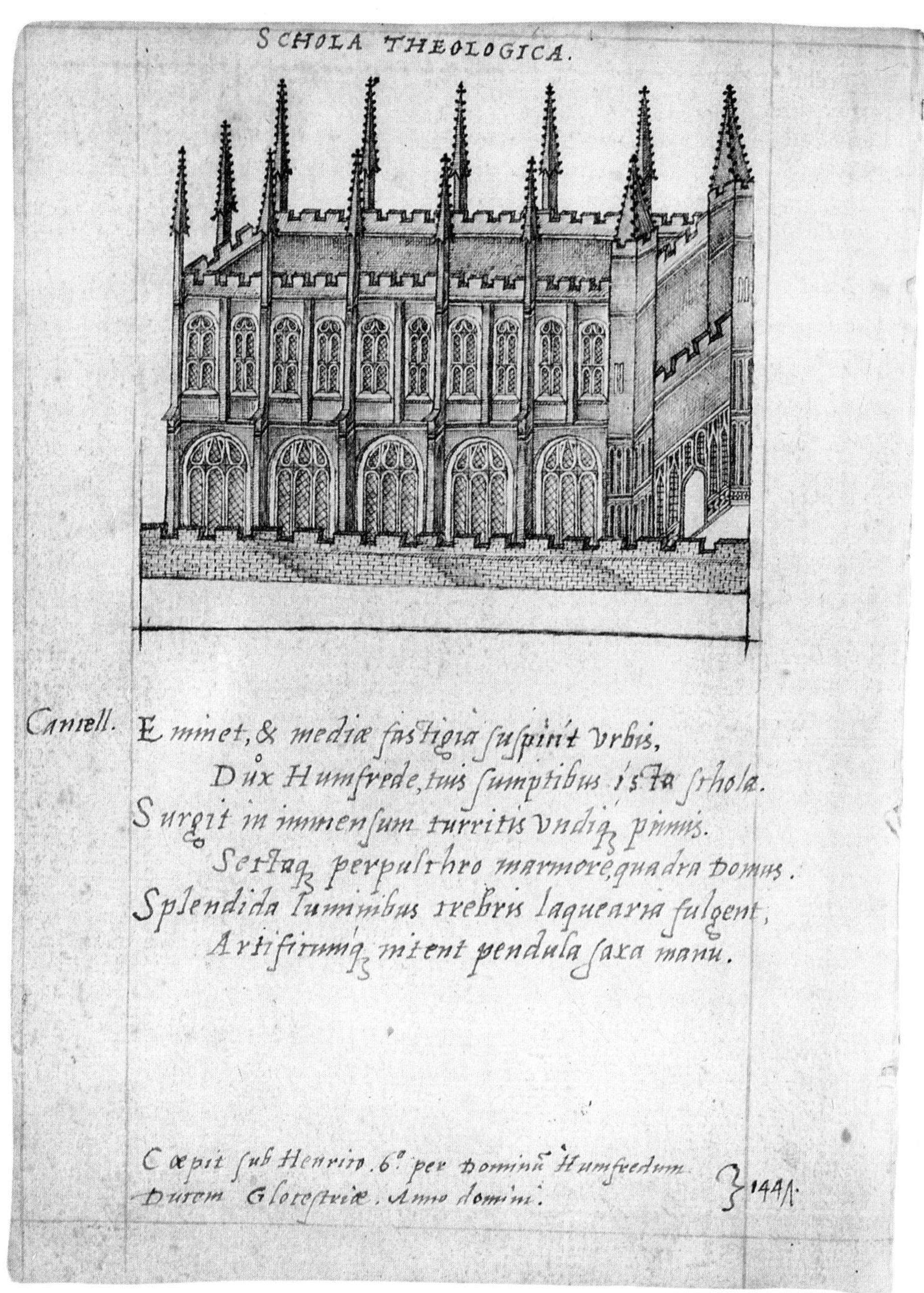
SCHOLA THEOLOGICA.
Cancell.
Eminet, & mediæ fastigia suspicit vrbis,
Dux Humfrede, tuis sumptibus ista schola.
Surgit in immensum turritis vndiq pinnis.
Sectaq perpulchro marmore quadra domus.
Splendida luminibus crebris laquearia fulgent,
Artificumq nitent pendula saxa manu.
Cœpit sub Henrico. 6° per Dominu Humfredum
Ducem Glocestriæ. Anno domini. 1441.

11. **The Divinity School, drawn by Bereblock, 1566**

Queen Elizabeth I made her first official visit to Oxford in 1566. The Oxford visit fitted into her policy of royal progresses in a special way; she could display her fabled erudition and support for learning, and remind Oxford men of the immense potential of royal patronage in University appointments and affairs. For a week, 31 August to 6 September, the University celebrated her presence. On Thursday 5 September, the Queen proceeded from her lodgings in Christ Church to St Mary's, the University Church, to hear the public disputations. On her way she was greeted in Hebrew by Thomas Neele, Regius Professor of Hebrew, and presented with two manuscript volumes of his own compositions. One still survives in the old Royal Collection in London. The second is said to have contained a 'topography of the whole University', in the form of a Latin verse dialogue with illustrations of Oxford buildings. A manuscript which exactly matches the description, written in the same hand as the other royal volume, is this book, given to the Bodleian Library in 1630 by John More, and there seems no reason to doubt that the Bodleian manuscript is the very book which was put into Queen Elizabeth's hands in the gardens of Christ Church in 1566.

The text which Neele composed for his royal guidebook to the Tudor University suited the elevated occasion and the elaborate literary conceits of his time. In ornate but vapid Latin elegiac couplets, he imagines a verse dialogue between the Queen and Robert Dudley, Earl of Leicester (the Queen's official host as Chancellor of the University); the scene is set at the palace of Woodstock, shortly before the royal party's departure for Oxford, and the Earl is made to describe the Colleges and University buildings in turn. The illustrations were drawn by John Bereblock, a Fellow of Exeter College; most of them are the earliest surviving views of Oxford buildings which are still recognizable today. That of the Divinity School shows it as still a free-standing hall; its upper floor (reached via the two turrets clearly visible at the west end) was by this date stripped of all its books and furniture.

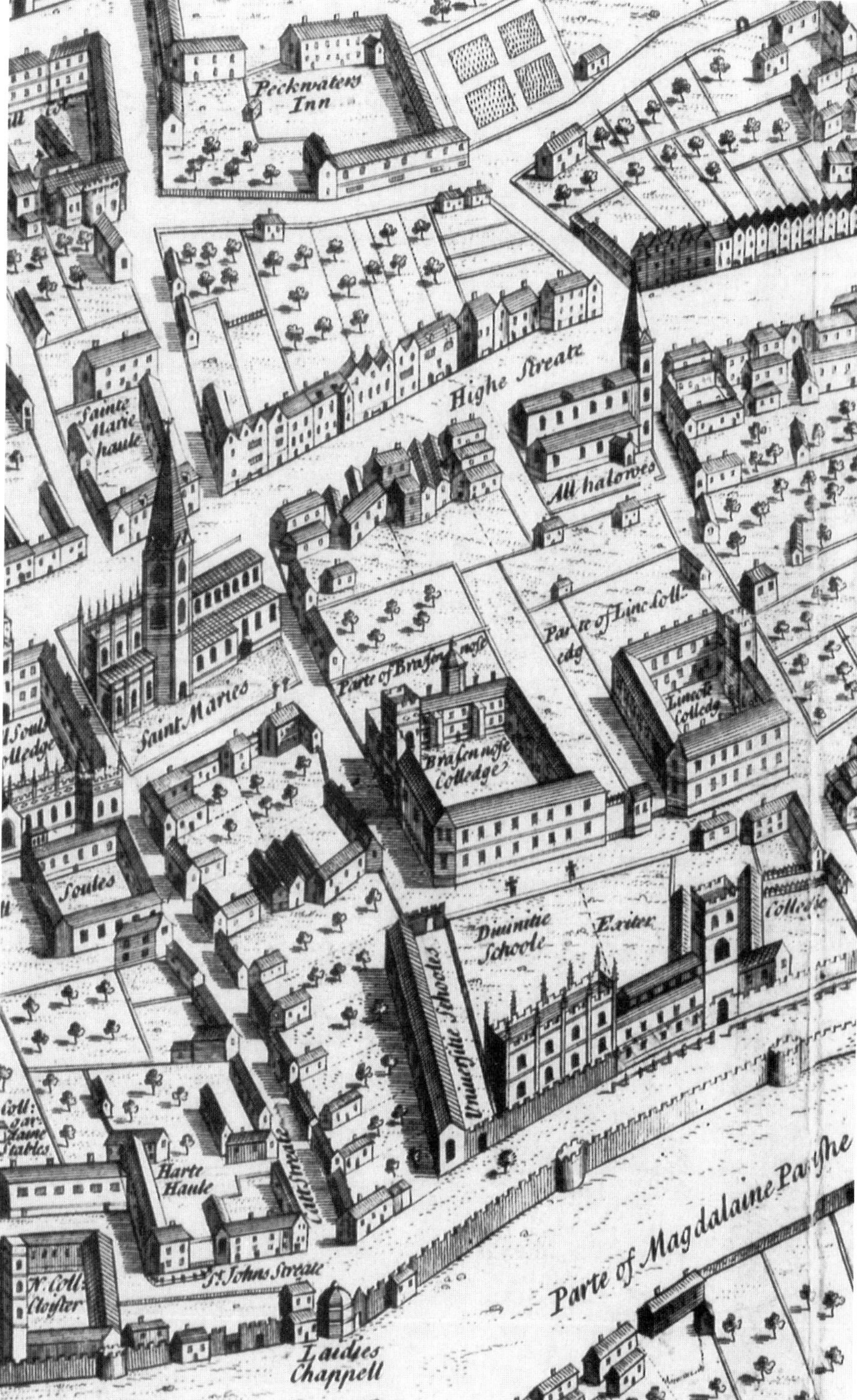

12. **The Divinity School drawn by Ralph Agas, 1578**

The centre of Oxford, including the University Church of St Mary and the Divinity School, from the bird's-eye map drawn by Ralph Agas, a talented land-surveyor, about 1578. This map was engraved in 1588 by Augustine Ryther on eight folio plates which together form a picture almost four feet wide and three feet high. The Divinity School is here shown in relation to adjacent buildings, at this time when much of central Oxford was open ground. Situated just inside the then still-existing city wall, its west end abuts onto the now vanished mediaeval buildings of Exeter College, while at its east end runs a single storey range of lecture-rooms here labelled 'University Schools'. By the early seventeenth century the University was planning to replace these dilapidated schools with a quadrangle of new lecture-rooms on the same site but stretching as far as Catte Street. Sir Thomas Bodley left money in his will to pay for an additional third storey for the new Schools Quadrangle to allow for future expansion of his Library.

This is the only other picture besides Bereblock's drawing (Plate 11) showing the mediaeval building as it was before it was added to by Bodley. The original print of the map formerly belonged to Thomas Hearne and later to Thomas Baker, the Cambridge antiquary. It was bequeathed to the Bodleian by Richard Rawlinson in 1755. Only one other copy is recorded. Because the original is badly discoloured, the detail shown here has been taken from the facsimile engraved in 1728 by Robert Whittlesey.

CHAPTER II

Sir Thomas Bodley and the Re-foundation

1598–1613

When he wrote to the University in 1598, offering to restore the Library at his own expense, a task which was to occupy the rest of his life, Sir Thomas Bodley was almost fifty-four years old, the very age at which he was painted by Nicholas Hilliard, the greatest miniaturist of his age (Plate 13), and had already retired from a remarkable career which had led him from the academic world to the diplomatic service.

Bodley was born at Exeter in 1544. Fearing persecution on the accession of Queen Mary, his strongly Protestant family fled to the Continent, settling eventually in Geneva. Here from the age of twelve Thomas, already well educated, studied divinity under Calvin and Beza, Greek under Beroaldus, and from Antoine Chevalier received lessons in Hebrew, proficiency in which was to be his lifelong pride. Shortly after the family's return to live in London on the accession of Elizabeth, Bodley entered Oxford as a student at Magdalen College. On graduating in 1563 he became a Fellow of Merton, where he undertook lectures in Greek at the same time as he was pursuing further studies in Natural Philosophy and 'sundry faculties, without any inclination to professe any one above the rest'. Public office also called him: at the age of twenty-five he was elected Proctor, and shortly afterwards Public Orator.

Bodley, however, from his childhood had European horizons, and now both ability and ambition led him to seek entry into public service in a larger sphere than that offered by the University. In 1576 he embarked on a period of foreign travel, intending to increase his knowledge of languages and his experience in the 'managing of affaires'. In 1585 he entered the diplomatic service of Queen Elizabeth, being dispatched on missions to assist the Protestant interest in Denmark, Germany and France, and becoming finally in 1588 the Queen's permanent representative at The Hague. Here he acquitted himself conscientiously in the frustrating task of maintaining the 'contract' between England and the recently founded United Provinces. He seemed naturally destined for still higher office, but his ambitions were compromised in the rivalry between the Cecil family and the Earl of Essex, each side seeking to associate the possibility of his preferment with their own political aims. Eventually his disenchantment with this 'throng of Court contentions' led him in 1597 to take his 'full farwell of State imployments'.

Bodley describes the beginning of the next and greatest phase of his career in a well-known passage of his autobiography: '. . . yet withall I was to thinke, that my dutie towards God, the expectation of the world, my naturall inclination, and very moralitie, did require, that I shoulde not wholly so hide those little habilities that I had, but that in some mesuer, in one kinde or other, I shoulde do the true part of a profitable member in the State: whereupon examining exactlye for the rest of my life, what course I might take, haveing sowght (as I thought)

13. **Nicholas Hilliard's miniature of Sir Thomas Bodley, 1598**

In May 1557 is recorded in the 'Livre des Anglois', preserved at Geneva, the arrival in that city of 'John Bodleigh', his brother, his wife, Thomas and two other sons, a daughter, three servants, with Nicholas Hilliard, and four others. The Bodleys and the Hilliards were among the leading citizens of Exeter and both were ardent supporters of Protestant reform, so it is not unlikely that the elder Hilliard took the opportunity of entrusting his twenty-year-old son to his departing neighbours.

The Bodleys returned to England immediately on the accession of Elizabeth, and there is no further recorded contact with the Hilliards except for this miniature, painted in 1598, the year Sir Thomas decided to devote himself to resurrecting his University's library. Nothing is known of the miniature's owners before its appearance in 1849 in Christie's sale of the Duke of Buckingham's collection of miniatures from Stowe. We next hear of it in 1897 when it was given to the Library by Canon H. N. Ellacombe. It is painted in oil on vellum over card and is preserved still in its original turned ivory box.

all the wayes to the wood to select the most proper, I concluded at the last to set up my Staffe at the Librarie-dore in Oxon; being throwghly perswaded, that in my solitude and surcease from the Commonwealth affayers, I coulde not busie my selfe to better purpose, then by redusing the place (which then in every part laye ruined and wast) to the publique use of Studients'.

It was this decision, proposed to the University in a letter dated 23 February 1598 and gratefully accepted by that body, that irrevocably involved the remainder of Bodley's life with the restoration of the Library. He clearly saw his own qualifications for the undertaking: his wide learning and knowledge of languages; his wealth, consolidated by his marriage to the rich widow, Ann Ball; a 'great Store of honorable freinds' in both academic and political worlds; and 'special good leasure to follow such a worke'. His experience of the 'management of affaires' gave him a thorough grasp of all the administrative and practical aspects of his new undertaking.

His first concern was to restore and refurnish the great room (Plate 8) above the Divinity School, where once had been Duke Humfrey's Library, though it had been long since stripped of all its contents and even of its furniture. For the restoration he enlisted an army of workmen whom he described unflatteringly as 'carpenters, joiners, carvers, glasiers and all that idle rabble' – he was neither the first man nor the last who fretted at the delays inherent in building works. The roof over Duke Humfrey's Library needed to be made good, and the result of the labours of his 'idle rabble' is still there to delight the eye (Plate 14). For construction and furnishings came timber from his old college, Merton, its Warden, Henry Savile, being his closest friend and adviser in the whole restoration undertaking. With typical thoroughness Bodley took care that his timber was properly seasoned, and himself minutely oversaw the installation of shelving and seating, which was completed within two years. The lay-out according to which the Library was now refurnished owed much to innovations which had taken place in college libraries during the sixteenth century. The great increase in college holdings of books had necessitated an evolution from the mediaeval lectern press: now, tall, three-storey cases with shelves above and later, when need arose, also below the reading desks, projected at right angles between the windows where formerly the lecterns had stood. The two-sided stalls which thus replaced the old chained lecterns accommodated vastly more books in the same space, and it seems natural that Bodley, seeking for the most modern way of shelving his Library, should have looked to the example of his own college of Merton, where such an installation had been completed only ten years earlier. Because its scale was determined by the size of the room over the Divinity School (Plate 8), the new Library was much bigger and more impressive than any mediaeval college

continued on page 28

14. **The painted roof of Duke Humfrey's Library**
Sir Thomas Bodley's restoration of the decayed mediaeval roof, completed by 1599, was both a structural and a decorative one. Many of the supporting roof timbers had to be replaced; those that were left visible were elaborately decorated with painted scrollwork, and much of the original ceiling was hidden behind a series of flat wooden panels each of which bears a painted shield of the arms of the University. At the intersections of the ribs which frame these panels are set small escutcheons with Bodley's personal arms. Only the modern installation of hidden floodlighting has enabled the variegated richness of this ceiling to become fully apparent.

15. **The arms of Thomas Sackville, Lord Buckhurst**
These are the arms of the first recorded benefactor, Lord Buckhurst, the University's Chancellor from 1591 until his death in 1608. They are found impressed in gilt on the covers of most of the 177 works bought from abroad by Bodley's agents out of the sum of £100 which Lord Buckhurst gave in 1600. Recording this gift, the Benefactors' Register added a marginal note in manuscript that he had since been created Earl of Dorset; this occurred in 1604, but the Garter motto which surrounds his arms dates back to 1589, the year he was sent on an embassy to the Low Countries, at the same time that Thomas Bodley was ambassador at The Hague. The brass stamp used here was one of several made for the Library to record for posterity certain outstanding donations; other stamps are illustrated in Plates 16, 17, 20, 35 and 52b. In 1605 the Earl presented the bust of Sir Thomas Bodley (Plate 46) which still stands at the entrance to Duke Humfrey's Library.

16. **The badge of George Carey, 2nd Baron Hunsdon**
Unlike many of the recently-published purchases credited to other principal donors, which had arrived unbound, the Hunsdon books, more than 200 in all, appear to have been received already bound, mostly in a distinctive tawny calf. Onto these existing bindings the Library added either his coat of arms or, as here, his family badge of a swan, surrounded by the Garter motto.

The donor's father, Henry, the first Baron, was Queen Elizabeth's first cousin and had been her Lord Chamberlain, a post which his son George afterwards held from 1597. Both father and son were patrons of the Players' Company to which Shakespeare belonged, known as the 'Chamberlain's Men'.

17. **The arms of Sir Robert Sidney**
Sir Robert Sidney was the younger brother of the more celebrated Sir Philip, later to be commemorated in the Bodleian Painted Frieze (see Chapter III). In 1600 Sir Robert gave the Library £100, which was spent entirely on foreign printed books, fifty-five in number. All these were folios in Greek or Latin, except a quarto and two folios which were in Arabic. The Benefactors' Register names him sixth in the roll of donors, noting in the margin that he was made Baron Penshurst in 1603, and Lord Lisle in 1605. The volumes bought with the money he gave were marked by the Library with this elaborate armorial stamp proudly displaying his sixteen quarterings.

18. **The upper cover of the Benefactors' Register, 1604**
Just as the vaulted ceiling (Plate 6) of the Divinity School had displayed the badges of important donors towards the cost of that building, so Sir Thomas Bodley in his turn was resolved, as he wrote to the Vice-Chancellor in 1600, to 'conserve a perpetuall remembraunce of every giver and his gift' by means of 'a Register Booke' of Library benefactors. As was his wont, he took personal responsibility for every detail, providing a large folio of vellum leaves, but because in his opinion no one (even in that age of professional calligraphers) came up to the standard of script he required, he caused the opening pages, which listed donations from 1600 up to June 1604, to be printed in type at his expense by the Royal Printer, Robert Barker. The result was a piece of typography that can properly be termed 'unique' without qualification, there being no call for any other copy to be printed; it is perhaps also the first privately printed book in England. About the binding of the volume Sir Thomas took equal care, and although the Register has been much restored it is still in its original black calf covers with elaborate brass corner- and centre-pieces and with clasps which bear the inscription 'Anno 1604'. But its triangular floral ornaments are also found tooled on the second volume of the Register, which was begun in 1693, so they were doubtless added here at that later date. At the centre is an enamelled plaque of the arms of Bodley, with one of the earliest uses of his motto 'Quarta perennis'. The volume thus bound was therefore in place when King James I paid his first visit to Oxford and to the new Library in August 1605, and it is then described as kept always in a most conspicuous place (on a special reinforced desk), so that, as Bodley had intended, it might catch the eye of all who came to see the Library.

ANNO M.DCIIII. 91

Aſia Bapt. Grimaye. 4. Ant. 1604.
Jo. Hier. Pulucrinus de curandis ſingulis humani corporis morbis. fo. Ven. 1600.
Maur. Cordeus in 1. lib. Hip. de Morbis Mulierum. fo. Par. 1585.
Doctiſſimorum virorum Comment. in Catullum Tibul. & Propert. fo. Lut. 1604.
Philippi Scherbij Theſes Philoſophiæ. 4. 1603.
Gio. Marinello delle copie delle parole 2. vol. Ven. 1602.
Remigius Altiſſiodorenſis & Varlenius in Pſal. fo.
Ant. Butrius in 6. Decret. fo. Ven. 1575.
Q. Horatius cum Comment. Adr. Turnebi. fo. Par. 1605.
Di Bart. Dionigi parte 5. delle Hiſtorie di Tarcagnota. 4. Ven. 1603.
Meditationes in Theriacam & Methridicam Antidotum. 4. Ven. 1576.

Donum Roberti Barker Regiæ Maieſtatis Typographi.

Origenis Homiliæ ſuper vet. Teſtamentum. fo. MS.
The new Teſtament, with ſome parts of the olde in ancient Engliſh. fo.
The Mirrour of the world written by a Friar at the inſtance of King Philip of France. An. 1289. fo. MS.
Foure books of Honour Militarie & Ciuill. fo. Lond. 1602.
Fr. Gonzaga de Origine Seraphicæ Religionis Franciſcanæ. fo. Rom. 1587.

Donũ Guil. Ballow Academiæ Procuratoris.

Augustin⁹ de non iurando. f. MS. De trib. hostibus hoiem impugnatib⁹. De verbis Domini & Apostoli. Ad fratres in Eremo. Epistola ad Julianũ Comitem. De igne purgatorij. De 10. plagis et de 10. preceptis. De gaudio & supplicio damnatorũ. Stimulus conscientiæ. Sermo Aug. de tremendo Judicio. De ebrietate. De fuga mulierum. Sermo ad parochianos. Epistole variæ Hieronymi ad diversos. Notabilia excerpta de epistolis Hieronymi. Aug. de perfectione iustitiæ. De vita christiana. Eiusdem meditationes de dilectione Dei. De decimis reddendis. Expositio S. Bernardi super Magnificat. Stourton de laude B. Mariæ. Distinctiones bonæ per Alphabetum.
Aug. sup Gen. ad literam. f. MS. Boetius de hebdomadib⁹. Aug. de Trinitate. De vera religione. De libero arbitrio. De natura boni. De natura et gratia. Liber retractationũ. De presentia Dei ad Dardanum. De fide ad Petrum. De predestinatione. De gratia & libero arbitrio. Ad inquisitiones Januarij. De fide & symbolo. Sermo ad iuvenes. De cura gerenda pro mortuis. De moribus ecclesiæ et Manichæorum. Hypognost. Contra Epistolã Manichei. De mendacio. Contra mendacium. De duabus animab⁹. De videndo Deũ. Ad Macedonium. Solilog. De assumptione B. virginis. Ep. ad Volusian. De virginit. Sermo Ambrosij de assumptione. Sermones in monte. De adulterinis coniugijs. De utilitate credendi. De

19. A page of the Benefactors' Register
On the page here shown can be seen the transition from the first section, specially printed for Bodley, to the remainder of the volume, which thenceforward was continued in various successive written hands. Bodley, in search of a manuscript continuator whose hand could take over at this point, said in a letter to Thomas James in April 1605 'I have bin told of one in Corpus Christi College, that writeth faire and finely, but I can not learne his name. If it be so, I hope we shall prevaile so muche with him, as he will be contented, to spare a fortnightes time, for our Register booke'. The missing name was that of John Hales, 'the ever-memorable', then a scholar of Corpus, later Fellow of Merton and public lecturer in Greek, and afterwards the preacher chosen to give the sermon at Bodley's funeral in Merton chapel in 1613.

This page includes five gifts made by the man who had been employed for setting up the first ninety pages of the Register in type, Robert Barker, the Royal Printer; besides three manuscripts, he also gave one of his own publications. In addition to its function of listing benefactors, the fact that the Register also records the full titles and dates of the books given or purchased makes it a valuable source for Library history.

20. The arms of Sir Walter Raleigh
In 1603 Sir Walter Raleigh, who had been educated at Oriel College, gave £50 to the Library. He is described in the Benefactors' Register as Governor of Jersey, an office to which he had been appointed in September 1600, but of which he was deprived in 1603 prior to his trial in November of that year on a charge of conspiring against James I. His gift must therefore have been made early in 1603. It was used to buy some seventy-two works, on the bindings of which the Library caused this stamp of the donor's arms to be impressed.

library. Such was its fame by the time it opened that Bodley's shelving became, during the next hundred years, the definitive pattern for future library furniture both in Oxford, for example at Christ Church (1610), and also elsewhere, as at Hereford Cathedral (1611).

Bodley's 'purse-ability', which, allied to his practical genius, had made possible this magnificent housing, was next called upon for the provision of books to stock his waiting shelves. His own learning and his 'store of honourable friends' were of equal importance in determining his policy of acquisition. In June 1600 he writes that he will 'busy my selfe and my friends about gathering in Books, of such as will be benefactours'. All his diplomatic skill and energy were used to encourage gifts. In 1600 a Register of Benefactors was begun (Plates 18, 19), in which it became an honour to be inscribed, and benefactions began to flow in. Some came from notable figures in public life, others from academics. The first name in the Register is, understandably, that of the University's Chancellor, Thomas Sackville (at that time still Baron Buckhurst, later Earl of Dorset), dramatist and statesman. He was one of that 'store of honourable friends', many of them formerly Bodley's associates in the affairs of the Low Countries, who were prominent among the first benefactors. Besides the entries in the Register, detailing the titles of books either given, or bought out of sums given, by each benefactor, several brass stamps were specially cut and used to impress the donor's arms or crest on the covers of volumes so acquired. Such stamps visibly record the gifts of Sackville himself (Plate 15), of the third named benefactor, Lord Hunsdon (Plate 16), of Sir Robert Sidney (Plate 17) and of Sir Walter Raleigh (Plate 20) among others, while the gifts of the second listed donor, the Earl of Essex, are generally distinguishable because they bear the arms of the Portuguese bishop to whom they had originally belonged (Plate 21).

Most of these earliest listed donors had given substantial sums of money, but the gift of Essex was the first *collection* ever given (since the re-foundation) and it inaugurated at the very beginning a feature which has been characteristic of the Bodleian's growth ever since. Other donors, too, gave groups of volumes chosen from collections which they had themselves formed or had been given; of this kind were the gifts of the High Steward of the University, Lord Lumley, probably the greatest English book collector of his age, and of other men who, like him, belonged to a group of historians and antiquaries which included William Camden, Sir Robert Cotton and Bodley's close friend Henry Savile. Two other especial cronies of the Founder, both also mentioned in his will, were William Gent, of Gloucester Hall, who gave many books, chiefly medical, and Thomas Allen (Plates 22, 23) of the same Hall, mathematician and astrologer. The twenty manuscripts given in 1601 by the latter, who was described by the Founder as 'a most careful provoker and solicitor of

21. **The arms of Bishop Mascarenhas** Robert Devereux, Earl of Essex, the favourite of Queen Elizabeth, was the second recorded donor, after the Chancellor, in the Benefactors' Register. He had studied at Cambridge, but was incorporated M.A. of Oxford in 1588, when his step-father, the Earl of Leicester, was Chancellor of the University, a post which Essex himself unsuccessfully sought after the death of Leicester in that year. His gift to Sir Thomas Bodley, an intimate friend of his, was made in 1600, presumably after his release in August of that year from confinement at York House following his failure in Ireland, and while plans were being prepared for the rising early in 1601 which led to his downfall and execution. It was long thought that the books brought back by him from his expedition to Spain and Portugal in 1596, and recorded in the Benefactors' Register as given by him to the total of 222 items (including one manuscript, the first to enter the newly restored Bodleian) had originally formed the library of Jerome Osorio, a noted Portuguese writer and the first Bishop of Faro, who translated his see thither from Silves in 1577 and died in 1580. It was indeed at Faro, where Essex landed on his voyage home after the sacking of Cadiz, that he took on board the local Bishop's library, but nearly one hundred of these books, now in the Bodleian, are uniformly bound and have on their covers the armorial stamp of Ferdinand Mascarenhas, who became the fifth Bishop of Faro in 1594 and died in 1628 as Grand Inquisitor of Portugal; apparently he never discovered what had become of his treasured books.

sundry great persons to become benefactors' were but a first instalment; other gifts of his followed in 1607 and still more came later through his friend and pupil Sir Kenelm Digby (Plate 73). Allen's important donation of mediaeval manuscripts was matched by the forty-seven volumes given in the same year by Sir Walter Cope (Plate 24) and a year later by no fewer than eighty-one manuscripts from the library of Exeter Cathedral (Plate 25), a donation from Bodley's own native city made at the suggestion of his brother Lawrence, who was a canon there. Further large groups of manuscripts, many from the English monastic libraries despoiled seventy years before, came in, for example, from Sir George More (1603), William Burdet of Sonning (1608) and the Dean and Chapter of Windsor (1612), so that by the time of Bodley's death in 1613, about 800 manuscripts in all had been either presented or bought. This collection laid a solid base for the Bodleian's eminence as a treasure-house of the Middle Ages, and justified its description by Bodley's friend Francis Bacon, made in a letter accompanying a presentation copy of his *Advancement of Learning* in 1605, as 'an ark to save learning from deluge'.

Not all gifts were large; smaller sums of money were contributed by the less rich, and individual books, and also other objects, arrived in a stream from a socially varied succession of donors within the University and outside – bishops and clergymen of all ranks, lawyers, doctors, knights and gentlemen, soldiers, widows, booksellers and merchants, among others. The gifts were as varied as the givers: a manuscript once presented to Cardinal Wolsey in 1519 now proves to be enclosed in the first surviving English gold-tooled binding (Plate 27); a poet gives his own collected *Works* with an added poem in celebration of the Bodleian as 'this goodly Magazine of witte' (Plate 26); another of the Founder's brothers presents astronomical instruments (Plate 28) and a London printer, who was also Bodley's principal agent in buying books abroad, sends a special hand-coloured copy of a herbal he has recently published (Plates 29, 30). One outstanding example of a single gift, great in value as it is in its physical size, is a huge Bible (Plate 31) which George Ryves, the Vice-Chancellor in 1601, doubtless persuaded the Chapter of Winchester Cathedral to present in that year. Bodley himself, in addition to financing many of the current acquistions from his own pocket, almost certainly paid for the purchase of, among others, three very distinguished manuscripts, forerunners of similar texts to be added over the coming centuries, an Apocalypse, a Bestiary and the celebrated *Romance of Alexander* (Plates 32, 33). Had anyone but the Founder himself been the donor of these three fine illustrated volumes, his name would surely have been preserved in the Register of Benefactors, but nowhere does this mention the name of Sir Thomas himself.

Gifts of money, small as well as large, provided around £1,700 in the

continued on page 42

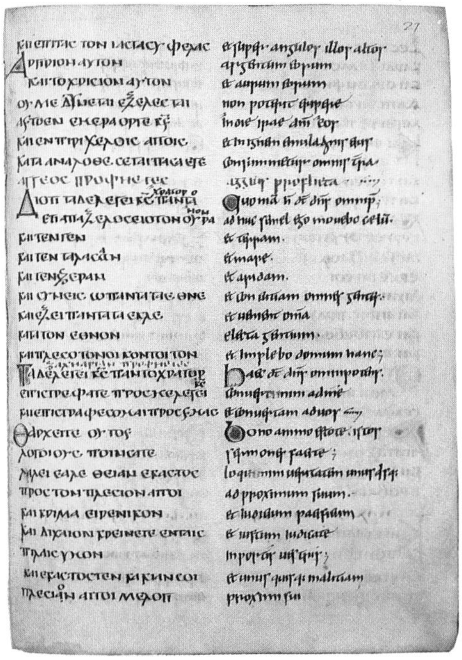

22. **A manuscript from Glastonbury used by St Dunstan**

Even without its association with St Dunstan, this celebrated volume would present rare and vital evidence for that darkest period in the intellectual history of Britain: the low point between the triumphs of Bede's time and the flowering of Anglo-Saxon culture in the tenth and eleventh centuries. Three of the four booklets bound together here were written independently in the ninth century and brought to England (and perhaps then united) during the tenth. The combination illustrates the twin sources of books available to the Anglo-Saxon reformers: imports from the Continent (especially France), and the vestiges of Insular culture still flickering in forgotten corners of the British Isles. Part I contains the start of a ninth-century copy, in decent Caroline minuscule, of a work on Latin grammar by the sixth-century author Eutyches. Since it is glossed with explanations in Old Breton, its origin on the other side of the English Channel is certain. Parts II and IV are both of ninth-century Welsh origin, as their Insular scripts unmistakably reveal. Part III takes its nickname 'Liber Commonei' from the person for whom it was apparently written. Its varied contents include a runic alphabet; a Paschal table for the years 817–832; computistical and astronomical extracts, for help in calculating the date of Easter, and, most importantly, bilingual sets of liturgical lessons and canticles in Greek and Latin, one of which is here illustrated. Pope Gregory the Great, in about the year 592, had laid down that some of these very lessons should be read out at the Easter Vigil service in both Latin and Greek; this manuscript seems to be unique evidence showing Gregory's decree still being followed in the ninth century in a remote outpost of the Roman church. The transliteration of some of the Greek into Latin letters suggests a faithful attempt to continue a practice which was beginning to lose its meaning. Part IV is one of the oldest surviving manuscripts of Ovid's *Ars amatoria* apparently copied from a recently imported Continental exemplar. It is equipped with typically Welsh 'construe-marks', to indicate the grammatical relationships between the words in difficult sentences. Despite his erotic themes, Ovid was regarded as a respectable model of good Latin.

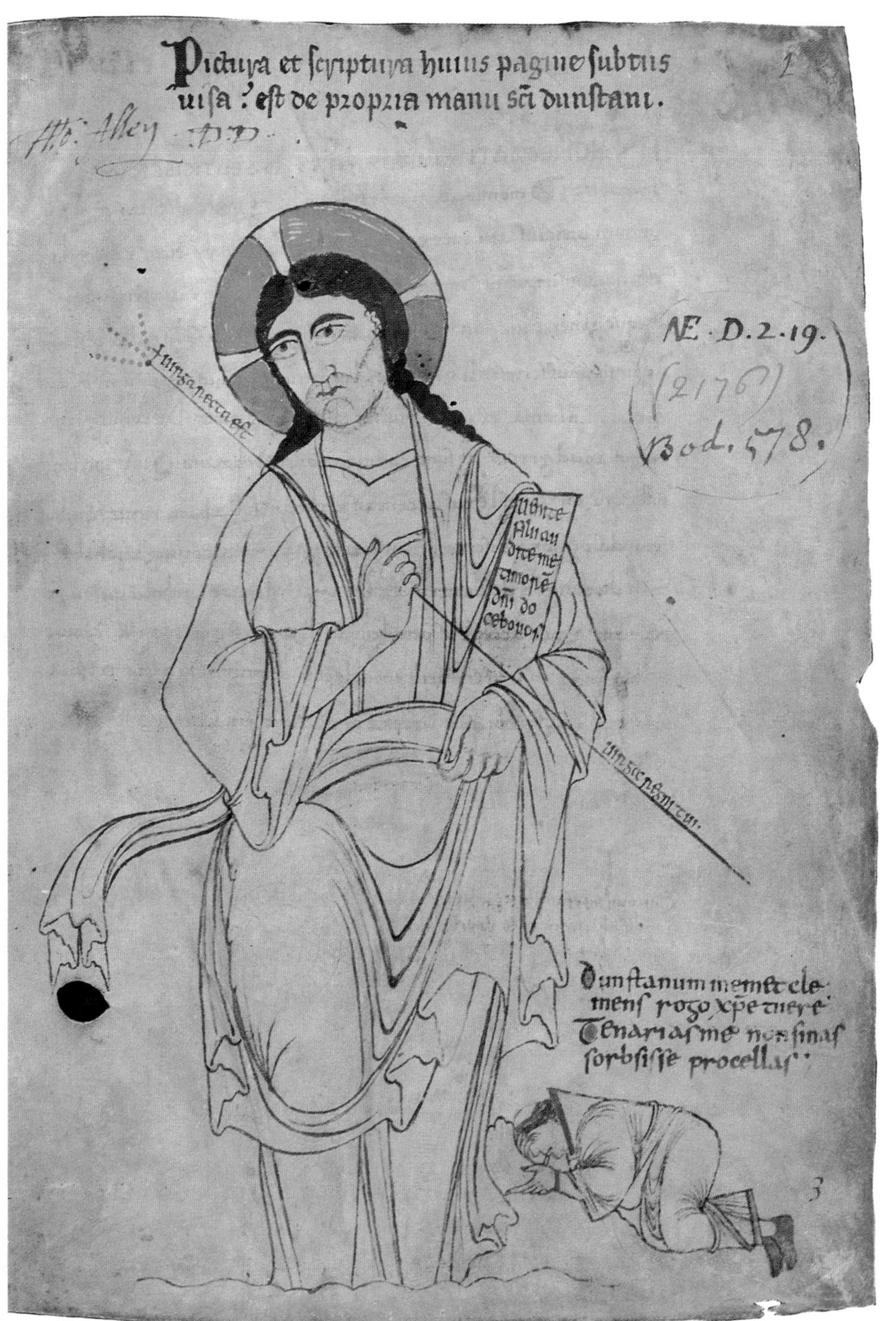

23. **Christ adored by St Dunstan, as drawn by the Saint himself**
St Dunstan, Archbishop of Canterbury from 960 to 988 and before that Abbot of Glastonbury, was one of the prime movers in the revival of English Benedictine monasticism and in the accompanying renaissance of English learning. On the first blank page of Part I of this manuscript (Plate 22) an accomplished English artist of the tenth century added a drawing of Christ with a kneeling monk. Above the monk an inscription in Latin hexameters reads: 'I beseech you, merciful Christ, to protect me, Dunstan; do not allow the infernal storms to overwhelm me'. The conclusion stated at the top of the page by a much later mediaeval hand is not unreasonable: 'The picture and the writing of this page, seen below, are in St Dunstan's own hand'. A similar tenth-century hand, perhaps identical with that of the Dunstan verses, added replacement leaves at the end of Parts III and IV of the manuscript. There is firm evidence that both Parts I and IV belonged to Glastonbury at the end of the Middle Ages, but in spite of their connecting links there is no firm evidence for the date when Parts I, III and IV were bound together, or for when Part II, which dates from the later eleventh century (it is the oldest surviving homily in Old English, on the Finding of the True Cross) was added. The combined volume was given to the Bodleian as a foundation present in 1601 by Thomas Allen.

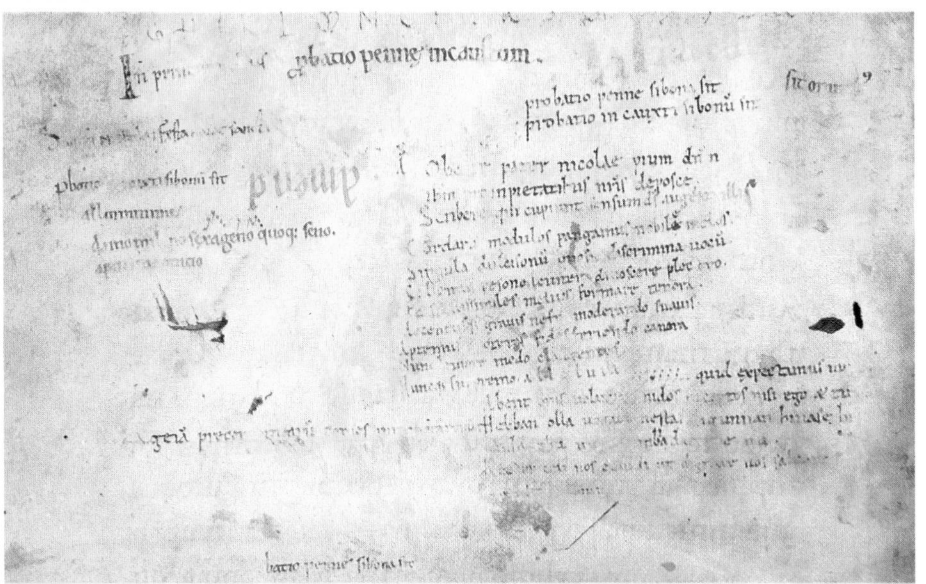

24. **Aelfric: *Homilies*, with 'the oldest specimen of the Dutch language'**
The circumstances under which a sentence in Netherlandish was scribbled on the final leaf of an Anglo-Saxon manuscript are unknown. The sentence reads 'Hebban olla uogala nestas bigunnan hinase hi [c]e [e]nda thu[. . .]', and it is obligingly preceded by a Latin version: '[H] Abent omnes uolucres nidos inceptos nisi ego et tu'. This phrase 'All the birds have their nests started, except you and I' is reminiscent of a saying of Jesus (Matt. viii, 20 and Luke ix, 58): 'Foxes have holes, and birds of the air have nests; but the Son of Man hath not where to lay his head'.

Palaeographically, the additional hand cannot be much later than the end of the eleventh century; it is not necessarily English. The next oldest instances of Netherlandish are from the thirteenth century. The manuscript was certainly at Rochester in the mid-eleventh century, probably written there in the early eleventh, and there is no reason to suspect that it ever left the Cathedral Priory until the end of the Middle Ages. Various instances of contact between Anglo-Saxon and Norman England and the Low Countries can be gathered from the historical records, and a certain international flavour is further attached to the scribe of the Netherlandish phrase by other references of his to the cult of St Nicholas of Bari in southern Italy, whose relics were translated to Bari in 1087. But little more can be deduced beyond the presence of a polyglot scribe at Rochester in the late eleventh century.

This manuscript is in fact the first of a two-volume set of homilies in Anglo-Saxon. Most of the homilies are taken from the two series of *Sermones catholici* by Aelfric (c. 995–c. 1020), Abbot of Eynsham, the greatest scholar and literary leader of the English Benedictine revival in the generation following St Dunstan. His homilies represent a major effort to present church teaching in the native language: only the titles in this copy are in Latin. The sermons cover most of the occasions of the Christian year, starting with Christmas. The script of the main section is a handsome square Anglo-Saxon minuscule of the early eleventh century, while a Rochester hand of the mid-century makes numerous alterations and additions between the lines. The two volumes were among the manuscripts presented by Sir Walter Cope to the Bodleian in 1602.

Opposite:
25. **Boethius: *De consolatione philosophiae*; Persius: *Satirae***
The two late tenth-century manuscripts bound together in one volume are relatively little known, for they contain no miniatures and their texts are not of crucial value, yet they are masterpieces of English calligraphy. Two styles of script were available in Anglo-Saxon England: the Insular style used for all vernacular and some Latin texts; and Caroline minuscule, used for Latin texts, in imitation of books imported from the Continent. But just as their Northumbrian predecessors had done in the late seventh century, the tenth-century English scribes imbued their imitations with the abstract grace of Insular calligraphy. As these manuscripts show, by the end of the tenth century they had mastered and surpassed the book arts of their Continental models. It was not without reason that Edward Johnston, the founder of modern calligraphy, took English Caroline minuscule as the model for his revived 'foundational' script.

The leather of the binding was added in the sixteenth century over late eleventh-century boards, so the combined volume was never cut down by later binders: the margins are beautifully proportioned (but possibly made extra wide in order to take the glosses). Though executed separately, the two parts are so similar that they must derive from the same scriptorium at the same date. They have been attributed to St Augustine's Abbey, Canterbury, a major centre responsible for the majority of surviving Anglo-Saxon copies of Latin classical texts. Boethius's *De consolatione philosophiae* had already been available in England in time for King Alfred to make his translation of it, but the Persius (a classical satirist of the first century A.D.) must have been a recent import since its accompanying gloss is a version of the so-called 'Cornutus'

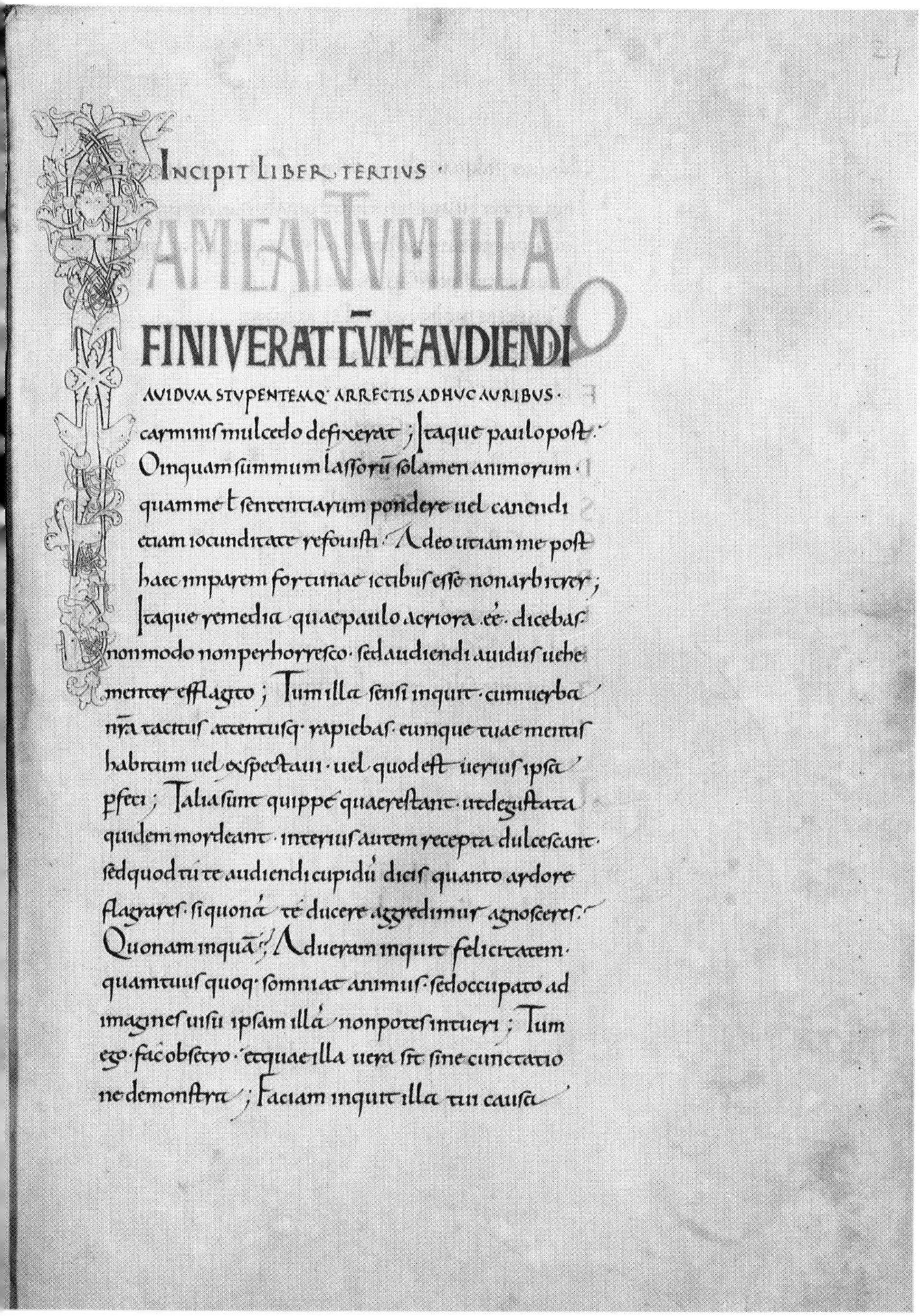

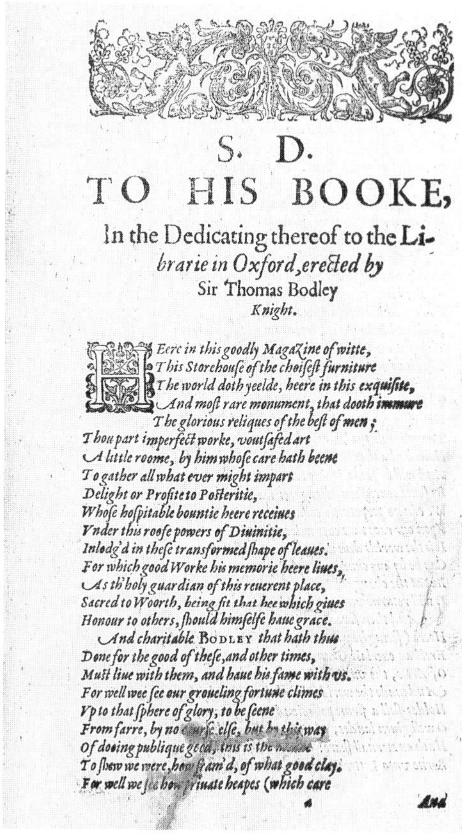

S. D.

TO HIS BOOKE,

In the Dedicating thereof to the Li-
brarie in *Oxford, erected by*
Sir Thomas Bodley
Knight.

Eere in this goodly Magazine of witte,
This Storehouse of the choisest furniture
The world doth yeelde, heere in this exquisite,
And most rare monument, that dooth immure
The glorious reliques of the best of men;
Thou part imperfect worke, voutsafed art
A little roome, by him whose care hath beene
To gather all what ever might impart
Delight or Profite to Posteritie,
Whose hospitable bountie heere receives
Vnder this roofe powers of Divinitie,
Inlodg'd in these transformed shape of leaves.
For which good Worke his memorie heere lives,
As th'holy guardian of this reverent place,
Sacred to Woorth, being fit that hee which gives
Honour to others, should himselfe have grace.
And charitable BODLEY *that hath thus*
Done for the good of these, and other times,
Must live with them, and have his fame with vs.
For well wee see our groveling fortune climes
Vp to that sphere of glory, to be seene
From farre, by no course else, but by this way
Of dooing publique good, this is the meane
To shew we were, how fram'd, of what good clay.
For well we see how private heapes (which care

And

26. **Samuel Daniel praises Sir Thomas Bodley**

Extremely few books of English literature were bought by the Bodleian in its opening years, Sir Thomas concentrating mainly on acquiring the manuscripts and latest printed texts of Latin, Greek and oriental authors, which he considered most suitable for a learned library. Gifts were, however, always acceptable and the poet Samuel Daniel (1562–1619) an Oxford man and tutor at Wilton of William Herbert, the future third Earl of Pembroke (Plate 71), presented to the Library (at some date after 18 April 1604 when Bodley had been knighted) a copy of his own collected *Works*, issued first in 1601, though at that date the poet had many years of creative writing still ahead of him. Into this presentation volume is inserted a specially printed leaf, unique to this copy, containing a new poem written in praise of the Founder and of his 'most rare monument'.

commentary, a Carolingian compilation. The decoration of the Boethius (shown here) consists of initials in a 'wiry' style which is plainly linked to the Insular past and is characteristic of fine Anglo-Saxon manuscripts of this period – snapping heads, interlace, acanthus foliage. Some of Boethius's poems are annotated here with musical neums.

The two manuscripts, still separate, were bequeathed by Leofric, Bishop of Exeter (1046–72) to his cathedral library, and bound together soon afterwards. They remained at Exeter until 1602, when Sir Thomas Bodley's brother Lawrence, a Canon of the Cathedral, persuaded the Dean and Chapter to present this and eighty others to the Bodleian.

27. **The earliest English gold-tooled binding, c. 1519**
Like the abstract designs seen on many early book covers, the technique of applying gold-leaf to bindings came from the East, reaching Italy in the fifteenth century and then spreading across Europe. Although the practice did not become common in England until the 1550s, the brown calf covers of a manuscript of Latin epigrams addressed by the celebrated Oxford grammarian Robert Whitinton to Cardinal Wolsey in 1519, were decorated with deeply impressed stamps of St George slaying the dragon and of Tudor royal emblems. From their position across the covers it would appear that these stamps were probably originally made for use with other forms of leather work; they are reminiscent of the ornamentation of some of the gilt coach and horse harness displayed in the Royal Mews at Buckingham Palace today. Experts believe that the stamps were made of wood and the gilding done without the use of heat. It is curious that this early example is not paralleled in England for several further decades, even though the gilt tooling of book covers was already by that time in frequent use in France and in Italy.

The manuscript reached the Bodleian between 1603 and 1605.

28. **Armillary sphere presented by Josias Bodley**

The armillary sphere is the oldest known instrument from the astronomy of antiquity. Constructed according to the planetary system of the Greek astronomer Ptolemy (c. 100–170), it shows the earth, represented by the gilded ball, surrounded by the great circles of the heavens and the ecliptic, but no fixed stars are indicated. The stand of this instrument, made up of three rampant lions, is engraved with the names of the four cardinal points and was originally orientated by means of a compass, which is now missing. On the broad ecliptic band, engraved with the signs of the zodiac, the vernal point coincides with 10 March, which shows that this armillary sphere was constructed before the introduction of the Gregorian calendar, which in most countries was adopted in 1582, though not until 1752 in Britain.

Used as demonstration models for teaching astronomy, many such instruments were masterpieces of craftsmanship. The present example is certainly that; it is made of brass, and measures about two feet in diameter; unfortunately it bears no date or maker's name. The base is engraved with the insignia of Henry Percy, ninth Earl of Northumberland, the 'Wizard Earl' (Plate 35), including the Garter, which was conferred on him in 1593. This points to his ownership of the instrument up to eight years before it passed, by some means not known to us, into the possession of Captain (later Sir Josias) Bodley, who presented it to the Library in 1601. With it he also presented three other astronomical instruments, including the celebrated and beautiful 'geometric quadrant' made by the Augsburg craftsman Christopher Schissler in 1579. That instrument, made of gilded brass, was kept in a cupboard in the wooden stand under the armillary sphere. When shown to the German traveller Zacharias von Uffenbach in 1710 by the Under-Keeper Joseph Crabb, it was described as made of 'pure gold'. Uffenbach formed a low opinion of Crabb's general ignorance, and stated that his interest in gold was chiefly in getting his tips from showing visitors the collection of curiosities.

Both instruments can be viewed in the Museum of the History of Science (Old Ashmolean), to which they are on permanent loan from the Bodleian Library.

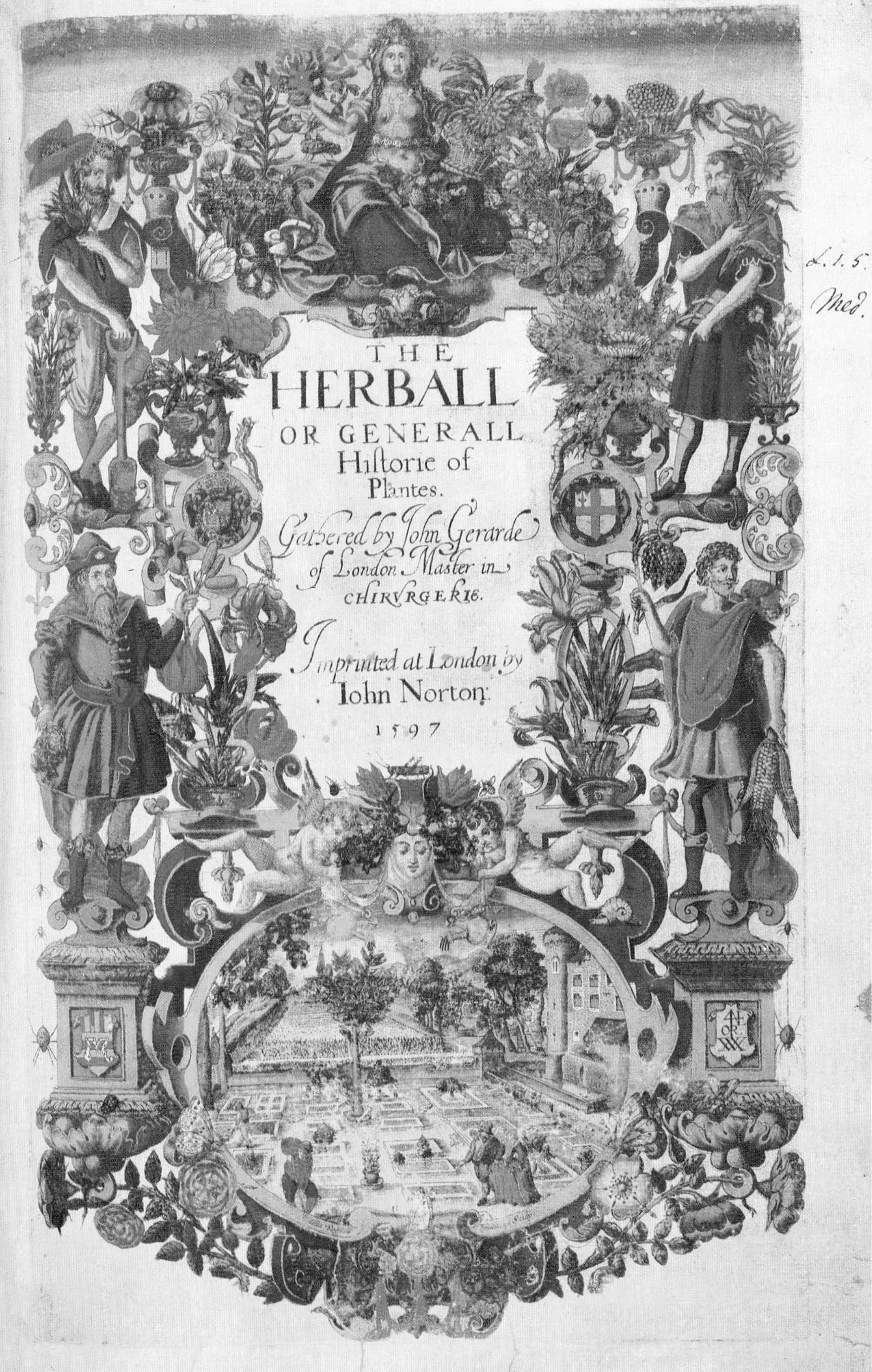
THE
HERBALL
OR GENERALL
Historie of
Plantes.
Gathered by John Gerarde
of London Master in
CHIRVRGERIE.
Imprinted at London by
Iohn Norton.
1597

29. **The titlepage of Gerard's *Herbal*, 1597**

Though for the past two centuries book-collectors have preferred uncoloured copies, it is a fact that early books illustrated with woodcuts or engravings were generally intended by their publishers to be coloured individually by hand to the owner's taste. A magnificent example of contemporary colouration is this copy of the first edition of Gerard's famous *Herbal*, given to the Library in 1601 by its publisher, John Norton, in a special presentation binding. The entry in the Register actually specifies 'Gerard's Herbal coloured'. Not only is the ornamental titlepage richly painted, as is the fine portrait of the author (Plate 30), but also the hundreds of woodcut illustrations of plants which adorn this celebrated and beautiful English herbal have been carefully painted in their correct natural colours. The donor, John Norton, had procured most of the woodblocks for this edition from Frankfurt; he was one of the leading London printers of the time and, as the then Master of the Stationers' Company, was a signatory to the enforcement document drawn up in 1612 (Plate 40). When the Library recommenced, Norton was also Sir Thomas Bodley's principal agent for the supply of foreign books.

30. **Portrait of John Gerard, the herbalist**

The engraved portrait of the author of Gerard's *Herbal*, facing the first page of text, in the specially coloured copy presented to the Library by the publisher in 1601. It shows Gerard at the age of fifty-three, in 1598, and describes him as born in Cheshire, and surgeon in London. Gerard is shown holding a spray of the potato plant; in the *Catalogue* of plants growing in his own garden at Holborn, which he originally published in 1596, he became the first man to record the potato in print. This portrait is signed with the initials of the engraver William Rogers, who also designed the titlepage of the book (Plate 29). Although that engraved titlepage is dated 1597, the date of this portrait suggests that the book was not completed for publication until the following year.

on erit fuga eis. fugiet. & ñ
eis qui fugerit. Si descende
nfernum: inde manus mea
si ascenderint usq; ad celum:
n eos. Et si absconditi fuerint
neli: inde scrutans auferã
ierint se ab oculis meis in
ibi mandabo serpenti. &
Et si abierint in captiuitatẽ
suis: ibi mandabo gladio &
ponam oclos meos sup eos
n bonũ: ait dñs ds exercitu
it terrã & tabescet: & luge
abitantes in ea. Et ascend&
nnis: & defluet sicut fluui
ificat in celo ascensionẽ suã.
ũ sup t͠rã fundauit. Qui
naris. & effundet eas sup fa
nomen eius. XV.
non ut filii ethiopũ uos estis
i israel ait dñs: Nunquid
scendere feci de terra egipti
e capadotia. & syros de cyre
li dñi dei sup regnũ peccans:
lud a facie terre. Veruntam
nterã domũ iacob: dic dñs.
mandabo. & concutiã in
b; domũ israel: sic concutit
ro. & ñ cadet lapillus sup
lio morientur omš peccato
r: qui dicunt. ñ appropinquabit

uineas: & bibent uinũ earũ. Et facient
hortos: & comedent fructus eorũ. Et
plantabo eos sup humũ suã: & ñ euellã
eos ultra de terra sua quam dedi eis: dic
dominus deus tuus.

EXPL AMOS PPHA
INCIP ABDIAS PPHA

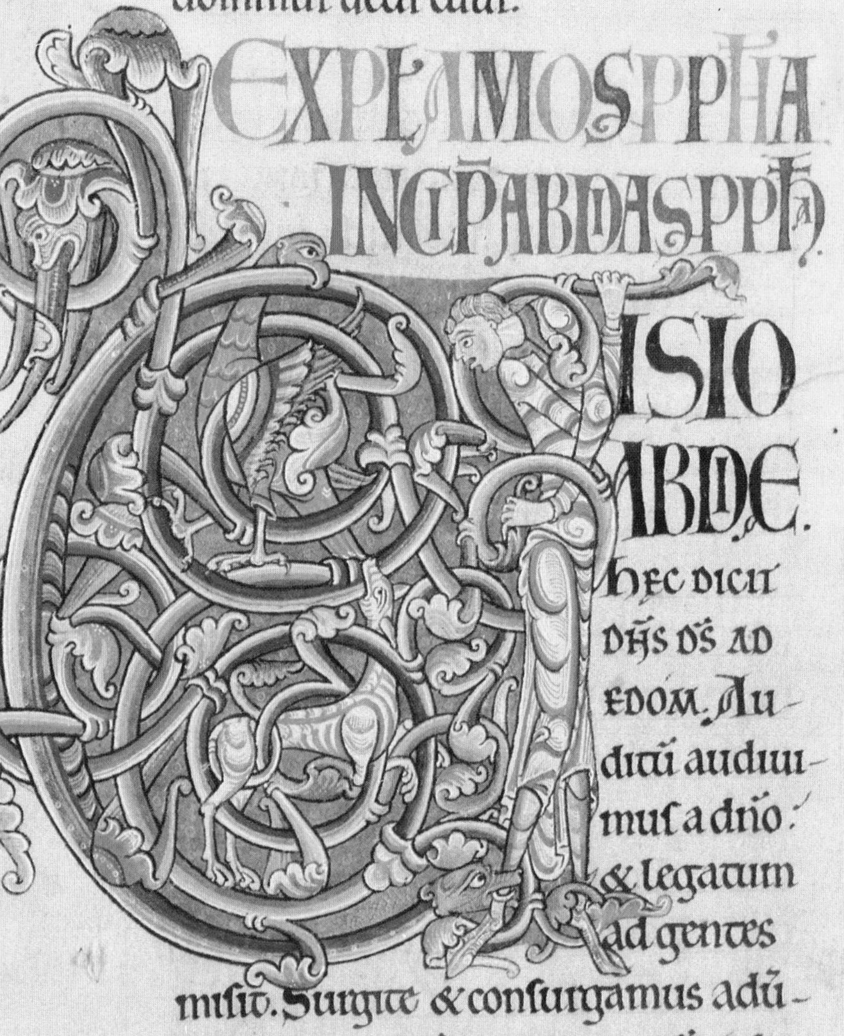

VISIO
ABDIE.

Hec dicit
dñs ds ad
edom. Au
ditũ audiui
mus a dño:
& legatum
ad gentes
misit. Surgite & consurgamus adũ
sum eũ in prẽliũ. Ecce paruulũ te de
di in gentib;: contemptibilis tu es ual
de. Supbia cordis tui extulit te: ha
bitantẽ in scissuris petre. exaltantẽ
soliũ tuũ. Qui dicis in corde tuo. Qs
detrahet me in t͠ram: Si exaltat fue
ris ut aquila: & si inter sydera posu
eris nidum tuũ. inde detrahã te: dic
dñs. Si fures introissent ad te: si la-

31. **An illuminated initial from the 'Auct. Bible'**

The tradition of giant bibles can be followed back through the magnificent Carolingian bibles of the early ninth century, and the *Codex Amiatinus* with its lost Northumbrian brothers of c. 700, to the Greek *Codex Sinaiticus* in the fourth century. They will normally have been lectern copies, used for public recitation in church or monastic refectory. The eleventh and especially the twelfth centuries produced many 'great bibles', in Italy, the Moselle basin region and England. By contrast, the characteristic thirteenth-century bible is a tiny copy designed for personal use by the growing student population of the newly-founded universities.

Although only a few of its decorated initials include figures, the two-volume 'Auct. Bible' can stand alongside the Lambeth, Bury and Winchester Bibles as one of the major triumphs of English Romanesque book-production. Its text-script is stately and regular, and the simple coloured capitals of its titles have an expert confidence of spacing and design. Care was taken to establish a full and accurate text, both in original conception – e.g. a double set of chapter-tables to Kings – and in later corrections. The major initials, gradually filled in by various artists in different styles over a long period, show the 'arabesque' type at its highest level of quality.

The writing of both volumes and the decoration and rubrication of the first volume have most recently been dated to c. 1140–50, perhaps carried out at Winchester rather than (as previously suggested) at St Albans. The Bible was certainly at Winchester during the second half of the century, at which time the rubrication and initials of the second volume were completed. Some of the later artists who worked on it also worked on the famous Winchester Bible, and at this period the texts of the 'Auct. Bible' and the Winchester Bible were 'intercorrected' by a single hand to bring them into mutual harmony. The difficulty of localizing the earlier work is due to the increasing realization among modern scholars that the top-flight artists were no longer monks, tied to one scriptorium, but professionals who moved from place to place and even from country to country.

The life of St Hugh of Lincoln relates a story of how King Henry II tricked the monks of Winchester Cathedral Priory into giving him a recently completed refectory bible, which he then presented to St Hugh at his Carthusian Priory of Witham; and how St Hugh, learning the true circumstances, insisted on returning the Bible to Winchester, without the King's knowledge. St Hugh was Prior of Witham from c. 1180 until his consecration as Bishop of Lincoln in 1186, and the story described the Bible as recently decorated and corrected, so it is likely that our 'Auct. Bible' was the very book involved.

After its return to Winchester Cathedral, the 'Auct. Bible' remained there until 1601, when George Ryves, who was both Warden of New College and also a Canon of Winchester, must have persuaded the Chapter to present the Bible to the Bodleian as a foundation gift. The two volumes received their present bindings at this time, and Sir Thomas Bodley mentions in a letter of 22 January 1602 the name of the man who made the elaborate clasps: Richard Haydock, a fellow of Ryves's own college and an admirer of Bodley. In a letter of 1604, Bodley cites 'one of Dr Ryves's great volumes' as the archetype of a heavy book, and the two volumes remain among the very heaviest in the entire Library. The nickname 'Auct. Bible' refers to its shelfmark, which is taken from its former home in the 'Auctarium'. This was an additional Library-room (formerly the Anatomy School) designated by the Curators in 1789 as a special repository for 'Mss and books of an early date relating to Greek and Latin Learning'.

32. **Marco Polo leaving Venice**
'Undeniably one of the great picture books of the Middle Ages' was M. R. James's verdict on the complex and lavishly illuminated volume which contains this picture. The core of the manuscript is a Flemish copy of *The Romance of Alexander*, illuminated between 1338 and 1344. Half a century or so later, in England, it was supplemented with further Alexander material and a copy of Marco Polo's *Travels*; these additions also encompass important miniatures. The connecting theme is 'travellers' tales': the Wonders of the East encountered by Alexander the Great in India and transmitted via Pseudo-Callisthenes to form the basis of the mediaeval Alexander-legend; and the adventures of Marco Polo in China.

The *Alexander* text of Part I, in essence a mediaeval romance of chivalry, is in French verse (rhymed 'Alexandrines', a term possibly derived from this very romance) in the Picard dialect of Flanders. It is built up of successive accretions by various authors: Lambert le Tort and Alexandre de Paris (de Bernai), Jean le Nevelon (le Venelais), etc. The section containing 'Vows to the Peacock' (*Voeux du Paon*), a popular concept of fourteenth-century chivalry, was grafted into the narrative by Jacques de Longuyon around 1310. *Le Restor du Paon*, a supplement by Jean le Court (Brisebarre), includes a song, here complete with its tune. At the end the scribe records the date when he finished writing: 18 December 1338. Below, a note in gold letters records that the illumination was finished on 18 April 1344 by Jehan de Grise: perhaps the master of a workshop (at Bruges ?), since two or more different painters are involved. Although there are many glittering miniatures illustrating the Alexander story (mainly battle scenes), today our main interest focuses on the scenes along its lower margins: cooking (Plate 33), games, puppet-shows, animals, and other vignettes of everyday life or fabulous invention, in endless profusion. While many of these are not so entirely unconnected with the text as has sometimes been supposed, they certainly provide us with a visual source for our understanding of everyday mediaeval life. Changes of plan in the degree of lavishness are discernable; at some point, the client seems to have demanded more pictures.

An English owner of c. 1400 decided to add a missing episode, Alexander's communications with the Brahmans of India. The result, Part II, is the unique manuscript of a version of the incident, in Middle-English alliterative verse (West Midlands dialect), with a cross-reference added at the appropriate point in the main French text. The same English scribe also wrote Part III, a remodelled French prose version (French may well have been the original language) of Marco Polo's *Li Livres du Graunt Caam*. The miniatures of Part II are lavish but crude. Those of Part III are much more expert: the frontispiece is the famous large miniature (here reproduced) showing the departure of the Polo family from Venice by ship, in which still-existing landmarks such as the four horses of St Mark's are carefully depicted. The name of the principal illuminator (most of the other miniatures are by his workshop associates) is written in gold into a miniature: *Johannes me fecit*. This Johannes is recognized, along with John Siferwas and Herman Scheerre, as one of the masters who established the International Gothic style in early fifteenth-century England. One of Johannes's men returned to Part I to add its present frontispiece, probably to replace a damaged Flemish original.

The volume's first certain owner was Richard Woodville, first Earl Rivers, who boasts engagingly that he bought it in London in 1466 'in the second year of the coronation of the most virtuous Elizabeth' – his own daughter, Edward IV's factious consort. After Woodville's execution in 1469 the manuscript had a succession of later owners and finally entered the Bodleian about 1603–4. Its source is not recorded, which suggests that the unnamed donor of such a spectacular manuscript was Sir Thomas Bodley himself. Centuries later the Bodleian entry-books record that it was consulted (on 27 April 1857) by William Morris, then a young B.A. of Exeter College; a few months later, he and his Pre-Raphaelite Brethren started their famous painting campaign to mediaevalize the walls of the Oxford Union.

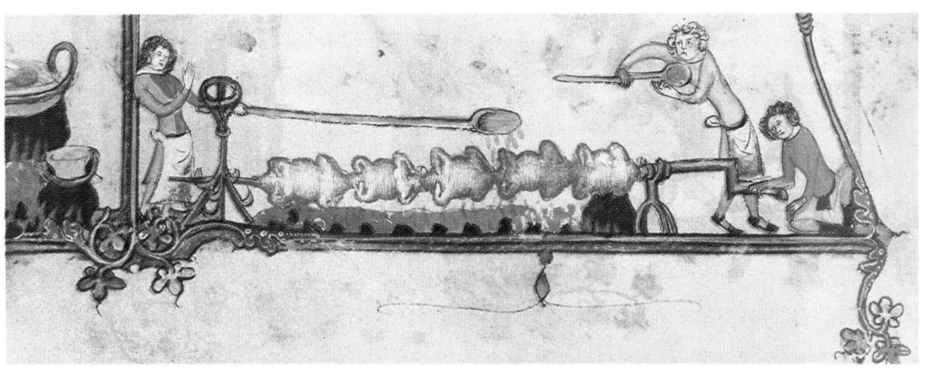

33. **Spit-roasting**
Roasting fowl on a spit; a marginal detail from *The Romance of Alexander* (Plate 32).

five years 1601–05, to augment Bodley's personal resources, and thus helped to finance the purchase of printed books on a remarkably comprehensive scale. The pages of the Register furnish lists of the books bought with the money given by each donor. These lists go part way to document the wide-ranging acquisition policy employed in building up the Library's foundation collections. They also illustrate how far these sums could then go in paying book bills. For example, the £100 given in 1605 by the Earl of Southampton (the patron to whom Shakespeare dedicated *Venus and Adonis* and *Lucrece*), purchased more than 400 titles, many of them in French, Italian and Spanish, including a notable 'first' – the copy of *Don Quixote* bought by Bodley's agent in Spain in the very year of its original publication. It can safely be asserted that no other copy of this rare first edition has been sitting (with its original shelfmark) on the same library shelf since 1605 – the year in which the book was first published and began to capture the imagination of Europe.

The Founder's breadth of vision did indeed call for a universal library with books in all faculties. If Theology held pride of place, with an emphasis on the works of the Reformers (reflecting Bodley's personal outlook) yet Jurisprudence, Medicine and the Arts, subjects of the traditional mediaeval *Trivium* and *Quadrivium*, were also substantially represented, and Bodley's own special interest in languages ensured that books were sought from the whole world. Two of the leading London booksellers, John Bill and John Norton, were commissioned to travel with *carte blanche* to exercise their judgment in acquiring books published on the Continent, from which Bodley himself then made his own selection of what to send up to Oxford. These early years also saw significant purchases of oriental books, and not only in Hebrew, Bodley's own special interest: about 1608 he had requested Paul Pinder, an Oxford man who was then consul of the Company of English merchants at Aleppo, to collect 'bookes in the Syriacke, Arabicke, Turkishe and Persian tongues, or in any other language of those Esterne nations, bycause I make no doubt but in processe of time, by the extraordinairie diligence of some one or other student they may be readily understoode'.

No less impressive, as indicating to what far-distant horizons in space as well as in future time the Founder's interests stretched, are his purchases of books in Chinese. Although in his lifetime there was probably no one in England (and very few in Europe) who could read literary Chinese, by the year 1613, when Bodley died, as many as forty-nine volumes (fascicles) had already been purchased by his Library, apparently at an average cost of £1 apiece. Chinese acquisitions are first mentioned, as being on their way from Bodley's London house, in a letter written to his Librarian in 1607, which adds 'because I cannot give their titles I have written on every volume the

continued on page 44

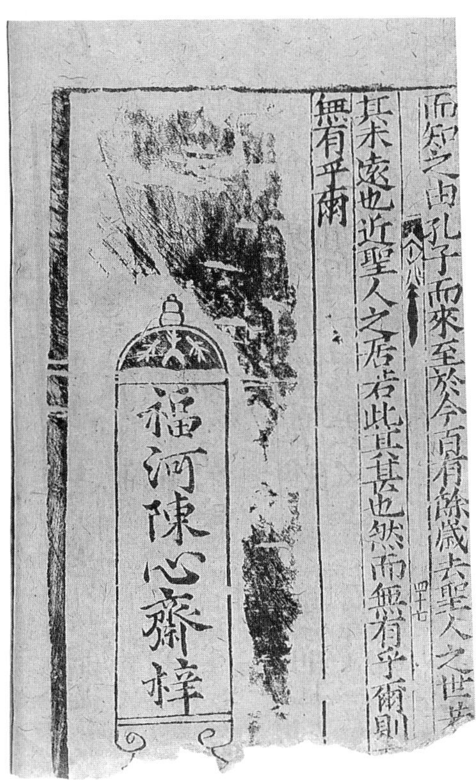

Donū Henrici Percey
Comitis Northumbriæ.
Aº. 1604.

34. **The first Chinese book purchased, with Bodley's autograph inscription**
It mattered little that when this book was bought there was no one around who could read it; Bodley's principle was sound and forward-looking: material was to be acquired and incorporated even in exotic languages and scripts, against a future day when scholars in those languages should arrive and identify what the Library owned. The two-way process of discovery and enlightenment mutually between the Library and its readers was thus begun, and has been going on in various fields ever since. Before this printed Chinese book was sent down from London where he had acquired it (perhaps ultimately through some sailor back from the East) Bodley picked up the volume, which had by then already been given its present limp vellum cover, and wrote in Latin in his own hand on a fly-leaf that it was the gift of the Earl of Northumberland in 1604, meaning that its cost had been charged against the Earl's £100 given a year earlier. Understandably enough, Bodley had in fact held the book upside down, and therefore written the inscription we see here wrong way up and at the back. Further, because neither he nor his Librarian could tell what the book was about, it was not entered among the other purchases listed under the Earl's name in the Benefactors' Register, nor could it find a place in either of James's two printed Bodleian *Catalogues* of 1605 and 1620. With various other Chinese volumes, each awaiting an identity, it was long kept in a gilded Limbo – one of the 'grates' or Archive cupboards with their doors of blue and gold lattice metalwork which still delight the visitor's eye on both sides of the entrance to Duke Humfrey's Library, and in which even today manuscripts of special value are preserved.
When in 1687 a Chinese scholar catalogued this and the other volumes in that cupboard, this one was found to be part of a text (without commentary) of the Confucian 'Four Books', in fact chapters 4–6 of the Analects of Confucius, with the whole of Mencius. The crudely decorative colophon, here reproduced, states that the blocks from which the book was printed, were 'cut by Ch'en Hsin-chai of Fu-ho'. This proves, therefore, to be a copy of a section of one of the cheap, commercial editions, produced (for a popular market) at Chien-yang in Fu-chien province during the Wan-li period, the last quarter of the sixteenth century. At home in China scholarly book-collectors would not bother with such cheap products, so that they are now rare and survive, if at all, outside China, mainly in Japanese or European collections.

35. **The badge of Henry Percy, Earl of Northumberland**
The famous crescent-moon badge of the Percys was stamped by the Library on the covers of books bought out of the sum of £100 given in 1603 by Henry Percy, the ninth Earl of Northumberland, who, like so many other early benefactor friends of Bodley, had also seen service in the Low Countries. Two years after this gift Northumberland was one of those created M.A. on the occasion of the royal visit to Oxford in 1605, but later in that year he was sent to the Tower, allegedly on suspicion of being concerned (Protestant though he was) in the 'Gunpowder Plot', through having in his employment Thomas Percy the conspirator, who was a distant cousin. He spent the next sixteen years in prison; his friend Raleigh (Plate 20) occupied his time in the Tower writing his *History of the World*, while Northumberland in the same prison enjoyed a large library of his own and congenial scholars had access to him; his keen interest in scientific experiments earned him the nickname of the 'Wizard Earl'. The armillary sphere given to the Library by Bodley's brother Josias (Plate 28) has Northumberland's insignia engraved on its base.

36. **Portrait of Thomas James, the first Librarian**
First in the series of portraits of Bodley's Librarians which today are hung round the walls of the room where the Curators hold their meetings is that of Thomas James. The inscription across the foot of the painting resembles those on the portraits of the next Librarians, and was doubtless added later when there began to be a series of such paintings. It states that after twenty years he chose to resign his post in May 1620; since it does not mention the sitter's date of death it seems possible that the portrait was commissioned after 1620 and before James's death in 1629. The painting, which is first mentioned in a list drawn up by Thomas Hearne in 1705, is not signed; in the present century it has been attributed to Gilbert Jackson, who was active from 1622 to 1640, an artist who remained unaffected by the style of portraiture favoured at Court.

James, who had accomplished prodigies of work during those twenty years of his librarianship, was not idle during the nine years of his retirement. He threw himself into the continuation of projects he had long cherished, mainly a single-handed crusade to prove that Roman theologians had falsified the writings of the Fathers. During his tenure of office he had assembled on Bodley's shelves a dozen or more different editions of the Spanish and the Roman *Index* of forbidden books, which he considered to be a guide to what were, in his view, books most desirable for the Library to possess; among several works published during his retirement was an edition of the Roman *Index* actually reprinted by him at Oxford in 1627. He was probably only about fifty-six years old when he died.

name of the giver'. Hence the example here illustrated (Plate 34) bears Bodley's autograph inscription (written in fact upside down inside the *back* cover) that it was given (out of money provided) by Henry Percy, Earl of Northumberland, in 1604 (Plate 35). These first Chinese acquisitions turn out to be almost all medical, and the few non-medical ones were very probably all ultimately also from the library of a single Chinese physician. Bodley's pioneering initiative in this field continued to be followed, so that by 1697, the year when Edward Bernard's *Catalogi* described them together in print, the number acquired from various miscellaneous sources had risen to seventy, and there were additional Chinese volumes in the collections of Laud, Selden and Thurston. Ten years previously (in 1687) the Library had paid a native

37. **Autograph letter of Bodley to Thomas James**
A single manuscript volume preserves no fewer than 231 letters, all written in Bodley's own hand, addressed to his first 'Keeper', Thomas James. From Christmas Eve 1599, more than a year before James actually entered on his duties as Librarian, until the month of the writer's own death in January 1613, this correspondence ranges over every aspect of Bodley's intimate and tireless personal supervision of the foundation and development of his Library, and provides detailed documentation of the thinking of the two men as they confronted the manifold problems presented by their great undertaking.

The letter here reproduced, dated 10 June 1602, begins 'I hope those litle wormes about ye covers of your bookes, come by reason of their newnesse and that heerafter they will away . . .' an attitude to bookworms which would make the modern conservationist gasp. The letter mentions several donors or possible donors, and refers to entering gifts 'on my Register', the Benefactors' Register (Plates 18, 19) which was then already in course of compilation. The correspondence reveals frequent differences of opinion between the two men, but Bodley, who was many years James's senior and anyhow in a position to be dictatorial in Library matters, clearly appreciated his Librarian despite the real or supposed shortcomings he found in him, and there are frequent touches of genuine cordiality; he ends this letter 'my very best wishes to your welfare Your affectionate friend Tho Bodley'.

The whole correspondence was published in 1926 and reprinted by the Bodleian in 1985.

Chinese scholar to visit Oxford to catalogue the whole collection. It is interesting to note that the later seventeenth-century additions, in contrast with the earlier medical acquisitions, were mostly novels.

As the late Ian Philip has pointed out in his definitive Lyell Lectures *The Bodleian Library in the Seventeenth and Eighteenth Centuries* (published in 1983), the very catholicity of the acquisitions made during the Library's first decade serves to refute the view, often repeated since it was expressed by Thomas Hearne, that Bodley's concern was to found an institution designed to defend a world view in accord with extreme English Protestantism. Bodley's own experience of life, and the

38. The interior of Duke Humfrey's Library, looking west

The restored Duke Humfrey's Library was finally opened by the Vice-Chancellor in 1602 on 8 November, a day still commemorated by its choice for the formal Visitation made each year by his modern successors. This picture of the Library as it is today gives a vivid impression of the sight which greeted the eyes of the first readers when the restored Library was re-opened. Standing with their backs to the great east window they could view, as modern readers still can, that noble procession of book-presses down both sides of the spacious centre aisle, and the vivid colouring of Bodley's restored roof (Plate 14) and its supporting beams. Apart from the large window in the distance, which belongs to the later-built Selden End, nothing structurally has since changed. True, the set of portraits (largely imagined) of College Founders on the walls is a later addition, and comfortable modern chairs have replaced the ruder seating of Jacobean days, but the books which face today's readers as they settle to their work are very largely the actual volumes placed on these shelves through the efforts of Bodley and his friends; like the proletariat, they have lost nothing but their chains.

diversity of the sources from which he welcomed help and advice, transcended any such narrow sectarian view.

Such a view might with more justice be attributed to the man whom Bodley chose to be the first Library-Keeper. Thomas James (Plate 36) was uniquely qualified for the post. From a background similar to Bodley's (his parents had also sought exile during the reign of Mary), a scholar of Winchester and a Fellow of New College, he was known as a prodigy of learning, and was to become known as a fierce Puritan polemicist, who recommended using the *Index* of books forbidden by the Roman Church as a Library desiderata list, and devoted himself to unmasking Romish errors in the interpretation of the Fathers. He had already edited the first English printing of that classic text of library management, Richard de Bury's *Philobiblon*, a re-issue of which in 1599 he dedicated to his future employer Bodley, and in 1600 he produced, in his *Ecloga Oxonio-Cantabrigiensis*, the first published survey of manuscripts held by the colleges of those two universities. Bodley's earlier choice of him was officially ratified by the University in 1602, and until 1620 James was to labour unremittingly as the builder of Bodley's great design. Working under constant direction from Bodley, who, now living in London, made his wishes known by frequent correspondence (Plate 37), James received the new acquisitions, classified, handlisted and catalogued them, and arranged them on the shelves. From the opening of the Library in November 1602 (Plate 38), it was James who assured its opening hours and services to readers, assisted at first only by a Janitor and then from 1606 also by an Assistant Keeper.

In 1605 James produced, and Bodley with some reluctance himself financed, one of the earliest ever published library catalogues, which was to spread the Bodleian's fame throughout the learned world. In its compilation, as in many other matters (such as his salary, and whether in breach of the Library Statutes he might be allowed to marry), James was not always in total agreement with his master. They differed over the arrangement of the 1605 *Catalogue*. This became in effect a classified shelf-list, following the order (based on the four-fold division of the faculties in the mediaeval university) according to which Bodley had insisted the Library should be arranged. Against James's advice, manuscripts and printed books had been mixed together on the shelves, and were so arranged in the printed catalogue too; the form of catalogue entry, using the genitive form of authors' names, was likewise at issue between the two men.

James also proposed, and later partly completed in manuscript, a subject catalogue, an aim which has haunted the dreams of librarians and readers alike ever since, but has always proved elusive of fulfilment. Bodley did not warm to another proposal by James, for an extension to cater 'for the younger sort' meaning probably Bachelors

continued on page 51

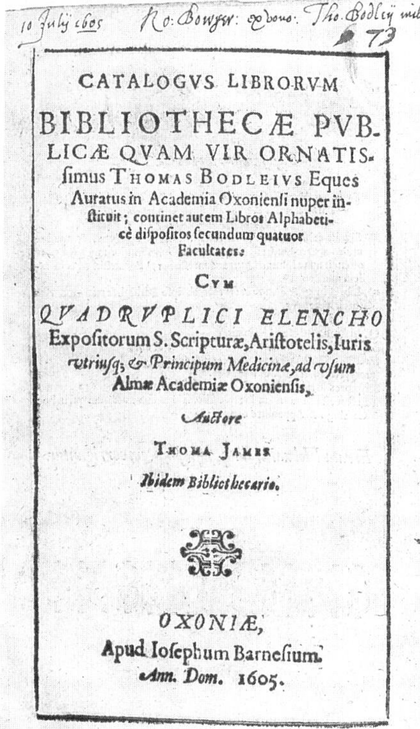

10 Julij 1605 Ro: Bowyer: ex dono: Tho: Bodley militis. 73

CATALOGVS LIBRORVM

BIBLIOTHECÆ PVBLICÆ QVAM VIR ORNATISsimus THOMAS BODLEIVS Eques Auratus in Academia Oxoniensi nuper instituit; continet autem Libros Alphabeticè dispositos secundum quatuor Facultates:

CVM

QVADRVPLICI ELENCHO Expositorum S. Scripturæ, Aristotelis, Iuris vtriusq; & Principum Medicinæ, ad vsum Almæ Academiæ Oxoniensis.

Auctore

THOMA JAMES

ibidem Bibliothecario.

OXONIÆ,
Apud Iosephum Barnesium.
Ann. Dom. 1605.

39. **The first printed *Catalogue* of the Bodleian, 1605**

If not quite the earliest, this was certainly the greatest general catalogue of the contents of any European library published up to that time. Its production grew out of a plan to print the 'Tables', which at first were placed in frames attached to the ends of the bookcases (as visible in Plate 38) listing the books contained on each shelf. As the Oxford printer Joseph Barnes was reluctant to undertake any larger venture on his own, Bodley himself promised in June 1604 to be 'at the charge of printing' a general *Catalogue* of the fast-growing collections, and even undertook to catalogue himself the books in Hebrew. Printing began at Oxford at the end of July and after a little more than two months 426 quarto pages, describing more than 6,000 titles, were in print. But when the stationer John Norton was shown the sheets, he pointed out that many books which he had himself supplied had not been included. In addition, he had 1,600 further books currently on offer to the Library, and further accessions from abroad were still flowing in. Bodley therefore decided to postpone publication until an Appendix could be prepared and printed, to include the newest accessions. The incorporation into the completed volume of that Appendix, arranged by Faculties as the main *Catalogue* had been, added over 200 further pages with 2,600 new entries, and led Thomas James to compile a massive author index to link the two parts of his *Catalogue* together. He also inserted subject lists he had compiled of writers on Scripture, on Aristotle, on Law and on Medicine.

Thomas James had no precedents to guide him in the organization and layout of his *Catalogue*. In essence he set out to list all the books, printed and manuscript alike, according to the order in which the folios stood, by Faculties, on the shelves of Duke Humfrey's Library, one page being allotted to each shelf. But difficulties beset him; what Sir Thomas called 'coupling' – the binding together of two or more works into one volume – caused interruptions to the alphabetical order on the shelves. Further, to avoid waste of space James felt compelled to use the remainder of each page beneath the listed folios both for inserting entries for smaller works in 4° and 8° either by the same authors already quoted or by others, and also for further cross-references to works shelved elsewhere.

Published in June 1605, and dedicated to the hopeful young Prince Henry, Thomas James's *Catalogue*, despite its discrepancies and difficulties in use, won deserved recognition for the riches of the new Library and for its laborious author. It soon circulated abroad as well as in Britain; among the copies now preserved in the Bodleian is the one bought and bound for the greatest French book-collector of his age, J-A. de Thou, who died in 1612. The titlepage here reproduced carries the only presentation inscription known on a copy of the *Catalogue*, recording in the handwriting of Robert Bowyer, who was Clerk to the Parliament, that this book was a gift to him from Sir Thomas Bodley himself on 10 July 1605. This copy was presented to the Library by one of its great benefactors, J. P. R. Lyell, in 1944.

40. Signatures of the Officers of the Stationers' Company, 1612

At a meeting held in Stationers' Hall in London on 28 January 1612, the Company decided to reinforce the agreement it had made earlier with Oxford University, to deliver to the Bodleian one free copy, in sheets, of every newly printed book. The new ordinance was signed by all those present, being the Master, the two Wardens, and the Assistants. Among the signatures, here reproduced from the document, are those of John Norton, currently the Master, and one of Bodley's principal agents in the purchase of books, who even before the agreement had himself presented the special copy of Gerard's *Herbal* (Plate 29); of Richard Field, the Senior Warden, who had printed in 1593 Shakespeare's *Venus and Adonis*; of Robert Barker, the printer of the first portion of the Bodleian Benefactors' Register (Plate 18), who was himself also an early benefactor; of Thomas Man, who sent the very first free book (Plate 41) and of William Leake, whose publisher's device appears on a pirated edition of *Venus and Adonis* (Plate 84).

41. The first book received under the 1610 Agreement, with Bodley's autograph inscription

As described on its titlepage, this is indeed a substantial treatise, here first printed anonymously and in an unauthorized text but reprinted for the same publisher in 1616 under the initials T. C., which are those of its author, the learned Puritan divine Thomas Cartwright, who had died in 1603. The copyright of the text had been entered on 28 November 1610 in the Stationers' Register to Thomas Man, Master of the Stationers' Company, with Jonas Man and Henry Clarke. Despite its more than 300 pages the book was in print less than three months later, for its arrival in Oxford, as the first fruit of the agreement signed in December 1610, was considered to be of sufficient importance to be announced at a meeting of Convocation on 22 February 1611. This announcement was no doubt prompted by the inscription (here reproduced) which Sir Thomas had added in his own hand facing the titlepage after he had received the book from one of its publishers and before he sent it down from London. But he was mistaken in describing Jonas Man as Master of the Stationers' Company; that dignity belonged from July 1610 to July 1611 to Thomas Man (senior) who was Jonas's father. Yet it was doubtless the Master himself who, in the name of the whole Company, selected as a suitable gift the book which he had just published and sent it through his son Jonas to Sir Thomas Bodley at Fulham. Once that agreement could be seen to be actually in operation, the University lost no time in sealing the deed, which was done in Congregation on 27 February 1611.

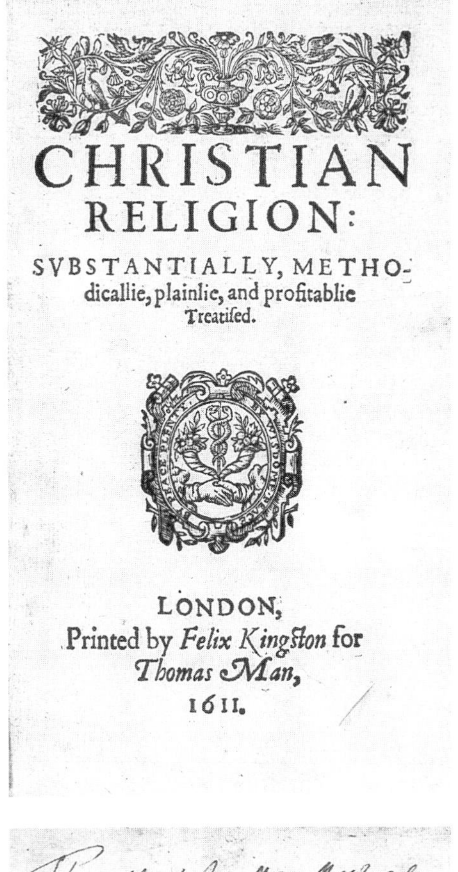

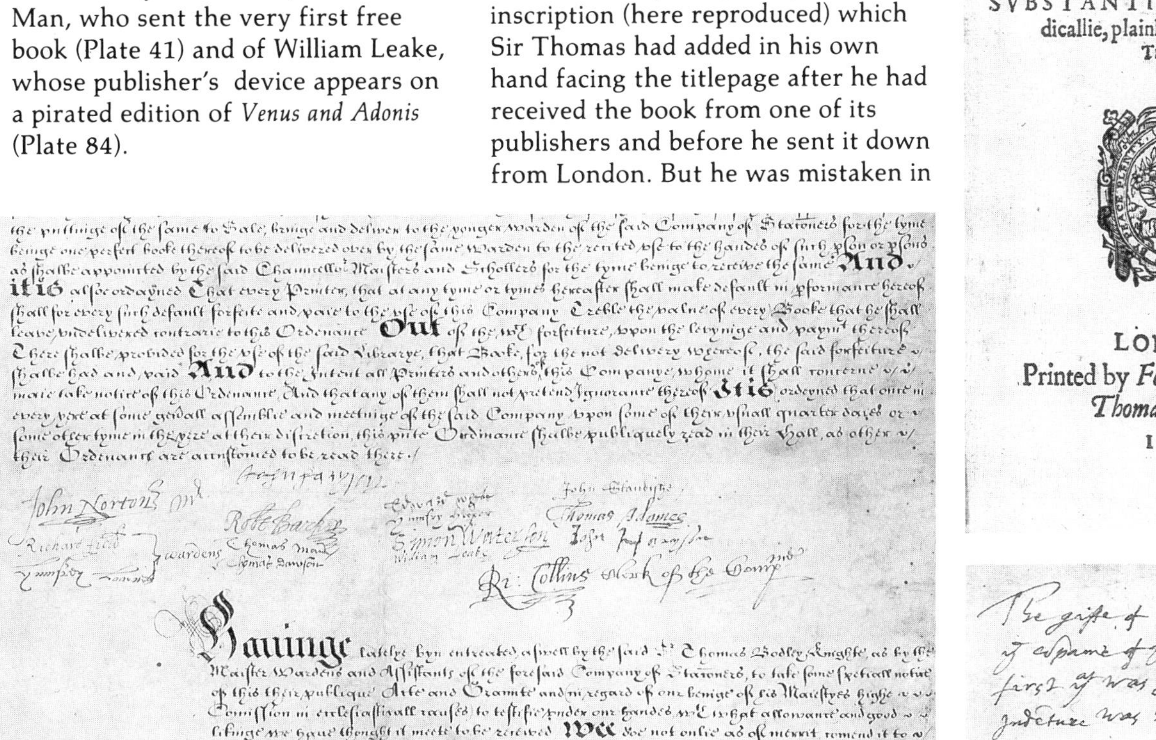

42. Arts End, looking north
Sir Thomas Bodley had taken over the shell, as it were, of Duke Humfrey's Library, which he restored and refilled without structurally altering it. His first original addition to the mediaeval edifice, completed and occupied just prior to his death early in 1613, was a great east wing, of which the upper floor is still called Arts End from being used to house the books of the Arts Faculty. Bodley raised the height of his new roof-ridge above that of the adjacent mediaeval library and also flattened its pitch, so attaining a greater overall height of wall. The large areas thus created along the inner and outer walls were intended for books, since it was the main purpose of the new wing to provide additional shelf-space. Furthermore, for the very first time in any English library the books were shelved against the walls, all the way up from the floor to where the rafters begin. The lofty effect created by these ascending tiers of shelves, with the larger books below and the smaller (which were never chained) above, is wholly satisfying to the eye. Though the design and details are already of the Renaissance, the pattern of its painted ceiling links up with that of the mediaeval one adjoining. The new wing is splendidly lit by its three huge windows.

of Arts of less than two years' standing, whom Bodley only admitted if they behaved with due reverence towards older readers. But he did act upon another suggestion of James's, with results which have remained to the present day of the greatest importance to the Bodleian, and also to other major libraries: this was his agreement made with the Stationers' Company of London in 1610.

Already by the year 1537 King François I had issued a decree to control the printing-press throughout France. By this law, licences to print had to be obtained for all books, and it was made a condition that a copy of every work so licensed and printed be deposited in the royal library, at that time kept in the Château at Blois. This idea of legal deposit was not immediately adopted in England, but during the reign of Queen Mary Tudor the English Crown likewise took control of its country's printing-presses by vesting their exercise in the Company of Stationers of London, whose members alone (excepting afterwards the two Universities) enjoyed the legal right to print. By endowing a trade guild with the management of this potentially lucrative monopoly in return for legal protection for its registered copyrights, the Tudor and later monarchs, through licensing by their bishops and other officers of state, aimed to keep a close censorship over all that was printed. When, therefore, Sir Thomas Bodley arranged a form of agreement between the University of Oxford and the 'Arte or Mistery of Stationers' of London for the latter to supply to his Library a free copy, unbound, of 'all new Books and Copies never printed before', he was placing the Bodleian in a position to receive, from the very source itself, and at no cost, virtually every authorized English-printed book issued from that date onwards 'for ever'.

Understandably, the outcome of this agreement did not fulfil all its initial promise. For a start, only a small part of the Stationers' output in Sir Thomas's time was likely to satisfy his own learned criteria of what was suitable for his Library, and since to begin with he himself operated the collection of copyright books (and others) at his Fulham residence, it seems he acted to exclude most of what he considered 'idle books, and riffe raffes' such, alas, as the vernacular plays and poems of Shakespeare, Marlowe and their contemporaries. Furthermore, some publishers (then and later, and a few even now) begrudged sending even the one agreed free copy, though in return they specifically enjoyed – as they still do – access for ever to their past productions when the need arises for a reprint. To meet the failures to deliver which marred the first year of operating the agreement, a second document was drawn up by the Company itself early in 1612 for its own members. Besides introducing fines for non-compliance, this 'Bye-law' (as it was termed by a later Bodley's Librarian) added to the range of material to be sent free a further category, namely books 'reprinted with additions' – a significant addition in itself and one

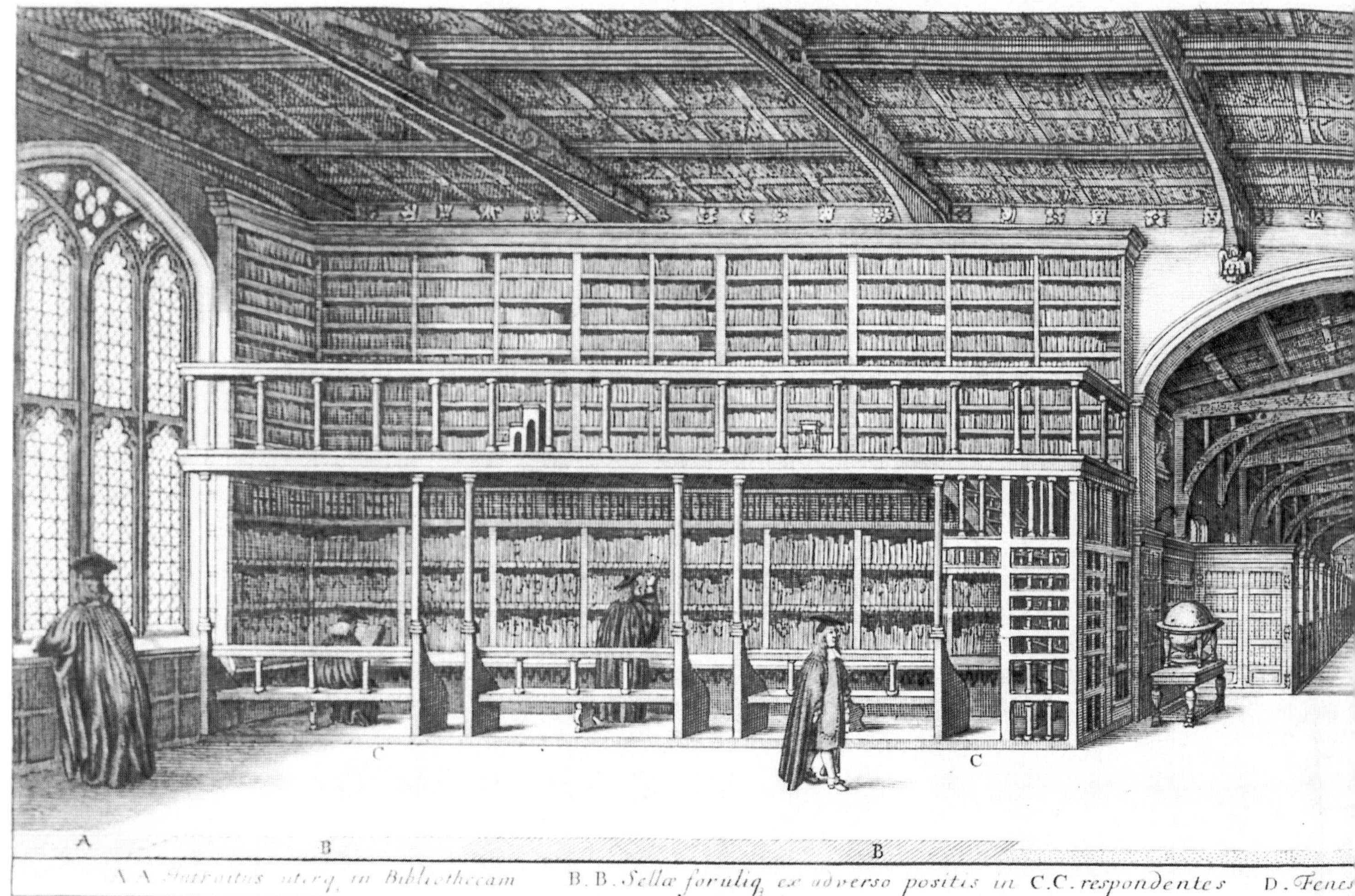

43. **Loggan's view of Arts End, 1675** This engraving, published in 1675, shows the view looking westward down the length of Duke Humfrey with Arts End occupying the foreground. It shows an interior that hardly differs from today's except for the pair of standing globes which have unfortunately since been taken away; such globes, one for the heavens and one for the earth, were formerly standard library furniture.

which initiated a principle which the Bodleian still uses today in its selection of which reprints to demand or not demand from publishers. This enforcement document of 1612 is signed (Plate 40) by the Master, Wardens and Assistants of the Company, and to add further weight to its authority the Archbishop of Canterbury and eighteen members of the Court of High Commission, a powerful state-appointed ecclesiastical body, have added their signatures, promising support.

But although several factors thus combined to limit the benefits which the Library actually derived from the agreement, its signing was a pioneering and far-sighted step, which led eventually to the passing into law of several Copyright Acts, by which the legal deposit of copies in the Bodleian and finally also in other major libraries, became a

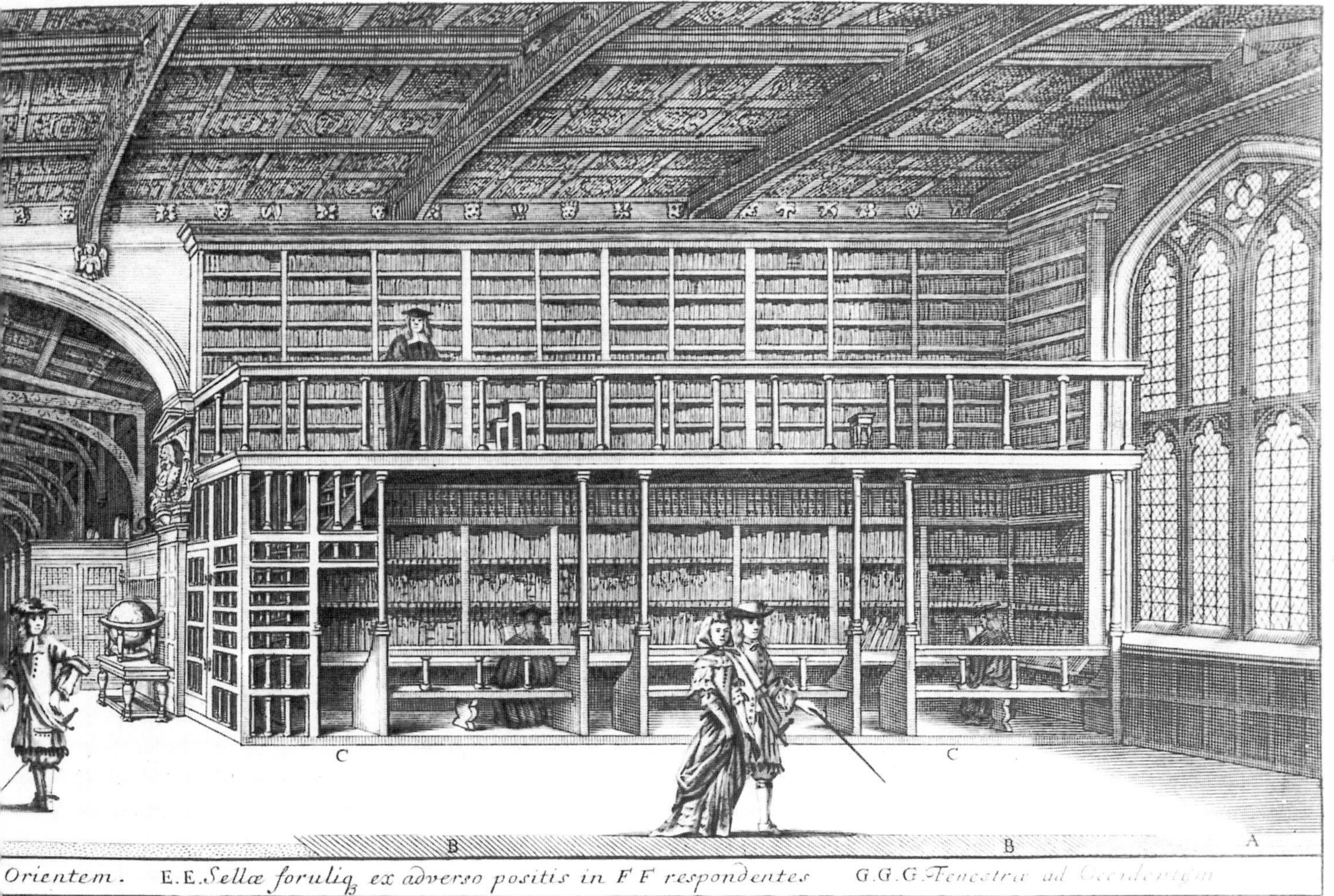

requirement under the Acts, with general and continuing benefit to the whole learned world. The identity of the first book presented, in 1611, under the terms of the newly-completed agreement, was considered worthy of mark by an autograph inscription in Bodley's own hand (Plate 41). His Library had now become what it remained for the next century and a half (until the founding of the British Museum by Parliament in 1753) – in effect *the* national Library.

Already by the time he wrote the preface to his first printed Bodleian *Catalogue* in 1605, which listed nearly 10,000 titles, Thomas James was expressing anxiety not about the influx of books but about the space for storing them. Fortunately the Founder, having so handsomely accomplished the initial task he had undertaken for the University of

44. **The bell-founder's device**
As early as September 1602 Bodley had mentioned in one of his letters to Thomas James, 'A Clocke and a Belle will be needefull for the librarie', and in another letter he refers in June 1604 to having sent a bell. But it seems that this bell did not give full satisfaction, for in 1611 he wrote again, 'As touching the bell, I would have it caste againe & if my frindes thinke it good, made somewhat bigger . . . I pray yow inquire, if the contrey therabout will yeld a bell founder'. It did, and the fruitful outcome of that enquiry was the dignified and sonorous bell we now hear, measuring 18 inches high and weighing approximately 2 cwt. Round its upper part, below the shoulder, runs a gilded inscription: 'SIR THOMAS BODLEY GAVE THIS BELL 1611', and further down is stamped a shield flanked by the initials W. Y., the mark of the bell-founder William Yare. Yare was a son-in-law of Joseph Carter, a noted founder who had bought the famous (and still existing) Whitechapel foundry in 1606 and had died in 1609. On his father-in-law's death Yare succeeded to the foundry at Reading, which was itself a direct successor of that established at nearby Wokingham early in the fourteenth century. His father-in-law had obtained, or copied, many moulding stamps employed by earlier founders, including the shield used here. It came from a Norwich foundry in the fifteenth century, but Carter added his initials I. C. on either side of the lowest bell on the shield. In the same year that he recast Bodley's bell, Yare recast one of the mediaeval bells which had been removed to Christ Church Cathedral from Osney Abbey, which formerly stood near the site of the present Oxford railway station; he also cast bells for the churches at the villages of Horspath (outside Oxford) and of Harwell, south of Abingdon, where three of his bells bear the same shield as the Bodleian bell. William Yare died early in 1617 and the Reading foundry was then closed down, though the same shield was later used again by the original foundry at Norwich.

At first hung outside, probably in some sort of bell-cote at the south-west corner of Duke Humfrey, as shown in Loggan's engraving, Sir Thomas Bodley's bell had to be rehoused in 1637 when Selden End was built, and just over a century later it was taken down and stored away, after which it was forgotten and its function usurped by a hand-bell. Then in 1866 the original bell was found beneath rubbish under the staircase, and was rehung on an iron frame in Selden End. Today it hangs again in the south-west corner of Duke Humfrey but beneath the roof instead of over it, and continues to be rung daily to mark the opening and closing times of the Library.

45. **Sir Thomas Bodley's personal seal** The autograph of the Founder, with the red wax impression of his personal seal, ratifying the deed drawn up in 1609 endowing his Library with the annual income from a farm in Berkshire and certain houses in Distaff Lane, London. The wax seal is still preserved in its round ivory box.

restoring, refurnishing and refilling its mediaeval library building, now showed his customary energy and foresight in meeting the new needs which his own recent success was bringing. Provision of further space to shelve the ever-growing number of books began in the summer of 1610. In the context of plans he himself had suggested to the University in 1611 to replace the tumbledown row of lecture rooms which lay to the east of the Divinity School (as seen in Plate 12), Bodley set about the building of a new wing lying centrally at right angles across the east end of Duke Humfrey's Library and opening directly onto it. The lower storey of the new wing is the high vaulted chamber known as the Proscholium, or entrance hall to the Divinity School, and above this Bodley constructed what became known as 'Arts End', after the books of the Arts faculties had been moved into it in 1612. It displays a transition from mediaeval to Renaissance library styles. Abandoning the chained stall system, the new room, following Continental models, introduces for the first time in Oxford, where it was to have no successors for a century, the system of a lofty room the walls of which were shelved from floor to ceiling, galleries reached by lattice staircases being added to give access to the upper shelves (Plates 42, 43).

The gallery shelves housed the increasing quantity of books of smaller format, which could not bear the weight of chains. Such books were fetched by the staff, the galleries with their unchained contents being closed to readers. The new wing was lit from both its north and south ends, but also principally by its large east window, modelled on the window it replaced which formerly gave light to the mediaeval library from this end. This great window was very soon to give its commanding view onto the new Schools Quadrangle which began to rise beyond. Together with Duke Humfrey's Library, Arts End gives eloquent architectural expression to Bodley's modernising spirit.

To the very end of his life, though distracted for a time by financial worries which fortunately proved to be only temporarily embarrassing, Bodley's personal supervision of all aspects of his Library's well-being continued undiminished. Besides providing it out of his own wealth – he had before starting on his public career taken the sound precaution of marrying a rich widow – with permanent endowment for its upkeep, he also drafted Statutes for its government, and thereby took steps to meet two weaknesses which he had discerned in the Library's mediaeval predecessor, namely the lack of continued funding and the permission (which was normal practice in collegiate life) for scholars to take books out. In his Statutes he expressly forbade the lending of books, a prohibition which to this day ensures that the resources of the Bodleian remain available at all times within its own walls. At the same time, looking back with approval on some aspects of the previous Libraries' ordinances, he drew up rules for the appointment of the Keeper; established the University's role in governing the Library by placing it under a body of Curators including always the Vice-Chancellor and Proctors, who among other duties were expected to count its contents at their annual Visitation; and required that each reader on first admission should take an oath binding him to observe the Library's rules.

In other smaller ways, too, Bodley continued to occupy himself with providing his Library with all that he considered necessary. Thus, as early as 1604 he had presented a bell, the ringing of which was to signal the opening and closing times of the reading room. But the original bell sent down from London did not give satisfaction, and in 1611 a country bell-founder cast for him a larger bell (Plate 44) which still carries out twice daily its donor's purpose.

CHAPTER III

Resources Doubled and Re-doubled

1613–1640

When Sir Thomas Bodley died on 28 January 1613, at the age of sixty-eight, he had already given his Library that permanent provision for its organization, maintenance, and growth which he rightly judged had been totally lacking to its predecessors. He had in fact completed the foundation of a new kind of institution, not merely a university library but, from the start, also a national one with a growing international reputation (350 foreign readers were registered between 1620 and 1640), characteristics which it has retained through later developments, which have in almost all cases been extensions of the Founder's principles. Its policy of acquisition by gift, purchase, and deposit was laid down, its government established, its funding assured, its expansion foreseen. In the autumn after his death, the highly personal supervision which Bodley had exercised over the Library was replaced by statutes, based on his own draft, which vested the control of the Bodleian in a body of Curators, a form of government which still operates. In the matter of finance, he had already in the year 1609 made a deed of endowment (Plate 45) providing a substantial annual income for book purchases out of the rents from landed properties in London and Berkshire. The massive iron chest containing the evidences for this endowment and for his other bequests to the University, was mentioned in Bodley's will and still survives (Plate 47). It was no fault of his foresight that within fewer than thirty years after his death the disturbances caused by the Civil War were largely to nullify this provision and reduce the Library's income to a level so inadequate that for centuries it was difficult to maintain the steady build-up of the collections and also to serve the needs of its readers. It is understandable, though regrettable, that a University made up of a group of self-governing and separately-endowed colleges should have been slow to devise adequate and continuing financial provision for a university institution which, unlike a college, of its nature could not remain roughly static in its size and its annual expenditure. However, for the decades covered by this chapter all seemed set for the full realization of the Founder's far-sighted vision.

By his will, though gossips suggested that his relatives and friends might feel disappointed at their largely token legacies, his bequests to the University were on a magnificent scale. The day after his funeral, the first stone was laid of the Schools Quadrangle, which in his lifetime he had urged the University to build on the site of the tumbledown little schools beyond his new Arts End. Here over the next six years was built, round three sides of a square – the existing Library forming its fourth and western side (Plate 48) – a range of rooms for University lectures; the names of the occupying faculties are still painted above the ground-floor doorways. With typical prescience, Bodley devoted one large part of his legacy to the expense of adding a third storey right

46. **Portrait bust of Sir Thomas Bodley, 1605**
From a handsome ornamental niche on the south side under the great archway leading from Arts End to Duke Humfrey this marble bust of Sir Thomas Bodley still keeps watch over the readers who enter and leave his Library. It was presented in 1605 by the Chancellor of the University, the Earl of Dorset (Plate 15), 'for the perpetual memory of the Founder' and is described as 'carved to the life by an excellent hand at London'. No identification of this 'excellent hand' has yet been suggested. Indeed, although it was already on public display when King James admired it during his first visit here in 1605, this fine contemporary portrait sculpture is still surprisingly unknown and apparently unstudied by art historians. No doubt because it has always been here, and because its lofty position does not allow close access, it has continually been passed by without special notice. It deserves more attention than it has yet received.

round the three new sides of the Quadrangle, to afford 'a very large supplement for stowage of Bookes'. The provision of an imposing entrance to the Quadrangle, as thus heightened, was achieved by constructing at the centre of its eastern range an imposing tower gateway (Plate 49). For much of the Quadrangle a quasi-Gothic style was felt to be suitable and most in harmony with the existing Library, but the ornamentation of the Tower, modelled on that which the same masons from Yorkshire had recently built at Merton College for Bodley's close friend Sir Henry Savile, made use of the contemporary vogue for the Five Orders of neo-classical architecture. An interesting side-light on this vogue is afforded by a gift made to the Library in 1620 by Sir Clement Edmonds, clerk to the Privy Council, of an alabaster geometric model, called at the time, 'a mathematical pillar' which incorporates five columns representing the Five Orders (Plate 50). Sadly, the soft Headington stone used for the original sculptures on the Tower was quick to decay in Oxford's damp climate, so that the seated figure of King James I now to be seen there is not exactly that which, double-gilt, so dazzled the monarch's own eyes on a visit he paid from Woodstock in 1620. Entrance into the Quadrangle from Catte Street was provided under the Tower through the Great Gate (Plate 51). Besides providing for the third storey of the Schools Quadrangle and its roofing, Bodley's bequests were also intended to

47. **Sir Thomas Bodley's 'blacke Iron Chest'**
The safekeeping of money and valuables posed obvious problems in the days before bank vaults and strong-rooms; it was common during the Middle Ages to use a really heavy metal chest, difficult for thieves to carry off unnoticed, and to fasten it with several locks, the various keys being held by different officials so that no one key-holder alone could gain access. Bodley's personal strong-box, containing the deeds of his properties and endowments, is mentioned in his will as 'my blacke Iron Chest', which he ordained should be painted, as can still be seen, in 'oyel coulers'. The University decreed in 1613 that it should be kept in Corpus Christi College along with the University Chest, which to this day gives its name to the University's administrative department. Bodley's Chest was finally brought to the Library in 1622 and continued in use as a safe as late as 1774, when it was found to contain only £25-worth of outdated guinea pieces. Nowadays it stands in the Divinity School and receives on behalf of the Friends of the Bodleian the donations of visitors, who can especially admire the beauty and intricacy of the metalwork of the locking mechanism under the lid.

make possible a link between the new Quadrangle and the eastern wing (Arts End) which he had added across the end of Duke Humfrey's Library. His will speaks of 'two Lobies or passages . . . to make a faire enterance into ye north & south corners'; it also speaks of making a 'faire storie case [staircase] to make ye ascent more easye & gracefull to ye first great Librarie', reminding us that while Bodley lived both Duke Humfrey's Library, and hence Arts End too, could still only be reached by means of the two mediaeval turret stairways at its far (western) end. Both purposes, that of linking up with the new Quadrangle, and that of making a more dignified, and less steep, means of ascent to the Old Library, were eventually achieved through Bodley's legacy by the building of the two staircases which stand out at the corners of the Quadrangle (Plate 48). Their ultimate completion enabled the turret staircases to be done away with when Bodley's third project, a wing

48. **The Schools Quadrangle, looking west**

This is the view to be seen on entering the Schools Quadrangle through the Great Gate (Plate 51). Opposite stands Sir Thomas Bodley's first addition to the mediaeval Library, his East Wing built in 1610–12. By way of modulating the transition to this partially Renaissance building from its Gothic neighbour, all its exterior walls are delicately ribbed with tall panels which take up the vertical tracery of the Perpendicular windows of the Divinity School and lead the eye upwards towards the aspiring row of crocketted pinnacles. These pinnacles, and the crenellated parapet from which they spring were repeated from the roof-line of the mediaeval building, and later were carried on round the roofs of the whole Quadrangle and also of the later West Wing. They crown the whole complex with a rich and unified skyline, well enjoyed in an aerial view (see the endpapers of this book).

The ribbing was continued on the outer walls of the two staircase projections jutting out at each end of the wing, which were added in accordance with Bodley's bequest to give access to the Library from the newly-constructed Quadrangle. In the rest of the Quadrangle the walls were left plain, but the vertical emphasis is here taken up by the tracery of the extremely large windows which give maximum illumination to the interior. These have proved especially valuable since most of the interior is occupied today by reading rooms. The centre of Bodley's East Wing is pierced by one huge Gothic window, lighting Arts End (Plate 42), and below it is the doorway giving access to the Proscholium and the Divinity School, which now forms the public entrance to the Old Library. Over the door a tablet was placed in 1622 commemorating Bodley's benefaction to the University and the world of letters. From this angle the doorway acts as a frame for the bronze statue of the Earl of Pembroke (Plate 71).

49. **The Tower of the Five Orders**
It was Sir Thomas Bodley's generosity and foresight in adding, at his own expense, a third storey right round the Schools Quadrangle that caused the first change of plan for the building of a tower gateway to give entrance to the Quadrangle from the street. At first, Bodley's Library, which formed its west side, was to be the Quadrangle's main feature, but the newly-added extra height of the other three sides called for a shift of the architectural centre of interest. Inspiration from Merton, and perhaps a desire to outshine nearby Wadham, led to a new plan for a five-storey tower of which the inner face should be richly ornamented, while the outer, facing into Catte Street, was to be left relatively plain. For its ornamentation the currently popular 'Five Orders of Architecture' were chosen, and by 1619 the five-storey Tower was already constructed. Before the ornamental carving was completed, however, King James presented the University with his *Works* (Plate 59) and this was made the occasion for another change, whereby an existing window on the fourth floor was replaced by a large canopied niche. Here the giving of the royal volume was enacted in stone; the seated monarch was portrayed handing one copy of his writings to Fame, who stands with trumpet at the ready, while the other hand bestows another copy on the suitably humble kneeling figure of the University. Although age and decay have robbed the whole design of the gilding and paintwork with which it once sparkled, the Tower of the Five Orders can still be enjoyed as a surprisingly successful marriage of the grave and sober Gothicising of Sir Thomas Bodley's structure with the exuberant overlay of his friend Sir Henry Savile's preferred neo-classicism.

across the western end to match the eastern wing Arts End, came to be undertaken, also at his expense, some twenty years after his death.

Proof has recently come to light that, for the interior of the splendid three-sided Gallery (now the Upper Reading Room) with which Bodley's bequest had adorned the top floor of the Schools Quadrangle, the ornamentation was planned, about the years 1616–18, by Bodley's partner in the creation of the Library, Thomas James (Plate 36) the first Librarian. Unfortunately, poor workmanship in the original woodwork and roof resulted later in centuries of progressive damage, until finally in 1830 Robert Smirke, the architect of the British Museum, felt compelled to advise the complete replacement of the original Gallery roof and ceiling. When this was done the richly painted wooden beams and panels, similar to those in Duke Humfrey (Plate 38) and Arts End (Plate 42) were destroyed (except for a few panels preserved by the intervention of Dr Bandinel, then Bodley's Librarian) and were replaced with the white plaster ceiling the Gallery now has. Further, Smirke's new plasterwork was carried down the walls to the level of the bookcases below, thereby obliterating the other feature which gave an additional richness to the original *décor*, its Painted Frieze. Most of what was known about this Frieze was preserved through the tireless note-taking of Thomas Hearne who had published in 1725 a list of more than two hundred heads in medallions which in his time still formed a continuous series along the top of the walls.

But in 1949 a chance repair to a patch of Smirke's plasterwork revealed that the original Frieze still remained, painted directly onto the wall surface and since hidden by the nineteenth-century plaster. Although it had been seriously damaged, the entire Frieze was uncovered and sympathetically restored over the next six years, and its layout at last became fully intelligible. Thomas James, using chiefly contemporary published collections of portraits such as Beza's *Icones virorum illustrium*, 1580, for the heads of Reformers, and Thevet's *Portraits des hommes illustres*, 1584, for the sages of antiquity and the early Church Fathers, arranged for the visitor (in what was to become the country's earliest public Picture Gallery) a panorama of writers chosen from among those whose works already reposed on the shelves of the adjacent Library. Along the southern wing his choice – and it is here that the influence of James is most unmistakably manifested – was intended to demonstrate a theological thesis: that from the sub-Apostolic church through the Middle Ages and Reformation up to Jacobean England there had been a continuity of written witness against the pretensions of the Roman Church, a thesis he had constantly reiterated in his own published books of controversy.

Along the north range he gathered the writers in the faculty of Arts, starting with Homer and ending with Sir Philip Sidney. Around the

Tower Room, which forms the centre of the whole design, are grouped prominent authors in the fields of Medicine and Law. The Frieze thus illustrates iconographically the layout of the books as they were placed in the Library alongside, classified according to the fourfold sub-division of the mediaeval faculties. In the Tower Room itself a further discovery revealed that above an elaborate plaster ceiling installed in 1753 still lay intact the beams and the thirty-six panels of the original Jacobean painted ceiling. Modern engineering proved equal to the task of removing the fine plaster-work of 1753 bodily and re-installing it two floors up, so that it adds grace and dignity to what is at present the Upper Archives Room where the University keeps its own archives. The section of original ceiling thus revealed in the Tower Room, combined with the Frieze below it (Plate 54) gives the best idea we can form of the rich effect the whole interior must have presented when new.

Whereas the Frieze portraits of contemporaries (Plates 52, 53, 55, 56) are doubtless authentic likenesses, many heads representing persons of earlier centuries were derived from picture-books and have no claim to be other than imaginary. There are some exceptions, such as Chaucer, whose features had already long been familiar to the public. Understandably, the men (Sappho is the only woman in the Frieze) of the previous century such as Humphrey, Bodley's tutor, tended to be more authentically portrayed (Plates 52, 53, 55, 56). One pleasant example shows remarkable fidelity to what was then accepted as a portrait from life: a manuscript presented to the Library in 1620 by Sir Henry Savile contained what was in fact a miniature by a fifteenth-century French artist in which the Oxford friar Roger Bacon, who died in 1294, was depicted deep in thought, head in hand (Plate 57). This was faithfully copied, pose and all, by whichever painter represented the head of Friar Bacon for the Frieze; this painter's name, and those of two or three others whose handiwork can be distinguished, have unfortunately not been discovered. Time has treated the Frieze unkindly, and its condition remains precarious. But although there have been losses, damage, and some poor repainting in the past, nevertheless the general effect of this decorative procession of illustrious writers starting in Classical Antiquity and ending with contemporaries who had personally helped Bodley and James, is still striking indeed. It was never a great work of art, but it remains a monument, without parallel in Britain, to the tastes and attitudes of the Library's founding fathers.

Besides the Frieze, with all the detailed planning and supervision it must have involved, Thomas James also brought to completion an even more elaborate and important undertaking, the publication in 1620 of the second printed *Catalogue* of the whole Bodleian collection of books. It can have fallen to the lot of few men in any age to have

50. **'The mathematical pillar', showing the Five Orders**
A five-sided pillar, 22 inches high, of carved alabaster, representing on each side one of the orders of classical architecture: Tuscan, Doric, Ionic, Corinthian, and Composite. It is surmounted by a large alabaster skeleton dodecahedron (the Platonic symbol of the heavens) enclosing a semi-circular brass solid of sixty faces, made up of a dodecahedron or a truncated icosahedron, with five equilateral triangles on each side of its pentagonal faces. The pillar was originally surrounded by ten Platonic or Pythagorean solids, including a cube, a pyramid, a dodecahedron, and two halves of an octahedron; three are now missing. The whole is supported on a heavy wooden base with two large wrought-iron carrying handles.

This model, now on display in the Museum of the History of Science, was presented to the Bodleian in 1620 by Sir Clement Edmonds (?1564–1622), Clerk of the Council and Fellow of All Souls. For centuries this enigmatic object was one of the treasures of the Bodleian; it was shown, for instance, to Uffenbach in 1710, who made special mention of it without divining its meaning. Significantly, this gift was made close to the time of the foundation of the Oxford Professorships of Geometry and Astronomy by Bodley's friend, Sir Henry Savile, in 1619. There may also be a connection with the Tower of the Five Orders (Plate 49), with its ascending sets of columns depicting the same classical orders of architecture. In the Tower two rooms were assigned to the two Savilian Professors, and here were kept the books, manuscripts and instruments given for the Professors' use by Sir Henry Savile himself.

The pillar may have been used to facilitate studies in solid geometry and in perspective, and it has been suggested that the two uppermost geometrical figures represent the celestial and sub-lunary spheres, expressing harmony and discord, concord and dissonance. The same ancient ideas of cosmic harmony, expressed in music and by the Pythagorean solids, were the building bricks of the universe described in Johann Kepler's *Harmonia Mundi*, which appeared in 1619; they were also the inspiration for his three famous Laws, on which rests the foundation of modern astronomy.

51. **The Great Gate leading to the Schools Quadrangle**
As part of its grand ceremonial entrance through the Tower of the Five Orders (Plate 49), the University fitted this ornate pair of oak doors to the Great Gate which faces into Catte Street and opens a passage through to the new Schools Quadrangle. Made of sturdy oak from Wytham Woods, its panels bear painted shields including those of the King and of Charles, Prince of Wales, and also of all the then-existing colleges, including nearby Wadham, so recently completed in its impeccable Jacobean style. The gate was formerly kept closed on all except special University occasions, for which it is still used. It also served as a public noticeboard for solemn University pronouncements, for example the sentence of Convocation depriving a notorious offender of his degree. Today, visitors and readers can enter the Quadrangle through its wicket-door, which is open daily.

52a. **Frieze portrait of Richard Eedes**
52b. **Arms of Richard Eedes**
52c. **Crest of Richard Eedes**

Educated at Westminster School and Christ Church, Eedes in his younger years had made himself such a reputation as a Latin poet as to be included by Francis Meres in a celebrated passage in his *Wit's Treasury*, published in 1598: 'These are our best for Tragedie, the Lord Buckhurst [Plate 15] . . . Doctor Edes of Oxforde, . . . Marlow . . . Kid, Shakespeare, Drayton, Chapman, Decker and Benjamin Johnson . . .' Nothing of Eedes was published, however, except six sermons in 1604 and a further three in 1627. By the date of Meres's tribute Eedes had become a noted preacher, and had been made a chaplain to Queen Elizabeth and appointed Dean of Worcester Cathedral, where ultimately he was to be buried after his death in 1604. King James I also made him a royal chaplain and nominated him as an Oxford divine to join the panel to which was allotted large portions of the New Testament to be translated for the King James Bible, or Authorized Version, eventually published in 1611. But Eedes was prevented from taking any part in this task by his death at the age of only forty-nine. It was obviously his reputation as a divine and a preacher, and his early benefaction to the Library, which earned him his presence in the Bodleian Frieze. His portrait (Plate 52a) is placed between that of his own father-in-law, Bishop Herbert Westphaling (also a benefactor to the Library in the same year as Eedes) and that of Thomas Sparke (Plate 53). Eedes's own gift of £13 6s 4d had been made in 1601 and was used to purchase fourteen folio volumes, on the covers of which the Library caused to be stamped in gilt a shield with his arms on it (Plate 52b). That he formed a library of his own is indicated by the presence on Bodley's shelves of several volumes with his autograph in them, as well as at least four in limp vellum bearing the lion's paw crest (Plate 52c) which is found on his tomb in Worcester Cathedral. Oddly, despite his appearance in the gallery of writers, Eedes's 1604 volume of sermons, printed just before his death and without his permission, figures in no Bodleian printed catalogue before 1674, while the posthumous edition in 1627 of three further sermons was not acquired by the Library until 1931.

53. **Frieze portrait of Thomas Sparke**
The portrait of Dr Thomas Sparke, another Oxford divine, preacher and writer, occupies the place in the Frieze next to that of Dr Richard Eedes (Plate 52a). Sparke was born in Lincolnshire and educated at Magdalen College and it was no doubt his reputation as one of the leading divines of the Puritan party within the Church of England which caused Thomas James to choose him for inclusion here. Appointed Rector of Bletchley in Buckinghamshire in 1578, he died there just over thirty-eight years later, and the date of his death, 1616, entered on the inscription round his portrait, provides a valuable indication of the period at which the Frieze was being painted, since no other of its persons bears a later obit. Two of his works, both printed at Oxford, were added to the Library between 1605 and 1620, about the time this portrait was painted.

published two complete but separate catalogues of a single great library, and both those by James are pioneer works, of importance also in the whole history of library development. Whereas his 1605 *Catalogue* (Plate 39) had been principally a shelf-list, by subject and size, with a lengthy author-index, his new *Catalogue* was a single alphabetical arrangement by authors and its size reflected the enormous growth of the contents of the Library, the entire Bodleian holdings having more than trebled since his earlier *Catalogue* of fifteen years before. The publication of the 1605 *Catalogue* had been paid for, somewhat reluctantly, by Sir Thomas Bodley himself; the expense of printing the new *Catalogue* was to be recouped, so the Curators hoped, by an ordinance that all future readers must buy a copy. At two shillings each this was not an unrealistic levy, and in the first two years the Librarian sold 270 copies, but unfortunately time has rendered it a condition of entry which it is no longer practicable to enforce.

With its nearly 600 pages, including items added while printing was in progress, the new *Catalogue* was going through the Oxford Press in the summer of 1620, just after its compiler Thomas James had at length resigned his arduous duties as Bodley's Librarian in May of that year and had been succeeded by John Rous, a Fellow of Oriel. While it was still printing, King James sent the University a copy of his *Opera* – the Latin translation of his collected works – bound in red velvet stamped with the royal arms (Plate 59). The gift was brought to Oxford by the Royal Librarian, Patrick Young, whose father had contrived to circumvent the promise the King had once made to let Sir Thomas Bodley choose what books he wished out of the libraries of the various royal palaces. The royal volume was received with great ceremony at a special Convocation in St Mary's Church, whence it was carried in procession on a cushion by the Vice-Chancellor, to be locked in a safe cupboard at the Library. The new Librarian, Rous,

54. **Painted ceiling and Frieze in the Tower Room**
A corner of the Tower Room, here pictured, shows the only portion of the original painted wooden ceiling panels which still survives in place in the Schools Quadrangle. The entire range of what is now the Upper Reading Room, which formerly housed England's earliest picture gallery, was once covered with this type of ceiling, while the continuous band of the Painted Frieze ran along the walls below it. In 1753 this Tower Room was given a false ceiling of decorative plasterwork, and it was only thus that, after the rest of the ceiling had been replaced in 1830 and the whole Frieze covered up, this one fragment alone remained, though hidden. The recent removal of the plaster has now revealed this precious glimpse of the splendidly rich effect which the combination of ceiling and Frieze must once have produced right down the three spacious lengths of the Old Library's uppermost floor.

55. **Frieze portraits of Matthiolus and Vesalius**
As seen in Plate 54, the Frieze series of portrait heads in oval frames is linked together by a band of continuous background against which are represented very often books, open or closed, but also objects symbolic of the adjacent writers' own special distinctions. Thus, in the pair here reproduced we can see on either side of the head of the great Sienese physician and botanist Pietro Andrea Mattioli an open herbal, a bottle, and a hand grasping a spray of foliage, to call to mind that the study of botany (as exemplified in the collected works of Matthiolus himself published at Frankfurt in 1598, a copy of which was already in the Library when the Frieze was being painted) was chiefly inspired by the wish to describe species for their medicinal usefulness.

Next to this botanist is pictured one of the most celebrated anatomists of the sixteenth century, the Flemish Andreas Vesalius, two of whose works are duly to be found in the printed Bodleian *Catalogue* of 1605. His portrait (a likeness certainly copied from the engraving by his fellow-countryman, Philippe Galle, in his *Virorum Doctorum Effigies* of 1572, a copy of which was available, before 1620, among the Arts books in the Library alongside) is very appropriately accompanied by a skull and other human bones.

greeted the acquisition with 'a verie prettie Speech' reported Young 'and placed it *in archivis* . . . with a great deale of respect'. The King felt pleased and flattered, the more so, a contemporary gossip alleged, because a similar gift to Cambridge had evoked only an adulatory letter from her Public Orator, the poet George Herbert. But Oxford's expressions of gratitude went further; the royal gift was given an entire page to itself in the Benefactors' Register, while at the Press those pages of the new *Catalogue* already printed with the details of the monarch's published writings as then held by the Bodleian, were cancelled and two new leaves inserted (Plate 60) to allow added typographic emphasis to the royal entry. There was a change of mind, too, in the decoration chosen for the still uncompleted Tower of the Five Orders (Plate 49), where in the fourth storey a window facing westwards into the Quadrangle was now blocked out. In its place was substituted a niche containing the now familiar sculptured group representing the King in the act of bestowing his *Works* on the University. Here the King's likeness was based on the engraved portrait of him by Simon van der Passe which had adorned those *Works*, and the original sculpture was double-gilt. But, alas, for once flattery had overtopped the royal appetite for it and James ordered the statues to be whitewashed and repainted in ordinary colours.

Meanwhile, the Bodleian still continued to arouse a pleasingly widespread interest and support. The Benefactors' Register records gifts and bequests not only from the learned and the wealthy but also from persons in many different walks of life: manuscripts, coins, printed books in various languages, and sums of money were given, for example, by two London scriveners, a professor from Leiden, the University carrier, various merchants and country clergymen, one of Bodley's own personal servants, and the Town-Clerk of Oxford. Some

56. **Frieze portraits of John Rainolds and Laurence Humphrey**

Though Sir Thomas Bodley was already dead before the Frieze was conceived and executed, a place was made in it for Laurence Humphrey, the Regius Professor of Divinity who was his Oxford tutor at Magdalen College when the Founder matriculated there in 1560 at the age of fifteen. Humphrey, a friend of Bodley's father and a fellow-exile during Queen Mary's reign, became President of the College and D.D. during young Bodley's time there, and later Dean of Winchester. He was a noted orator, patristic scholar, and a prolific Puritan controversial writer; the three works of his recorded in the 1605 printed Bodleian *Catalogue* had doubled in number before the second *Catalogue* was printed in 1620, even though Humphrey had died thirty years earlier.

His companion on the Frieze, likewise represented in the 1605 *Catalogue* by three of his writings, was Dr John Rainolds. This portrait occupies the place of honour over the Tower Arch and is derived, as are other near-contemporary versions, from the half-length effigy on his monument in the chapel of Corpus Christi College, where he was President from 1598 till his death in 1607. Like Humphrey, Rainolds was also a noted biblical scholar, controversialist and divine of strongly Puritan convictions; although he had apparently acted in a woman's part in front of Queen Elizabeth on her first visit to Oxford in 1562, his tract *Th'Overthrow of Stage-Playes* shows that long before her second visit in 1592 he had publicly attacked all theatrical performances, even those university dramas which were acted on royal occasions at Oxford. On this visit Queen Elizabeth is reported openly to have rebuked Dr Rainolds for his 'obstinate preciseness' (i.e., Puritan intransigence); later, James I chose him as the leading Puritan spokesman at the Hampton Court Conference in 1604, the chief outcome of which was the translation which became the King James's Bible or Authorized Version, in which Rainolds took a prominent part. After his death in 1607 his large and valuable library was widely distributed under the terms of his will; the Bodleian received forty volumes and many others went to enrich the libraries of his own College of Corpus and of the other colleges to which he had belonged in his long Oxford career. Finally, after bequests of books to many friends and former pupils, the residue was distributed to promising Oxford students, nearly 300 in number, chosen by his executors.

57. **Portrait miniature and Frieze portrait of Roger Bacon**
It shows the early strength of the Bodleian holdings in English mediaeval learning that by the time the Frieze was completed the Library contained at least nine volumes at different shelfmarks embracing various works of Roger Bacon, the thirteenth-century Oxford Franciscan philosopher and natural scientist, whose name later passed into popular legend. Six of these volumes were manuscripts, but curiously the three printed editions then held did not include the two medical works edited in 1590 at Oxford from the press of the printer of the 1605 *Catalogue*.

When choice was to be made for a portrait of Bacon for the Frieze, someone, probably Thomas James himself, lighted on a manuscript of his treatise on old age, which must have belonged at the time to Sir Henry Savile, though shortly afterwards, in 1620, presented by him to the Bodleian. A miniature in this manuscript, drawn in two colours by a fifteenth-century French artist, shows the Friar seated at the doorway of his convent, deep in thought. The Frieze painter has copied this original most exactly, except that in the resulting portrait the Friar himself has benefited from his own prescriptions and has gained a younger and fresher complexion.

donors were, of course, figures of eminence in public life, such as the poet and former diplomat Sir Henry Wotton, then Provost of Eton, who had already given a manuscript Koran in 1604; in 1633 he gave two books doubtless acquired during his own long sojourns as English ambassador at Venice, the one a manuscript which had formerly belonged to Cardinal Bembo, the other a copy of Tycho Brahe's *Astronomiae instauratae mechanica*, 1598 (Plate 61) which the Danish astonomer had presented, with autograph additions, to the Doge. Another eminent donor was Francis Bacon. In 1605 he had sent his friend Sir Thomas Bodley his newly published treatise *Of the . . . Advancement of Learning* with a letter greeting the Founder as a fellow worker in that enterprise, but this presentation volume was evidently discarded as a duplicate after Selden's library brought in another copy, and that Bacon gift is no longer in the Bodleian. Misfortune also befell the copy of a 1613 edition of his *Essayes*, of which the sheets received from the Stationers were found at Oxford to be incomplete and so could not be bound, nor was there any procedure for its replacement. But when Bacon translated his *Advancement of Learning* into Latin and published it in an expanded form in 1623 as the first volume of a projected edition of his collected works, he presented a copy to Oxford University richly bound in velvet (Plate 62) and bearing a special, very characteristic inscription (Plate 63).

Sir Thomas Bodley's general misgivings about books in English being suitable for the great institution of international learning he was planning to found – very few people outside England could in those

continued on page 80

PARTHENIA
or
THE MAYDENHEAD
of the first musicke that
euer was printed for the VIRGINALLS.
COMPOSED
By three famous Masters: William Byrd, Dr. John Bull, & Orlando Gibbons,
Gentilmen of his Ma:ties most Illustrious Chappell.

58. **The first engraved music in England, c. 1613**

The virginals, the earliest of the harpsichord family of musical instruments, were possibly so named from their frequent use for domestic chamber playing by young ladies, a connection further underlined by the title of this book, *Parthenia* (Maiden's songs). One such young player was Dorothy Evans, here charmingly pictured by the engraver William Hole whose volume, if not the first printed music for this instrument (as claimed on the titlepage), was certainly the earliest music in Britain printed from engraved metal plates. From this period copperplate engraving gradually came to supersede typesetting in music publishing all over Europe.

Parthenia consists largely of Pavanes and Galliards, written by three of the most celebrated English musicians of the day. Its titlepage bears no date, but as the first issue, printed for Dorothy Evans herself, included a leaf of dedication to Frederick, the Elector Palatine, and 'his betrothed Lady Elizabeth', daughter of King James I, who were married on 14 February 1613, it must have been in print before that wedding date. It has not hitherto been known how much later the book was made more publicly available, having its former dedication leaf now discarded, and instead the words 'Dedicated to all the Maisters and Lovers of Musick' fitted onto the title plate while its imprint was altered from the private one 'Lond: print: for Mris Dor: Evans' to the more general one here shown. This Bodleian copy, however, probably received in sheets direct from the Stationers' Company under the recent agreement, is listed in Library Records as sent out to a local Oxford bookbinder, Christopher Barber, for binding on 7 February 1614, a date which finally establishes that the public issue must have followed the private one within less than a twelvemonth.

59. **Presentation binding on King James's *Opera*, 1620**

Velvet, despite the tendency of its nap to wear away if much handled, has nevertheless often been chosen as the material for binding books of special value or importance. So the volume containing a 1620 issue of the Latin translation of King James's collected *Works* was clothed in red velvet for presentation by its royal author to Oxford University. The University had already received a copy of the 1619 issue of this translation, bearing, besides the King's autograph, a flattering inscription in the hand of Sir Robert Naunton, the King's Secretary of State. The olive-green morocco binding of this earlier gift is quite unlike that of the 1620 gift, here illustrated. It was this second copy, likewise autographed by the royal donor, and inscribed this time by Sir Giles Calvert (who had succeeded Naunton as Secretary of State) which was solemnly carried in procession from the University Church to a special place in the Bodleian. Certainly the original condition of this volume has been preserved notably well; the binding, employing a technique of leather onlays, tooled in gilt and painted, which are very unusual on a velvet binding, can be recognized by the tools (including the thistle stamped at each corner direct onto the velvet) as the work of a craftsman only recently identified. This was John Bateman, who, with his son Abraham, had received in 1604 a life appointment to 'the office of Bookebynder to his ma[jes]tie within the Realme of Englande' at a fee of £6 per year.

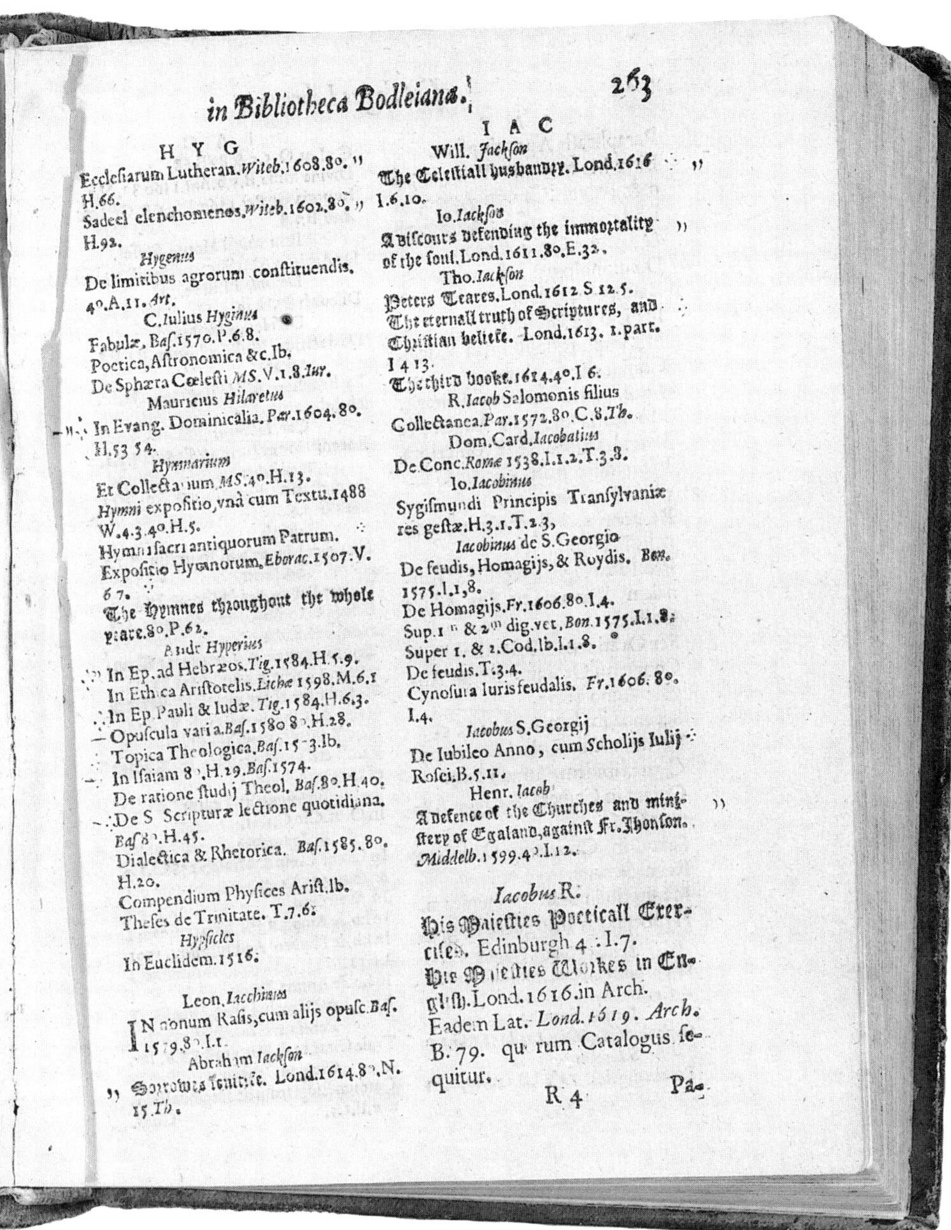

in Bibliotheca Bodleiana. 263

H Y G

Ecclesiarum Lutheran. *Witeb.* 1608.8°.
H.66.
Sadeel elenchomenos. *Witeb.* 1602.8°.
H.92.

Hygenus
De limitibus agrorum conſtituendis.
4°.A.11. *Art.*

C. Iulius *Hyginus*
Fabulæ, *Baſ.* 1570.P.6.8.
Poetica, Aſtronomica &c. Ib.
De Sphæra Cœleſti *MS.* V.1.8. *Iur.*

Mauricius *Hilaretus*
In Evang. Dominicalia. *Par.* 1604.8°.
H.53 54.

Hymnarium
Et Collectaneum *MS.* 4°.H.13.
Hymni expoſitio, vnà cum Textu. 1488
W.4.3.4°.H.5.
Hymni ſacri antiquorum Patrum.
Expoſitio Hymnorum, *Eborac.* 1507.V.
67.
The Hymnes throughout the whole yeare. 8°.P.62.

Andr. *Hyperius*
In Ep. ad Hebræos. *Tig.* 1584.H.5.9.
In Ethica Ariſtotelis. *Lichæ* 1598.M.6.1
In Ep. Pauli & Iudæ. *Tig.* 1584.H.6.3.
Opuſcula varia. *Baſ.* 1580 8°.H.28.
Topica Theologica. *Baſ.* 15‑3. Ib.
In Iſaiam 8°.H.29. *Baſ.* 1574.
De ratione ſtudij Theol. *Baſ.* 8°.H.40.
De S. Scripturæ lectione quotidiana.
Baſ. 8°.H.45.
Dialectica & Rhetorica. *Baſ.* 1585.8°.
H.20.
Compendium Phyſices Ariſt. Ib.
Theſes de Trinitate. T.7.6.

Hypſicles
In Euclidem. 1516.

Leon. *Iacchinus*
IN nonum Raſis, cum alijs opuſc. *Baſ.*
1579.8°.I.1.

Abraham *Iackſon*
Sorrowes ſeuitiue. Lond. 1614.8°.N.
15. *Th.*

I A C

Will. *Jackſon*
The Celeſtiall husbandry. Lond. 1616
I.6.10.

Io. *Iackſon*
A diſcours defending the immortality
of the ſoul. Lond. 1611.8°.E.32.

Tho. *Iackſon*
Peters Teares. Lond. 1612 S 12.5.
The eternall truth of Scriptures, and
Chriſtian beliefe. Lond. 1613. 1. part.
I 4 13.
The third booke. 1614.4°.I 6.

R. *Iacob* Salomonis filius
Collectanea. *Par.* 1572.8°.C.8. *Th.*

Dom. Card. *Iacobatius*
De Conc. *Romæ* 1538.I.1.2.T.3.3.

Io. *Iacobinus*
Sygiſmundi Principis Tranſylvaniæ
res geſtæ. H.3.1.T.2.3.

Iacobinus de S. Georgio
De feudis, Homagijs, & Roydis. *Bon.*
1575.I.1,8.
De Homagijs. *Fr.* 1606.8°.I.4.
Sup. 1^m & 2^m dig. vet, *Bon.* 1575.I.1.8.
Super 1. & 2. Cod. Ib. I.1.8.
De feudis. T.3.4.
Cynoſura Iuris feudalis. *Fr.* 1606. 8°.
I.4.

Iacobus S. Georgij
De Iubileo Anno, cum Scholijs Iulij
Roſci. B.5.11.

Henr. *Iacob*
A defence of the Churches and miniſtery of England, againſt Fr. Ihonſon.
Middelb. 1599.4°.I.12.

Iacobus R.
His Maieſties Poeticall Exerciſes. Edinburgh 4°.I.7.
His Maieſties Workes in Engliſh. Lond. 1616. in Arch.
Eadem Lat. *Lond.* 1619. *Arch.*
B. 79. quorum Catalogus ſequitur.

R 4 Pa-

60. **A cancel leaf of the 1620 Bodleian printed *Catalogue***

Just as the presentation to the Library by King James I of his collected *Works* (Plate 59) had led to an alteration of the ornamentation of the Tower of the Five Orders (Plate 49) to allow for the insertion of a seated statue of the King in the very act of presentation, so, too, alterations to the second *Catalogue* of the whole Library, which was then currently at the press, were made as a direct reaction to the same royal gift.

Thomas James had retired from his post at the beginning of May 1620, just before the gift was received. On the titlepage of his new *Catalogue* he therefore describes himself as 'lately Chief Librarian' (a Sub-Librarian had first been appointed in the year 1606) and proudly, but justifiably, claims his work would be of use to librarians and private collectors throughout Europe. It was indeed a great advance on his earlier *Catalogue* of 1605; when Bodley died, James was able to shelve manuscripts and printed books apart, as he had always wished to do, though both are here listed together in a single alphabetical sequence of authors, far easier to consult than the subject shelf-list *Catalogue* he had printed in 1605. Besides describing a much-enlarged total of volumes, this was the earliest such author catalogue of any great European public library ever printed, and it pioneered cataloguing procedures and set standards which were influential far outside Oxford.

Bodley himself had paid, albeit reluctantly, for the publication of James's first *Catalogue* in 1605. This time the Curators had to finance the printing, which cost £112 10s, and they aimed to recoup the expense by legislating in 1621 that every reader admitted thenceforward should purchase a copy, price two shillings – an ordinance which has since unfortunately been dropped. In all but a handful of surviving copies the leaf as here pictured has been reprinted (as was the corresponding leaf in the 36-page last-minute Appendix which forms part of the 1620 *Catalogue*), so as to reset the entries in the bottom right-hand corner (and overleaf) under 'Jacobus R[ex]' in larger types than those used in the rest of the volume, thus offering a tribute of typographic flattery to the royal author and donor.

Opposite:

61. **Presentation copy of Tycho Brahe's *Astronomiae instauratae mechanica*, 1598**

After the death in 1596 of his patron King Frederick II, the Danish astronomer Tycho Brahe left his native country and moved with his instruments from his island observatory at Uranienborg to Prague where the Emperor Rudolph II had offered him a new home and financial means to carry on his work. On his way there he stopped at the castle of Wandsbek in North Germany where he summoned a printer from nearby Hamburg to produce this fine folio for him.

Dedicated to his new patron the Emperor, the book describes and

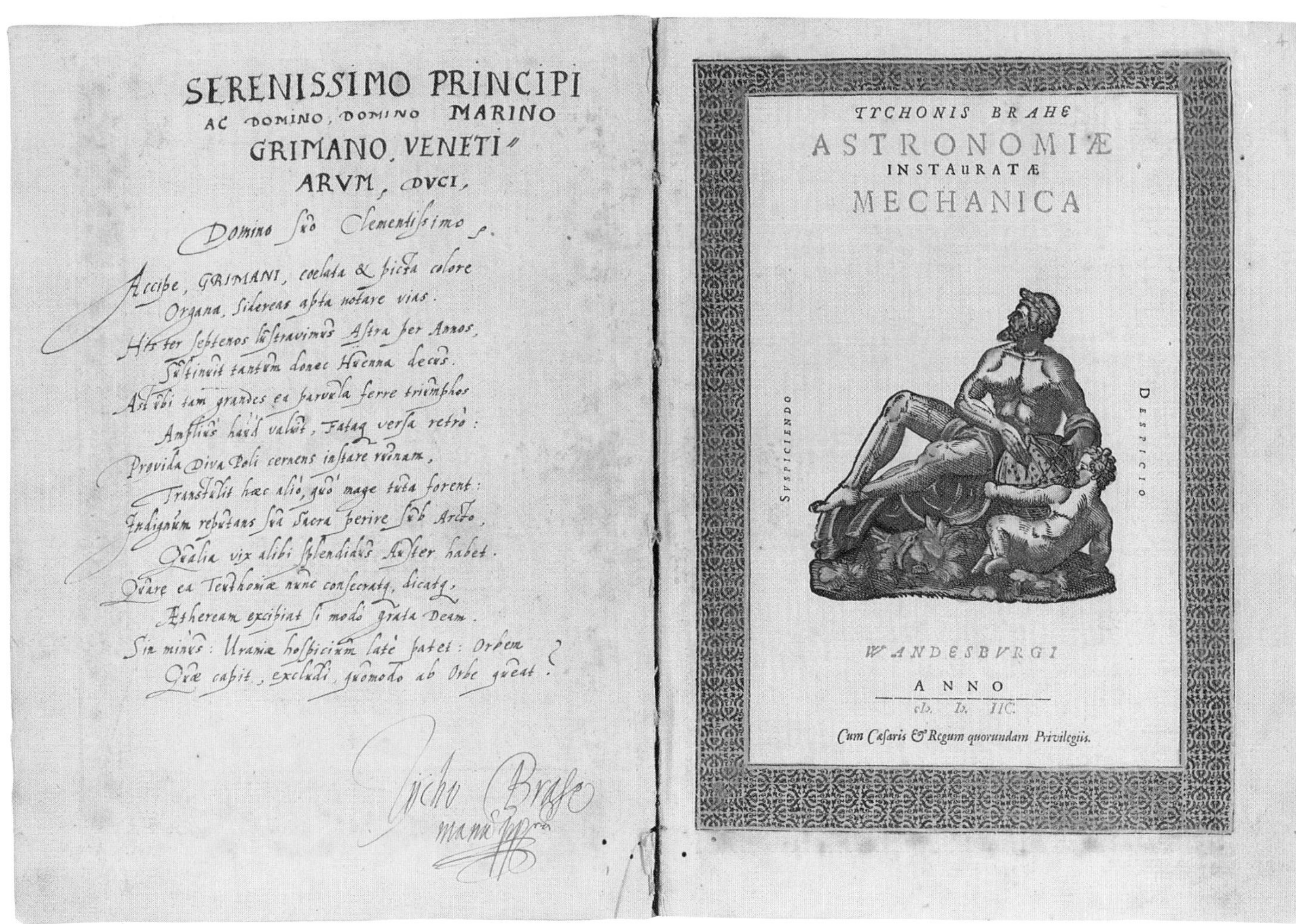

illustrates with plentiful woodcuts his astronomical instruments and also gives an account of his own life and his discoveries. Being privately printed and obviously intended principally to be given to friends, copies survive in various presentation bindings. The Bodleian copy has the cuts and borders all hand-coloured and is bound in green silk tooled with gilt stamps; opposite the title is this signed Latin poem, by Brahe himself, presenting to the Doge of Venice, Marino Grimani, these fruits of more than twenty years of observing the heavens, and also referring to the recent change in his fortunes. Following the printed book is a second Latin manuscript poem, also by Brahe himself, introducing to the Doge a further work; likewise dated at Wandsbek in 1598, this second book sets out, in forty-one pages of beautifully written manuscript tables, his own observations of the exact positions of 1,000 of the fixed stars. This important star catalogue, at which Brahe had toiled so long, was still unpublished when he died in 1601, and it devolved upon his assistant, Johann Kepler, who had joined him at Prague in 1600, to see it into print.

Sir Henry Wotton, poet and diplomatist, became Provost of Eton in 1624. From there he sent this volume to the Bodleian in August 1633, adding to it an elegantly penned inscription which explains that, though doubtless intended by Brahe for preservation in Bessarion's Library at Venice (the Marciana), it had chanced to come into Wotton's possession by purchase among other manuscripts. In a distinguished series of diplomatic missions abroad, Wotton had served three times as English ambassador at Venice and was actually resident there when the Doge Grimani died in 1605, so it is likely that he bought the volume there. For this gift and that of a manuscript (said to have once belonged to Cardinal Bembo) of the Acts of the Council of Constance, Wotton was formally thanked by the University in Convocation a fortnight later.

62. Presentation binding on Bacon's *De dignitate et augmentis scientiarum*, 1623

In 1620 Lord Chancellor Bacon had presented to the Bodleian a copy of the second part, entitled *Novum Organum*, of his great philosophical work, the *Instauratio Magna*. This second part was the first to be published and the presentation copy was bound in velvet of a deep purple colour with an old-fashioned version of the University's arms stamped in gilt on the upper cover and the author's own crest of a boar at the centre of the lower cover. When the first part, an enlarged translation into Latin of his earlier work *Of the Proficience and Advancement of Learning*, came out three years later in 1623, he presented this copy (Plate 63), which is bound in blue velvet but ornamented in a style totally different from his earlier gift of 1620 and from the King's gift (Plate 59) of the same year. The ornamentation, in raised gold and silver thread, is reminiscent of that employed in the previous century, except for a sprinkling of tiny metal spangles, which were just then coming into vogue. Such work would not be done by the bookbinders themselves, but by some of those professionals who produced the 'rare and curious covers of imbrothery and needleworke' which were popular especially in Jacobean and Caroline England; they are alluded to in a petition addressed by London tradesmen to Archbishop Laud in 1638 in which they describe books 'richly bound up for ye Nobilitie and gentrey . . . for whome . . . they are indeed most fitt'.

Franciscus Baro de Verulamio Vicecomes S^ti Albani
Inclytae Academiae Oxoniensi S.

Cum Almae matri meae Incl. Academiae Cantabrigiensi scripserim, deessem sane officio, si simile amoris pignus Sorori ejus non deferrem. Sicut autem eos hortatus sum, ita et vos hortor; ut Scientiarum Augmentis strenue incumbatis, et veterum labores, neque nihil, neque omnia esse putetis, sed vires etiam proprias modeste perpendentes, subinde tamen experiamini. Omnia cedent quam optime, si Arma non alii in alios vertatis, sed junctis copiis in Naturam rerum impressionem faciatis. Sufficiet quippe illa honori et victoriae. Valete.

63. Francis Bacon's presentation inscription

In 1605, the year of its publication, Francis Bacon had sent a copy of his *Advancement of Learning* to his friend Sir Thomas Bodley with a covering letter which said that Bodley's new 'ark to save learning' deserved a copy of any work by which learning should be improved or advanced. Similar thoughts recurred to Bacon's mind when, nearly twenty years later, he came to compose this Latin inscription for the specially-bound copy (Plate 62) of an enlarged Latin version of the same work, which he presented in 1623. His book aimed to widen the scope of learning by a new appeal to the observable facts of the natural world. In the same way this inscription urges Oxford, as he says he has similarly urged his own *alma mater* Cambridge, to fall to their common task, neither despising the labours of the past nor thinking them all-sufficient, but directing their united energies towards the increase of knowledge by confronting Nature with a continual reference to their own experience, however modest. This, he says, will indeed bring honour and success.

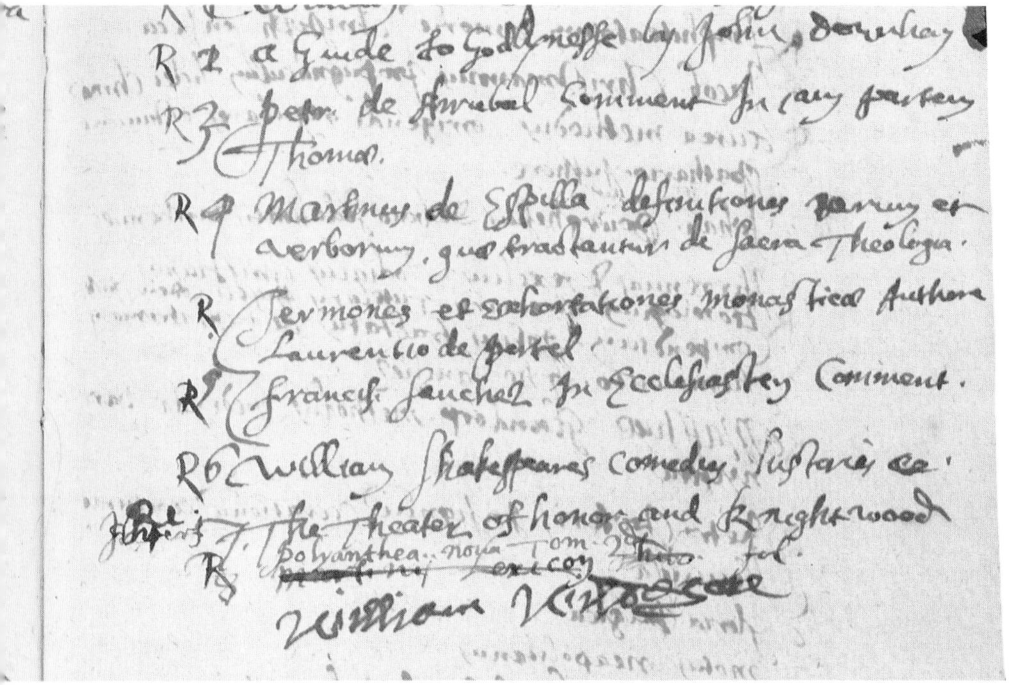
R 6 William Shakespeares Comedies, Histories, &c.
R 7 The Theater of honor and knighthood
William Wildgoose

64. **Binder's receipt for the Shakespeare First Folio**
Books received free under Bodley's agreement with the Stationers' Company such as the 1613 *Parthenia* (Plate 58) were, like new English and foreign purchases, most often acquired unbound, in the condition in which books then normally left the printer's workshop, namely as a set of loose sheets, sometimes stitched through from top to bottom in a rough paper wrapper to hold the pile together, the purchaser afterwards making his own arrangement for binding. After the sheets of a copy of the 1623 Shakespeare First Folio were delivered by the Stationers' Company to the Bodleian they were put into a batch of such unbound books which were entered in the current Library daybook (a kind of record journal kept by the Librarian) under the heading 'Delivered to William Wildgoose These bookes following to be bound 17 Febru. 1623 [1624]', a list which the binder signed when he took them away; the numbered entries were later checked in with a large R (i.e. returned) when he brought them back.

It was ultimately Wildgoose's binding habits that enabled Strickland Gibson, later a distinguished member of the Bodleian staff, and already then a pioneer in the study of bookbinding history, to recognize a somewhat dilapidated copy of the First Folio brought by an enquirer into the Library in 1905, as bound locally for some Oxford chained library. Gibson then found that consecutive waste leaves from the same early printed book which Wildgoose had used to line the covers of another book in that 1624 batch, were present in this First Folio, so proving that here was the original Bodleian copy. It was bought by public subscription and restored to the shelves from which it had once been sold as a 'duplicate'. This was probably in 1664 when the publication of the Third Folio had provided the opportunity to substitute a fresh edition (with *Pericles* and six spurious plays added) in place of what was by then the badly worn 1623 copy. Examination shows that two plays exhibit more thumbing than the others from the hands of the seventeenth-century readers whose attentions reduced this copy to its present state: most thumbing in *Romeo and Juliet* and next most in *Julius Caesar*.

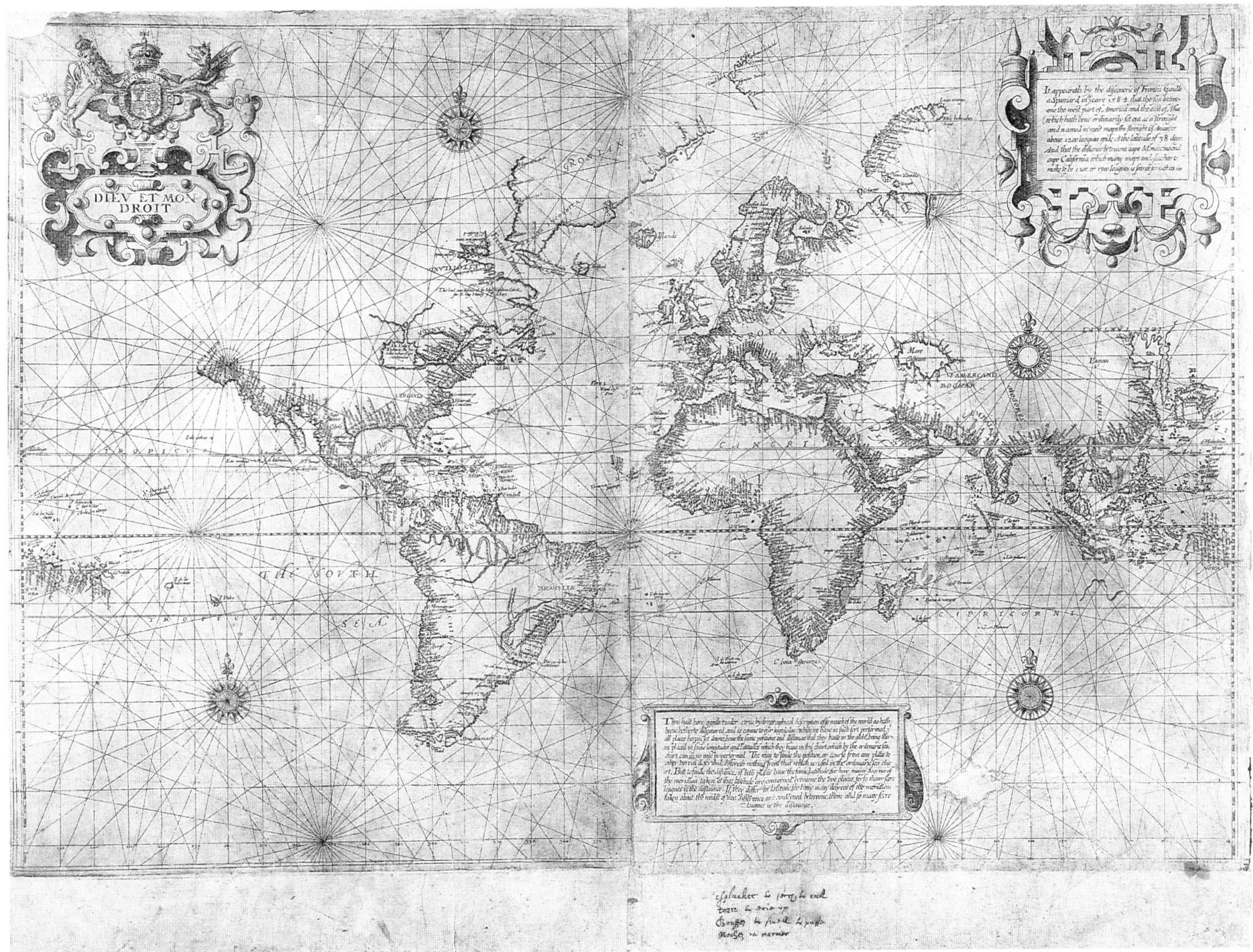

65. **Shakespeare's 'New mappe with the augmentation of the Indies'**
The most likely map to be that referred to by Shakespeare in *Twelfth Night* is this engraved sea chart of the whole world. It is undated and the engraver is unknown, but it was based on the researches of Edward Wright, a brilliant Cambridge mathematician, who, as a result of personal experience gained when he joined the Earl of Cumberland's expedition to the Azores in 1589, wrote an important book, *Certaine Errors of Navigation*, first published in 1599, setting out his conclusion that existing sea charts were inaccurate because of errors in the map projection then employed. Wright's chart was one of the first to use Mercator's Projection, and copies of it are occasionally preserved bound into the second edition of Hakluyt's *Principall Navigations* of the years 1598-1600. Yet it seems probable that it does not really belong to that book, since Hakluyt nowhere alludes to this map, and those copies of it found in his book could all have been added afterwards.

Furthermore, a chart bound within the pages of a three-volume folio work on sea exploration would be less likely to have caught the public eye than a separate map engraved and sold on its own by the printsellers. It therefore seems more likely that Edward Wright's chart was published about the year 1600, which fits with the state of geographical discovery shown in it. The earliest state of the plate, here reproduced, is without the added cartouche in the lower left corner which refers to the discoveries of Drake and Cavendish and was therefore probably put in later to bring the map more up-to-date and so to boost its sales. The large number of 'rhumb lines' engraved on this chart as aids to navigation further increases the likelihood that Shakespeare had this map in mind when penning his description of Malvolio's face all creased 'into more lines than there are in the new mappe . . .' A revised and even more scarce world chart of 1610 by Edward Wright is reproduced as Plate 96.

66. A page from a Mass by John Taverner
This set of six partbooks containing eighteen Tudor masses was originated by John Taverner during his period in Oxford from 1526 to 1530 as organist of Wolsey's new Cardinal College (later Christ Church). Taverner evidently intended them to provide a set of festal masses for the use of the College choir. The first section contains eleven masses, beginning appropriately with Taverner's own six-part mass *Gloria tibi Trinitas*, the College itself being dedicated to the Trinity. At the opening of this mass the initial E in five of the partbooks has been turned into a portrait assumed to be of Taverner himself – in three of the books, including the 'mean' partbook shown here, a ribbon issuing from the mouth also bears his name. Although the fine hand of this first section remains anonymous, Taverner was certainly responsible for the selection of the music, including masses by Fayrfax, Burton, Aston, Marbeck and others. With Taverner's departure from Oxford

days understand its language – meant that hardly any literature in English other than sermons and controversy came into the Library in his lifetime and indeed for more than two decades after his death. What, in fact, most preoccupied the presses of members of the Stationers' Company, publications which would, at least in theory, all have been available free to Bodley's Library, were predominantly ballads, romances, jest books and such popular productions, but these were in his eyes 'idle bookes and riffe raffes', among which he included English plays. Bodley did not discourage the acceptance and cataloguing of all plays as such, but felt that those in other languages could be useful for learning those languages and often had been written by internationally famous authors. The reputation of Shakespeare, born a year after Bodley became a Fellow of Merton and dying three years after him, was not to become international for another century and a half, and so his works and those of Marlowe, Ben Jonson and their fellow-poets and dramatists were not at first to be found on the Bodleian shelves. But one substantial volume of over 900 pages which did something to redress the balance, was received from the Stationers' Company in 1623. It was entitled *Mr William Shakespeares Comedies, Histories & Tragedies* and is one of the most famous existing copies of the so-called First Folio (Plate 64). Although it spent a protracted period outside the Bodleian, it has long been safely restored to its earliest home, and is of course the only copy of that celebrated book of which it can be said that it came direct from the original printers to its present in 1530, the books passed into the hands of William Forrest, a petty canon of the College, who, probably in the 1550s during the Marian restoration of the Latin rite, added the remaining seven masses, including a further two by Taverner. After Forrest's death c. 1581, the manuscripts passed to John Baldwin, 'a singing man of Windsor' and later a Gentleman of the Chapel Royal, who for some reason completed or recopied part of the sixth partbook. From Baldwin they passed to his fellow-Gentleman, William Heyther (or Heather) who in 1627 founded a Music Professorship at Oxford giving his own music books, including these partbooks, to form the nucleus of the famous Music School collection, which passed to the Bodleian in 1885. The Forrest-Heyther books, apart from constituting the unique source for much of the music they contain, are also remarkable in being one of the very few sets of English partbooks from the first half of the sixteenth century to have survived complete.

owners. The 1623 First Folio printed thirty-six plays for which Shakespeare's fellow-actors Heminge and Condell had been able to obtain a text they considered authentic; half of these had never been printed before, so at least in the shape of this first collected edition of his plays, Shakespeare as an author made a grand first entrance into a library which, despite containing at that date no previous work of his, was destined eventually to become one of the world's four chief repositories of Shakespearean material and of English drama and literature generally.

One of the plays first printed in the 1623 Folio was *Twelfth Night*. In Act III Maria says of the love-besotted Malvolio 'He does smile his face into more lines than are in the new mappe with the augmentation of the Indies', which obviously must refer to something well-known to Shakespeare's audience when the play was first performed in 1601. The Bodleian possesses a copy of the rare map to which Shakespeare is most probably here alluding (Plate 65), a map which is also noteworthy as the first sea chart of the whole world to be published in England.

Although music was a principal delight at all levels of Jacobean and Caroline society, with most composers writing with equal readiness for church and for secular occasions, published music seems to have been left to the professional musician and the amateur performer to collect and preserve, and for a long time was apparently not thought of as printed material to be sent regularly to the Bodleian. Indeed we might fairly question who could be expected to use such music books in a library devoted to silence and serious scholarship, where most volumes were kept chained. Nonetheless there were a few exceptions which are notable. For example, when the rejoicings over the marriage of the King's eldest daughter in 1613 gave occasion for the issue of the earliest English music book printed entirely from engraved copper-plates, namely the work by Byrd, Bull and Gibbons entitled *Parthenia* (Plate 58), a copy came at once from the publishers to the Bodleian in sheets and was issued for binding, as the Library's records now reveal, on a date which affords new evidence about this undated publication. And only three years later when, following a drive instigated by Thomas James 'for the due exacting of the Books of the Stationers' (who were already proving negligent about their agreement), a large consignment of recent books was received, it included two musical anthologies published in 1610 by the son of the lutenist John Dowland. The Bodleian copies of these two anthologies are among the exceedingly few that have survived anywhere. It is significant that although *Parthenia* was entered in the 1620 Bodleian printed *Catalogue*, the two Dowland books are not to be found either there or in the Appendix which Rous published in 1635; some materials were undoubtedly considered of lesser importance and their presence in the Library was not made public by inclusion in the printed *Catalogues*.

Musical degrees had been awarded by Oxford University as far back as the fifteenth century, though they were notably few down to the end of Elizabeth's reign. But in 1627 William Heyther (or Heather), a friend and the executor of William Camden, the historian who had founded in 1622 a Professorship of History, himself in turn founded an Oxford Professorship, that of Music. Heyther was a Gentleman of the Chapel Royal who became an Oxford Doctor of Music in 1622; he laid down that his Professor was to lecture (in English) on the theory of music, with a subordinate, under the unique title of *Choragus*, to conduct music practices twice weekly. Heyther also endowed his Chair with his own instruments and his valuable collection of early music, which became the nucleus of the famous Music School collection. Although this collection long continued to function as what would now be termed a Faculty Library, the University finally passed its rich accumulations to the Bodleian in 1885. Among the treasures given by Heyther was a set of partbooks of early Tudor Masses which originated with John Taverner while he was organist at Wolsey's new Cardinal College in 1526–30. The initial letter at the start of one of Taverner's own masses has apparently been made into a portrait of that composer (Plate 66).

A form of gift bringing continuous benefit to any library is the setting up of a fund to provide income for the purchase of books. Other instances of this valuable practice have enriched the Library, but an early one, possibly the first of its kind in Bodleian history, was the gift of £100 by Margaret Brooke in 1633. Unlike most sums given by various benefactors down through the centuries which were spent once for all, her gift was made in order to bring an annual income of £5 for ever. The rent, from land in the Gloucester village of Wick Rissington, is still paid annually. The Library expressed its gratitude by causing a delightfully florid brass stamp to be cut (Plate 67) which was to be impressed in gilt on the covers of books for which her endowment had paid. It also presented her with a pair of gloves at the cost of £2. During the past 350 years her original benefaction has repeated itself more than sixteenfold, and her example still deserves imitation. As the commitments and expenditure of a great institution go on expanding, the existence of funds earmarked for such a specific purpose as book buying provides an element of certainty, stability and continuity which powerfully aids the steady pursuit of an accessions policy; without such accessions even the greatest collections can become fossilized.

Among those who contributed Latin verses to a volume published in 1613 by the University to honour Bodley's memory was the forty-year-old President of St John's College, William Laud (Plate 68). His college presidency was the first rung in a ladder of public offices which took him, by way of three increasingly important bishoprics, to the See of

continued on page 88

67. **Margaret Brooke's purchase fund commemorated**

In his own manuscript catalogue of the books which he had chosen for the Bodleian from Robert Burton's library, John Rous included a poem by a certain Robert Roche printed at Oxford in 1599. It is fortunate he chose it, since no other copy of the book has been preserved. Following the title, *Eustathia, or the Constancie of Susanna*, Rous added 'dedicate to Mistris Margaret Brook our Benefactrix'. This must have been information derived from his own personal knowledge, since the dedication as printed says only 'to Mistris M. B. wife to . . . D. B. Esquier', so the lady concerned has not elsewhere been identified. The D. B. of this dedication, her husband Duke Brooke, died in 1606, and in the Benefactors' Register she is described as his widow, of Temple Combe in Somerset. The £100 she presented in 1633 was invested in land at Wick Rissington in Gloucestershire, to bring in £5 annually for book purchases, as it still does today. In 1636 the sum of twenty-three shillings was spent for a brass stamp to be used on the covers of books bought out of her fund. The stamp was commissioned from a London engraver and is still in existence. The significance of its design, here reproduced from a gilt impression on one of her benefactions, would have been clear to the men of that time: a serpent devouring its own tail represents perpetual continuity in the form of a closed circle; two cornucopiae, symbolizing the pouring out of plenty, support a laurel crown, while a ribbon issuing from the serpent's mouth bears a Latin verse from Psalm 65, which the Authorized Version translates 'Thou crownest the year with Thy goodness'. Below this the bottom scroll explains '*Annuo reditu Margaretae Brooke quinque librarum*' – 'by the £5 yearly income of Margaret Brooke'.

68. **Portrait of Archbishop Laud**

The original of this portrait of Laud, for which he sat to the court painter Sir Anthony Van Dyck in 1635, has recently been identified as the canvas in the Fitzwilliam Museum at Cambridge. The Bodleian copy of it bears an inscription with the donor's name and the date of the gift, 1674. The donor, Sir John Robinson, was a nephew of Archbishop Laud, being the son of Laud's elder half-brother. He became a wealthy member of the Clothiers' Company and was Lord Mayor of London in 1662. From 1653 he owned the Nuneham Courtenay estate near Oxford.

INDICE
DE LIBRI GRECI
ANTICHISSIMI
SCRITTI A PENNA,
Che ſi trouano nella Libraria, che fù del Q.
Illuſtriſ. Sig. GIACOMO Barocci,
NOBILE VENETO.

IN VENETIA, MDCXVII.

69. A *Catalogue* of the Barocci Collection, 1617
A printed descriptive list of the Greek manuscripts owned by Giacomo Barocci, a citizen of Venice who died in 1617, this is a very early and rare example of a practice which became common in the next few centuries, that of publishing the catalogue of a collector's library soon after his death, in the hope of attracting a purchaser for the collection as a whole. Later, when book auctions became more frequent, such trial catalogues could be used as a basis for a piecemeal sale in lots, if no single buyer had been found.

This copy of the Barocci list came to the Library not with the Barocci manuscripts which were eventually bought by a London bookseller and presented to the Bodleian in 1629 by Lord Pembroke, but in 1659 with the library of John Selden (Plate 92) whose autograph and Greek motto are written in the top outer corner of the titlepage.

70. A thirteenth-century miscellany of Byzantine authors
The Bodleian's collection of Greek manuscripts is the largest in Great Britain. This has been true since 1629, when the 244 volumes of the Barocci collection and the twenty-nine Greek volumes of the Roe collection reached the Library. Laud gave ninety-four further Greek manuscripts between 1635 and 1641, and subsequent donations included groups of Greek manuscripts from Oliver Cromwell, John Selden (Plate 92), and later Richard Rawlinson. These holdings were further strengthened by a remarkable series of Bodleian purchases of scholarly collections, made during the first quarter of the nineteenth century – D'Orville (1804), Clarke (1809), Canonici (1817), Saibante (1820), Meerman (1824) – which were largely due to the far-sighted influence of Thomas Gaisford, who was playing a part in the affairs of the Library even before his elevation to an *ex officio* Curatorship through his tenure, between 1812 and 1855, of the Regius Chair of Greek. Besides the papyri, the greatest accession in the twentieth century has been that of the 116 manuscripts which formed the entire Greek collection of the Earls of Leicester at Holkham Hall, acquired by the Bodleian in the years 1954, 1956 and 1981. The Barocci collection had been formed by the mathematican Francesco Barocci (1537–1604), who lived for most of his life in Crete, and by his nephew Giacomo Barocci of Venice (1562–1617), who inherited and added to it. The manuscripts are wide-ranging in date and subject-matter, and many retain their early Greek or Cretan bindings. The example here illustrated, one of the most important Byzantine manscripts in the Bodleian, is a large miscellany of c. 1250–80. According to a recent analysis, it comprises 144 items, including a number of unique or rare texts by major Byzantine authors of the twelfth century, such as Michael Psellus. Eighty authors are named, and there are further anonymous works. The manuscript is an early example of oriental paper used for Western texts, and seems to have been built up over a longish period by no fewer than eight scribes. It is not known how the manuscript reached the Barocci collection.

Sir Thomas Bodley's wise statutes had laid down 'that the books are not to be taken out of the Library, nor to be lent by any means': but nevertheless this manuscript was lent to Patrick Young, a major Greek scholar who was librarian successively to Prince Henry, James I and Charles I. In a paper of c. 1654 in support of the Library Statute, the then Librarian Thomas Barlow cites this loan and says that 'above 60 or 100 leaves . . . were irrecoverably defaced' in transit. The manuscript is still, indeed, in a very fragile condition through the softening and decay of the 700-year-old paper at the edges and folds.

71. **Bronze statue of the Earl of Pembroke, by Hubert Le Sueur**

It is appropriate that this fine contemporary statue of one of the Bodleian's great early benefactors should today stand prominently in front of the main public entrance to the Old Library. But it was not until 1723 that it came to Oxford as the gift of the eighth Earl of Pembroke; legend tells that two Oxford scholars dining at Wilton, the Earl's Wiltshire home where the statue had remained since it was first made about 1630, learned of its impending presentation to the University and prevailed upon the donor to allow them to carry back with them the statue's head (which is indeed separately cast) – a safety precaution against damage in transit, and an earnest that the great bulk of the gift, which weighs about three-quarters of a ton, would follow.

Formerly this bronze stood in the Tower at the centre of the Picture Gallery, but being more than life size, it has gained greatly enhanced dignity and publicity since it was moved into its present position in 1951. Its sculptor, Hubert Le Sueur, was attracted over to England from Paris by King Charles I in 1625 and for more than a decade the King used his services continually. Probably the commission for our statue came from the Earl's brother Philip, who as Lord Chamberlain, actually paid out what the King owed to Le Sueur for his work. The dead Earl's likeness, traditionally based on a sketch by Rubens, was not the statue's chief purpose, which was to commemorate a public figure in the heroic mould favoured years before by the Queen's father, Henry IV of France: hence the elaborately rendered armour, which attests Le Sueur's position as both son and brother of Parisian master-armourers. Such armour reappears in the same artist's bust of Charles I (Plate 82).

بسم الله الحي الازلي

كتاب المجامع المقدسة المدعوة

كتاب قضايا الملوك المنصورين

Thomas Roe Eques auratus et Ser.mi Magnæ Britanniæ &c. Regis apud Turcarum Imperatorē Orator in gratitudinis suæ erga matrem Academiam perpetuū testimoniū, hunc Librum quem ex Oriente secum aduexit, publicæ Bibliothecæ. D.D. Anno Dom. 1628. /.

72. **An Arabic version of the early Councils of the Church**

Sir Thomas Roe brought this manuscript back with him from the East and gave it in 1628 (as the Latin inscription at the foot of the title reveals) as a token of gratitude to his *alma mater* Oxford, after his retirement from the post of English Ambassador to the Ottoman Emperor. Among the twenty-nine manuscripts he gave the Bodleian in that year (all but three of them Greek codices) he himself treasured this one above all; it had been a present to him from his friend Cyril Lucar, the Patriarch of Constantinople and former Patriarch of Alexandria. It is indeed a notable manuscript, being one of the earliest surviving texts of the collection of Canons of the early Councils of the Church as translated into their own language by the Melchites, the Arabic-speaking Christians of Syria and Egypt. Finely written on more than 350 leaves of paper, the volume is shown by internal evidence to have been certainly already in existence before the year 1390. Its importance was soon recognized in the West; by the middle of the seventeenth century it had been studied at Oxford (in 1672) by the Cambridge orientalist William Beveridge.

The first account book of the Library records under the year 1629–30 'Item to Mr Barnes for bindinge the Arabicke manuscript of the Councells £1 5s'. The craftsman who received this large payment was the Oxford bookbinder Roger Barnes, two of whose known roll stamps can be recognized on the covers of this great tome. Were this precise evidence not available, the style of the decoration could easily suggest a binding made half a century earlier.

73. The Oxford *Chanson de Roland*

The *Chanson de Roland* is the earliest surviving masterpiece of French literature. The Christian heroes Roland and Oliver win death and glory in a rearguard action against the infidel (in the year 778, at Roncevaux in the Pyrenees), and are avenged by Charlemagne, the sovereign lord: subject-matter to arouse all the ideals of patriotism and chivalry. From the twelfth century onwards, the legend had gathered a snowball momentum: later versions could be double in length and adapted to more recent developments in assonance and metre. But the Oxford manuscript, the unique witness, crystallizes the growing saga at a moment of crucial importance: in this manifestation, the *Song of Roland* is the earliest and finest of the entire genre of *chansons de geste*.

Though it stands at the start of the written vernacular literature, the *Roland* itself sums up generations of oral composition by *jongleurs*. As its name implies, the *Chanson* was composed for sung performance; but the manuscript preserves only the words, and the sole hint of performing practice (apart from the versification scheme itself) is the mysterious *AO*, a refrain (?) written at the end of many verses. Like the Homeric problem, that of the relationship of the author to the oral tradition has exercised modern scholars for over a century. How, they ask, were the historical events of the year 778 transmogrified into the glorious epic of three centuries later? How much of the Oxford text is due to the natural honing of tradition, how much to the decisive intervention of one genius? Does an awkward digression like the episode of Baligant suggest subsequent modifications between the genius's work and the manuscript record? At all events, there is a clear contrast between the *Chanson* and the monastic annals or monuments of sober Latin learning.

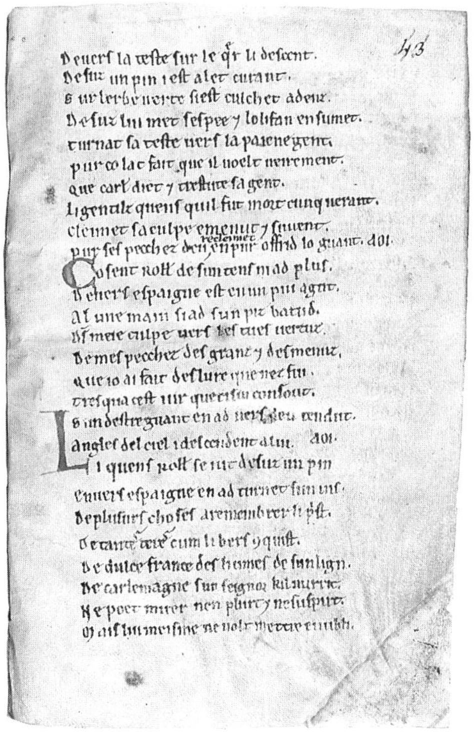

This contrast persists in the physical appearance of the manuscript itself. It is a 'scruffy' little book, in contrast to the handsome volumes which were being written to stock the monastic libraries of the time – even austere Cistercian ones. This scribe's lack of professionalism is shown in the unevenness of his work: his pen varies in sharpness, his ink in colour and his letters in size. He is perhaps trying to write more formally than is his usual style. The only decoration consists of plain red initials at the beginning of each group of lines; the initial on the first page is of slightly ornamented form. Palaeographically, the usual dating of 'second quarter of the twelfth century' is guesswork, and the scribe may have worked on either side of the Channel. Linguistically, the manuscript probably belongs to the English side, for the dialect is Anglo-Norman. But this raises further controversy: does the manuscript present an adaptation of a Continental composition, or was the earliest masterpiece of French literature composed in Norman England?

The last line of the *Chanson* is an enigmatic mixture of Anglo-Norman and Latin: 'Ci fait la geste que Turoldus declinet'. Turoldus might be the master-poet, or the scribe, or someone involved in any of the intermediate stages. The manuscript's later history is equally mysterious. It is now bound up after a twelfth-century copy, made in France, of Calcidius's Latin translation of Plato's *Timaeus*. The two manuscripts were made in quite separate circumstances: the Calcidius, a common academic text of the period, is a much more expert production. On the front flyleaf, an inscription records that the 'Thymeus Platonis' (without reference to the *Chanson*) had been bequeathed to Osney Abbey near Oxford by Master Henry de Langley. This cleric had studied at Oxford in the 1240s, held a benefice at Bridgnorth Castle, Shropshire, and probably was dead by August 1263. The present binding dates from 1632–4, and is the standard brown calf with the arms of the donor Sir Kenelm Digby, who gave this and other volumes in 1634. The two booklets were already together in their previous binding, for they were catalogued together in 1622 among the manuscripts of Digby's source, the long-lived Oxford collector Thomas Allen; but there is no internal evidence that they were together in the Middle Ages.

74. **Armorial book-stamp of Archbishop Laud**
With notably few exceptions, Laud's extensive gifts were sent down from his London residence in large batches already new bound in dark brown calf, stamped on both covers with the Archbishop's arms in gilt. These bindings were supplied by a London printer, Richard Badger, and two different stamps were employed. The design is the same in both, showing the personal arms of Laud on the right half of the shield, and those of the archiepiscopal See of Canterbury, to which he was translated from London in 1633, on the left. The stamp here reproduced is the smaller of the two.

Canterbury and a dominant position (the phrase specially fits his character) in both Church and State, two realms which, according to his thought, were necessarily interdependent. He was already Bishop of the wealthy See of London when in 1630 he succeeded Lord Pembroke (Plate 71) as Chancellor of Oxford University, which soon felt the impact of his reforming energies. But his massive contribution to the build-up of the Library's manuscript holdings did not wait upon his taking over the Chancellorship.

Already, even before his own years as a large-scale book purchaser began (he was never a collector in the bibliophilic sense), he had been responsible in 1629 for channelling to Oxford its first really large manuscript accession in a single language, a batch of no fewer than 242 Greek codices. A printed list of these manuscripts, collected by the Venetian family of Barocci, had been published at Venice in 1617 (Plate 69), no doubt with a view to a sale following the death of Giacomo Barocci in that year. Twelve years later the prize was carried off, to the chagrin of Continental rivals, by an enterprising London bookseller, Henry Featherstone, who at the time was also the main agent of the Bodleian for the acquisition of foreign printed books. When the collection reached England, Archbishop Ussher wrote from Dublin to recommend that the King should acquire these manuscripts, but Laud's diary records their delivery at his London house and adds 'These I got my Lord of Pembroke to buy and give to Oxford'. This gift (Plate 70) laid the foundation of the Bodleian's pre-eminence among British libraries in the extent of its Greek manuscript collections, a pre-eminence which it has maintained right up to the present day.

'My Lord of Pembroke', who gave these manuscripts, was William, third Earl, who had already given the Bodleian £100 in 1609. He became Chancellor of the University in 1617, and in 1624 Pembroke College was so named in his honour. A nephew of Sir Philip Sidney, and famed himself as a patron of art and letters, he was the elder of 'the incomparable pair of brethren' to whom in 1623 the First Folio of Shakespeare (Plate 64) was dedicated. His statue by Le Sueur (Plate 71) now stands before the main entrance of the Old Library (Plate 48). There was a sequel to the Pembroke gift; a further two dozen Greek codices, which had been retained in the Earl's collection, were bought by Oliver Cromwell and given by him to the Library in 1654.

The very same carrier's consignment which brought the Barocci manuscripts to Oxford from London House, Laud's residence, also brought a large trunk containing twenty-nine manuscripts given, as Laud wrote 'verye noblye and freelye bye Sir Tho. Roe, who hath long bine imployed in his Maiestyes service in Turkeye'. Roe had no need of introduction at Oxford, for he was a former member of Magdalen College and had already in 1620 presented a Persian manuscript to the

75. **The Laudian *Acts of the Apostles***
Oxford's most important biblical manuscript is a bilingual copy of the *Acts of the Apostles*, in Greek and Latin. Each page contains two parallel columns of text, Greek on the right, Latin on the left, with only a word or two in each line. To make the words match exactly, the word order of the Latin text (a pre-Vulgate version) has sometimes been altered. The manuscript was written c. 600 possibly in Sardinia (a Greek edict of a *Dux Sardiniae* was added at the end). The same scribe wrote both the Greek and the Latin, in uncial scripts which are identical for those letter-forms which are shared by both languages. The occasional lapse into Greek letter-forms in the Latin text – e.g. *P* for *R* – suggests that the scribe was more at home writing Greek. The format recalls the bilingual Virgils common among the fourth- and fifth-century papyri of Greek Egypt; like them, the Laudian *Acts* was perhaps intended for Greek-speakers less familiar with Latin, rather than *vice-versa*, though the format would help readers unskilled in either language. As a witness to the Greek text of the bible, this is the earliest surviving manuscript to include *Acts* viii, 37: 'And Philip said [to the Ethiopian eunuch], If thou believest with all thine heart, thou mayest [be baptized]. And he answered and said, I believe that Jesus Christ is the Son of God.'

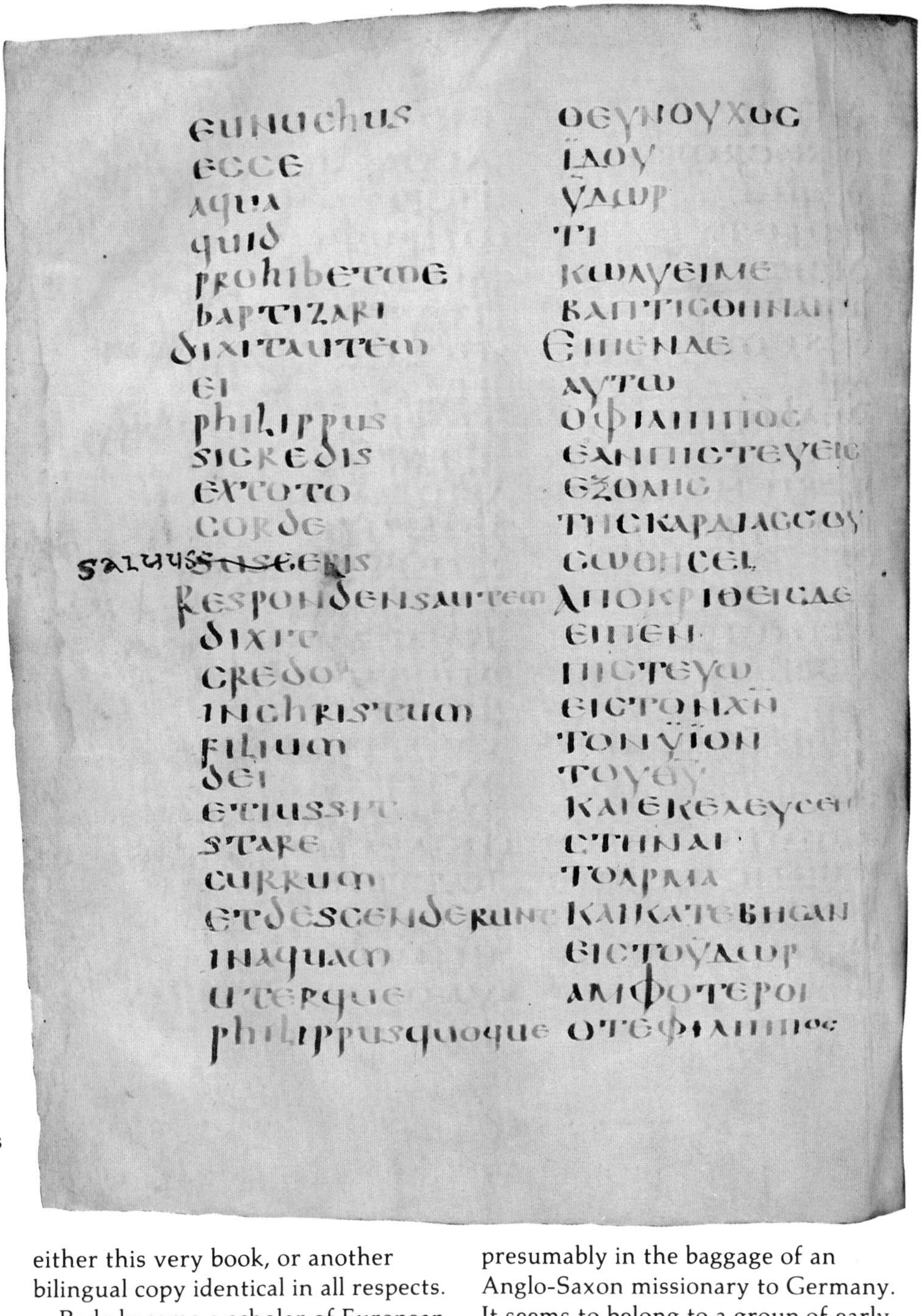

But the manuscript has another claim to fame, as a monument to early English learning: it is almost certainly one of the very copies used by the Venerable Bede for his two commentaries on *Acts* (His *Expositio*, composed c. 709–716, and his *Rectractatio*, after 731). The evidence for this lies in the fact that when Bede refers in his commentaries to the Greek text of *Acts*, he tends to give not a direct quotation in Greek but a Latin version which exactly mirrors the distorted Latin of the Laudian manuscript: Bede was using either this very book, or another bilingual copy identical in all respects.

Bede became a scholar of European stature without leaving his native soil, an achievement made possible only by the import of foreign books into Northumbria in the later seventh century. Imported uncial scripts, as in the Laudian *Acts*, had a major influence on the Irish-trained scribes of Lindisfarne and Wearmouth-Jarrow. Soon afterwards, the bilingual *Acts* must have re-emigrated, presumably in the baggage of an Anglo-Saxon missionary to Germany. It seems to belong to a group of early manuscripts which came into the hands of Archbishop Laud's agents in Germany from the library of St Kylian's Cathedral, Würzburg, an Anglo-Saxon foundation. In the flood of manuscripts which Laud presented to the Bodleian during the 1630s, the *Acts* arrived as part of a donation in 1636.

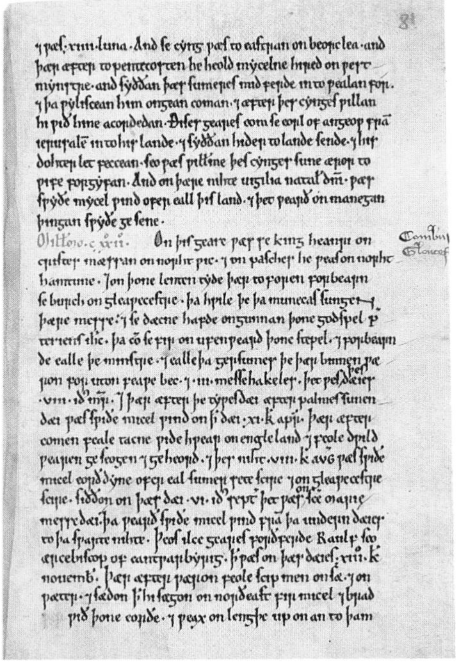

76. **'The Peterborough Chronicle'**
The historical value of the Anglo-Saxon Chronicle can scarcely be overrated: its near-contemporary accounts of events, year by year, set the basic framework of English history. Like the various sets of Irish annals, the manuscripts of the Anglo-Saxon Chronicle diverge increasingly as they progress to later events: each of its seven principal versions is a complex individual artefact.

The Bodleian manuscript, version 'E' of the Anglo-Saxon Chronicle, was written out at Peterborough Abbey. Events up to the year 1121 were transcribed by one scribe in a single writing campaign, so the main part of the manuscript dates from that year. As he wrote, he incorporated the chief events of his Abbey's history, in twelfth-century language which contrasts with the surrounding Old English: so his ultimate source was *not* compiled at Peterborough. Behind the block of text copied out so neatly in 1121 would have been a complex sequence of exemplars, into which successive annalists will have added their entries for the events of their times. The entries for the eleventh century – particularly fascinating when the Norman Conquest is described in the vernacular of the conquered race – present shifting local viewpoints, sometimes Northern (York ?), sometimes Southern (Canterbury ?). From 1079 on, 'E' is the sole remaining version of the Chronicle.

The events for 1122–31 are written in by the original scribe, but it is clear from changes in ink-colour and spacing that the entries were made in six successive blocks. The conclusion is that these entries were being written down more or less as they were composed, and indeed they are full of Peterborough material. This section therefore has a claim to be the earliest 'autograph' manuscript of any Middle-English text, and its precise date and origin make it as important for the history of the English language as it is for English history. It is the base manuscript for the study of the East-Midland dialect, and shows the cultural impact on the Anglo-Saxon language of the invasion of French.

The years 1132–54 are covered by a second scribe, whose work must have been done all at one stint at the end of that period. The section includes the famous description of the anarchy in King Stephen's reign under the year 1137. In the late thirteenth century a short Chronicle (in Anglo-Norman French) was added; not a continuation for events after 1154, the date at which the main annalistic entries end, but a skeletal summary of English history from the legendary Brut to Edward I. By 1565 the manuscript had come into the hands of Sir William Cecil (later Lord Burghley), and had already begun to attract a good deal of antiquarian interest; at one point Cecil lent it to Archbishop Parker. Its next recorded owner, William Lisle, a Cambridge scholar of Anglo-Saxon, had the volume interleaved with paper to take his copious notes. After Lisle's death in 1637 four of his manuscripts were presented to the Bodleian in 1638 by Archbishop Laud.

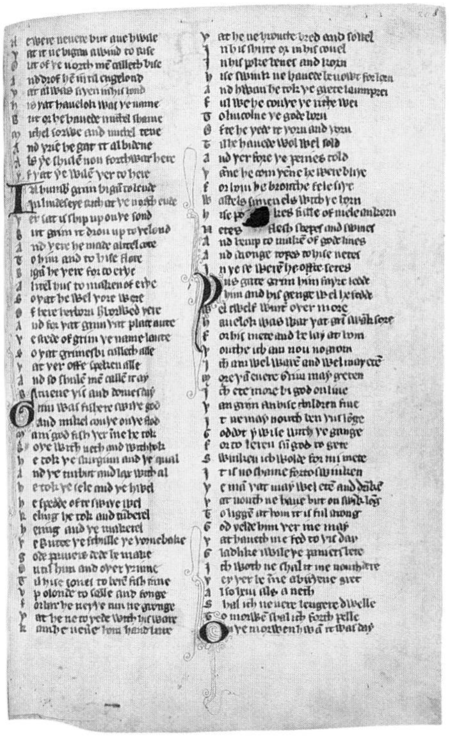

77. **The Middle-English *Lay of Havelok the Dane***
Verses describing the foundation of Grimsby from the unique surviving copy of *The Lay of Havelok the Dane* (except for a few fragmentary lines at Cambridge) are here accompanied by one of the three known copies of *King Horn*. These are two of the earliest Middle-English romances in date of composition: *King Horn* is put at c. 1225, *Havelok* c. 1280–1300. Their models may have been French Romances from the Anglo-Norman milieu, such as the *Chanson de Roland* (Plate 73), but their themes derive not from Arthur or Charlemagne but from the Viking period of English history. Havelok, a foundling prince of Denmark, undergoes a classic story-pattern of rejection and triumphant return and assumes the crowns of both Denmark and England; the settlement of his foster-father Grim the fisherman becomes the future town of Grimsby. *Havelok* is even further from the sober historical record than *Roland* is from the real Charlemagne, and indeed there is no Viking ruler with whom

he can securely be identified. Nevertheless the poem (intended for a popular audience) has a gritty realism which makes a marked contrast with the courtly illuminations of the rich or the theological abstractions of the scholar.

The two romances appear at the end of what is claimed to be the earliest surviving copy of a much commoner text, the *South English Legendary*. This collection of metrical Lives of saints seems to have been compiled for use in the preaching mission of the thirteenth-century friars, to be recited for the public instruction of the laity. The original arrangement, still discernible here, was in calendar order, with saints' days and 'temporal' feast-days combined. The copies of *Havelok* and *King Horn* are written in a hand of different texture from the *Legendary*, but perhaps as an addition to it rather than as a separate entity. The exemplar of the two romances had twenty lines to the page, and would have been much smaller and more portable. The variety of sources which lie behind this large corpus as it now stands is demonstrated by the different dialects of the original compositions: Lincolnshire for *Havelok* with its Grimsby connections, more southerly and westerly dialects for *King Horn* and the *Legendary*. Modern editors complain of the scribes' slovenliness in terms of accuracy of copying, but in terms of letter-forms their work had a modest professionalism, and there are penwork initials of reasonable quality.

Further saints' Lives were added after the romances, and the name of a fifteenth-century owner, Henry Perneys, is recorded at the end. The manuscript came in Laud's first donation of 1633.

Bodleian. After being sent to the New World by Prince Henry to explore for gold – he was the first Englishman to sail up the Amazon – he later became a highly valued and successful ambassador, first to the Mogul Emperor, with whom he negotiated a trade treaty important for the future of British India, and later, from 1612 to 1628, at the Ottoman Porte. It was through his friend the ambassador Roe that the Patriarch of Constantinople, Cyril Lucar, presented to King Charles I the precious fifth-century *Codex Alexandrinus*, now in the British Library. Lucar had earlier been Patriarch of Alexandria and another manuscript, also of Alexandrian origin, was given by him to the ambassador personally. This was an Arabic manuscript of early Church Councils (Plate 72) which Roe, who prized it even above the *Codex Alexandrinus*, described in his Memoirs as 'the jewel of the East'; after his return from Constantinople it came in the trunk with the rest of his gifts, which were mostly Greek manuscripts.

Sir Kenelm Digby, the son of a Gunpowder Plot conspirator, entered Gloucester Hall (now Worcester College) in 1618 aged fifteen, though as a Catholic he could not matriculate or take a degree. But with the seventy-seven-year-old Thomas Allen, who had taken up residence in that College nearly fifty years earlier, and who died there in 1632, this brilliant and wealthy young student began a close friendship which was no doubt the origin of his lifelong interest in natural science, bearing fruit in several original works in medicine, chemistry, and philosophy. In combining his public life – he was at various times traveller, courtier, diplomat, and naval privateer – with his consuming intellectual pursuits, Digby was a typical Renaissance figure. By 1629 he had made for himself a collection of manuscripts in addition to a considerable library of printed books. Then in 1632, under a codicil to Allen's will, he was bequeathed over 200 manuscript items from the latter's collection. These he rearranged, bound up and gave to the Bodleian, together with a catalogue, two years later. Once again, it was Laud who arranged the benefaction. In a letter to the University, Laud described the collection of 235 volumes, newly bound by Digby with his 'arms upon them', which Laud forwarded to Oxford 'in their several trunks as they were packed up by [the donor] himself'. More than half these manuscripts reflect the early history of science in England, including works by Robert Grosseteste, once the University's Chancellor, who left his books to the Oxford Franciscans, and by Roger Bacon (Plate 57), himself one of those Oxford Franciscans. A large number of the Allen/Digby manuscripts derived from former English monastic libraries, many of them from Oxford and the surrounding area. The collection also contained, besides a group of Arabic and Hebrew manuscripts, various historical and literary texts, mainly written in England, including a volume of four English mystery plays; most celebrated of all, he gave the earliest known manuscript of

continued on page 95

78. **Archbishop Laud's pre-Columbian Mexican Codex**
'Codex Laud' is the smallest, oldest and most mysterious of the five documents which, few as they are, make the Bodleian a place of pilgrimage for students of ancient Mexico. All five items reached the Library during the seventeenth century: 'Codex Bodley' is listed in the Library *Catalogue* of 1605, though its source is unknown; the 'Codex Laud' was presented by Archbishop Laud and 'Codex Selden', the 'Selden Roll', and the 'Codex Mendoza' by Selden (Plate 98).

Like the Selden and Bodley codices, 'Codex Laud' is in 'screenfold' format, whereby a long strip of material is folded concertina-fashion into square 'pages'. The resulting screenfold resembles the codex form of a European book except that it can still be unfolded completely. Both sides of the strip can be used. The strip is made up of pieces of deerskin pasted together and covered with a thick gesso-like layer of lime paste as a smooth white background to the painted figures.

Clues to the origin and date of 'Codex Laud' can be sought only in stylistic and iconographic comparisons with a few other codices (most notably the Vatican's 'Codex Borgia') and with archaeological finds. Attempts to reconcile elements which seem Aztec, Mixtec, even Mayan, have produced a geographical range of guesses from Western Oaxaca to the Gulf Coast of Vera Cruz. The general verdict on the date is that it is certainly pre-Spanish Conquest, perhaps fifteenth-century. The only hint of the screenfold's immediate history lies in its box, a tailor-made slip-case of red leather tooled in gilt: Continental, not English, probably sixteenth-century. The box is labelled 'Liber Hieroglyphicorum Aegyptiorum M. S.' in a seventeenth-century hand which is identifiable as that of Laud's servant William Dell. This shows that no memory of Mesoamerican provenance can have travelled with the manuscript. William Laud's concern to extend the range of languages available in the University Library is sufficent to explain why he included his strange 'Egyptian Hieroglyphic' find in his donation.

One undeniable aspect of 'Codex Laud' is its technical virtuosity: the designs are laid out with mathematical precision, the drawings have an unhesitating confidence, and the black outlines which surround the areas of brilliant colour are of an exactly uniform thickness. Artistically this is a masterpiece, alongside which the other four Mexican manuscripts in the Bodleian appear almost slovenly in execution.

Unlike Mixtec genealogies, 'Codex Laud' follows no detailed code of picture-writing. Its pictures are clearly religious in character and fill out both sides of the screenfold; they are arranged in sequences which are sometimes numbered with bar-and-dot or simple dot notations. The most striking sequence shows full-page images of supernatural beings (belonging recognizably to the Aztec-Toltec pantheon) in their various manifestations, benign or malignant: divinities such as Xochipilli the Flower Prince, Mictlantecutli the Death God, and Mayauel the Mother-goddess and Patroness of intoxicating liquor. In some series of smaller pictures, human beings make offerings or perform other ritual acts. Most sequences are accompanied by permutations of the twenty day-signs

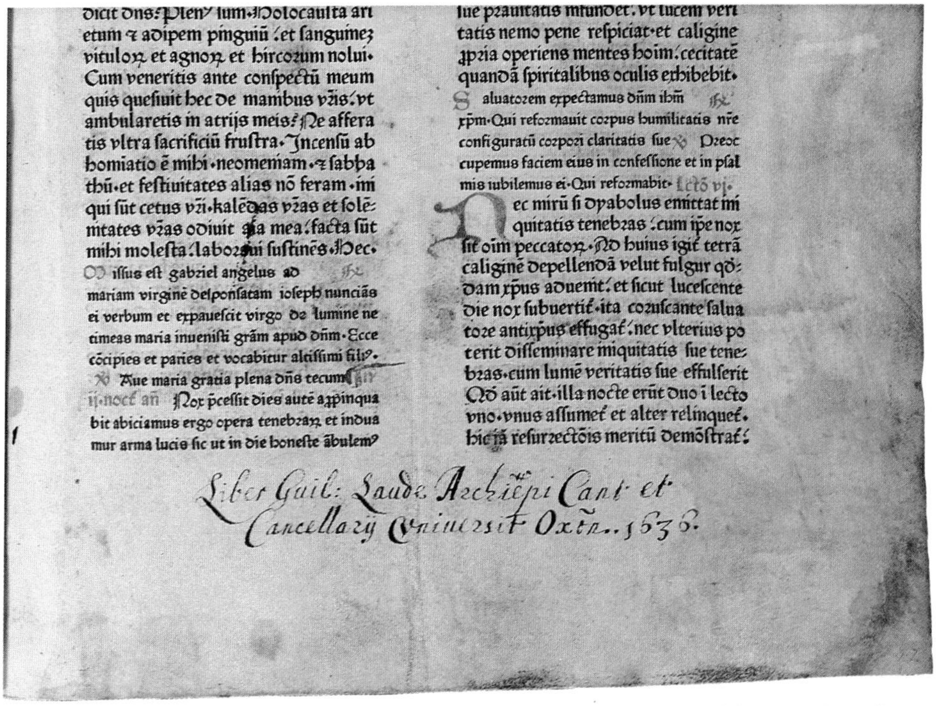

dicit dns: Plen' sum. Holocausta ari
etum et adipem pinguiu: et sanguinez
vitulorum et agnorum et hircorum nolui.
Cum veneritis ante conspectu meum
quis quesiuit hec de manibus vris: vt
ambularetis in atrijs meis: Ne affera
tis vltra sacrificiu frustra. Incensu ab
hominatio e mihi. neomeniam. et sabba
thu. et festiuitates alias no feram. ini
qui sut cetus vri. kalendas vras et sole
mitates vras odiuit aia mea: facta sut
mihi molesta: laboraui sustines. Dec.
Missus est gabriel angelus ad
mariam virgine desponsatam ioseph nuncias
ei verbum et expauescit virgo de lumine ne
timeas maria inuenisti gram apud dnm. Ecce
cocipies et paries et vocabitur altissimi filius.
Aue maria gratia plena dns tecum
Nox pcessit dies aute appinqua
bit abiciamus ergo opera tenebrarum et indua
mur arma lucis sic ut in die honeste ambulem

sue prauitatis mundet: vt lucem veri
tatis nemo pene respiciat. et caligine
ppria operiens mentes hoim: cecitate
quanda spiritalibus oculis exhibebit.
Saluatorem expectamus dnm ihm
xpm. Qui reformauit corpus humilitatis nre
configuratu corpori claritatis sue. Deeoc
cupemus faciem eius in confessione et in psal
mis iubilemus ei. Qui reformabit. Lectio vj.
Nec miru si dyabolus emittat ini
quitatis tenebras: cum ipe nox
sit oim peccatorum. De huius igit terra
caligine depellenda velut fulgur qo
dam xpus aduenit: et sicut lucescente
die nox subuertit. ita coruscante salua
tore antixpus effugat: nec vlterius po
terit disseminare iniquitatis sue tene
bras. cum lume veritatis sue effulserit
Qd aut ait. illa nocte erut duo i lecto
vno. vnus assumet et alter relinquet.
hic ia resurrectois meritu demostrat:

Liber Guil: Laud: Archiepi Cant: et
Cancellarij Universit: Oxon. 1636.

(death's head, rabbit's head, flint knife, etc.), which were used throughout Mesoamerica, in combination with the numerical coefficients 1 to 13, to form the divinatory almanac of 260 days known as the 'tonalpohualli'. These may indicate the purpose of 'Codex Laud' and the small handful of related 'ritual-calendrical' codices: to foretell the future and to predict whether a given day, under the influence of a Sun God or an Earth Goddess, would be auspicious or inauspicious. The similarities to the astrology or geomancy of mediaeval Europe are obvious, and indeed there are so many parallels between 'Codex Laud' and a near-contemporary set of English prognostic calendars which later reached the Library in Richard Rawlinson's collections – pictorial mode of expression, calendarial content, astrological purpose, even screenfold format – that their spontaneous generation in entirely independent cultures must indicate some universal human quirk.

These two facing pages represent (right) Tlazolteotl, Earth Goddess, Eater of Filth and (left) Tonatiuh, the red Sun God.

79. **The first book printed at Würzburg, 1479**

In many places throughout fifteenth-century Europe, the newly-invented art of printing was first introduced to meet the needs of some special patron. At Würzburg in Bavaria it was the Bishop, Rudolph von Scherenberg, who, in a letter dated 20 September 1479, written on behalf of his whole Chapter, granted a privilege to three named 'notable masters of the printer's art' whom he had summoned to his city to produce an edition of his diocesan breviary. Of the three, Stefan Dold is likely to have been the financial organizer, while the actual printer was George Reyser; Johann Beckenhub, a priest of the diocese of Mainz, was the press corrector, being an expert in liturgical work who had probably already partnered Reyser in several earlier service books issued at Speier. Together these men issued this, the first book printed at Würzburg, a substantial folio of 353 leaves, intended for use on a lectern in choir. Despite its bulk, the edition has largely perished; only four other copies are recorded, none of them perfect.

The copy presented by Laud to the Bodleian is printed on vellum, but is, like the others, incomplete. At the foot of the first page is added, in the hand of one of Laud's secretaries, the Archbishop's ownership formula as found on most of his gifts, with the date 1636, which is the date when Laud acquired it. It was among his massive acquisitions from Germany in that year and undoubtedly came, as did various other Laudian manuscripts, from Würzburg itself, which had fallen to the invading Swedes in 1631. A 1481 printed Würzburg Missal on vellum, also given by Laud in 1636, came from St Bartholomew's Church there, so the two volumes may from the beginning have been together.

אמנני
אצלו שכנני
ארם חקנני
יה קנני
בנון בערכי
כי עץ ירכי
בשעשועי ברכי
ראשית דרכי

80. The Laudian *Mahzor*
Not long after the appearance of the *mahzor* in book form in the various Ashkenazi communities of Germany and France in the second half of the thirteenth century, we find some of the more highly decorated volumes bountifully provided with illuminations for the best-known prayers and *piyyutim*. It was these which influenced the production of illuminated *mahzorim* in Germany in the fourteenth century. The two outstanding examples in this category are the 'Worms *Mahzor*' in the Jewish National and University Library, Jerusalem, and this 'Laud *Mahzor*' which is to be assigned to southern Germany and to be dated about 1290.

The full-page panel here reproduced encloses the beginning of *piyyut* for Pentecost showing the Giving of the Law (top), Moses sprinkling the Israelites with blood (below), and the baking of unleavened bread for Passover (bottom). This page also shows the birds' heads and blank faces (the features of the group on the right were added later) given to human figures, characteristic of the school from which this *Mahzor* originates.

the first surviving masterpiece of French literature, the epic poem of the *Chanson de Roland* (Plate 73).

Following the valuable collections of Barocci, Roe and Digby which he had been a principal agent in acquiring for the Bodleian, Laud began endowing the University with large gifts of manuscripts which he had himself managed to assemble. Even before he became its President he had made occasional gifts to the library of his own College, St John's, a pointer to the probability that he had begun to acquire manuscripts himself, both by purchase and through donations from friends, many years before he became Archbishop of Canterbury in 1633. By then he owned quite a sizeable collection, numbering 303 manuscripts, and the thrust of his collecting now became apparent, for nearly all of these formed part of his first gift to the Bodleian, which he sent to Oxford in May 1635, amounting to a total of 461 manuscripts. Though most of these were in Latin, there were also large and important groups in Arabic – he founded Oxford's Arabic Professorship in 1636 – and in Greek and English, the latter including the early Middle-English poetry manuscript here illustrated (Plate 77); for a man so immersed in public affairs as Laud had already long been, the overall scope of this donation was astonishingly wide-ranging, embracing as it did books in a total of seventeen different languages, eleven of them oriental. This diversity was further increased by his later benefactions, bringing the ultimate total of languages represented to more than twenty, over half of them non-European.

A second gift followed in a little over a year after the first. Dispatched in June 1636, it comprised a further 184 manuscripts, all but a handful of them collected, as the donor's accompanying letter claimed, within the previous twelve months, 'not' he added, 'without expense'. To this second donation, which included two important early Irish volumes and Laud's single, and very mysterious, Mexican Codex (Plate 78), he added the fine bronze bust of King Charles I (Plate 82) which faces that of Sir Thomas Bodley (Plate 46) across the archway at the entrance of Duke Humfrey's Library, and also five cabinets of coins, the foundation of what soon became England's earliest comprehensive coin collection – something felt by earlier scholars to be a necessary adjunct to any serious historical library.

The year which saw the dispatch of the second donation also saw Laud begin a series of extensive and important new acquisitions from Germany. Not a few of these, as Laud himself reveals, were given him by Thomas, Earl of Arundel, who in 1636 went to Vienna on an embassy, and on his travels was also collecting manuscripts and objects of art on his own account. But most were bought by Laud himself, though tantalizingly little has yet come to light about the channels through which they were obtained. What is evident is that the disturbances caused by the Thirty Years War made large numbers of

هندول

81. An Indian miniature from the Laudian album

Among the large and distinguished Bodleian collection of Indian miniature paintings from various periods is a remarkable album of paintings and calligraphic samples, apparently representing the interests of a single collector, which was presented to the Library by Archbishop Laud in 1639 or 1640, and was one of the first such works ever to come to Europe. Of the thirty paintings in this Laudian album, eighteen are from a set of *ragamala* icons, illustrations of Indian musical modes. It has been argued by some art historians that these paintings, which can be dated approximately to the early seventeenth century, are of Deccani (Southern Indian) origin, but it is now considered more likely that they are of similar origin to that of the rest of the paintings in the album, that is to say 'popular Mughal', from one of the courts in Northern India.

The miniature shown here is of the *raga* called *Hindol*. The icon for this *raga* commonly depicts a young nobleman, or the god Krishna himself, sitting on a swing in the company of one or more lady consorts. The name of the *raga* (meaning 'swing') is here written in Indian *Nasta'liq* script above the painting. The album is attractively bound in contemporary reddish brown leather.

manuscripts suddenly available in Germany and this accounts for the presence among Laud's acquisitions of large groups from churches and religious houses at Würzburg and Mainz, two cities which had fallen to the invading Swedish armies of Gustavus Adolphus in 1631, and no fewer than seventy-five manuscripts from Eberbach, a Cistercian monastery near Wiesbaden, plus a score of others deriving from the celebrated early scriptorium at Lorsch. Germany's loss was certainly England's gain; many splendid Carolingian manuscripts, the like of which had scarcely been seen in this country for the previous 700 years, were included in the Archbishop's third donation, made in the summer of 1639. Pre-eminent among all in age and value was the Laudian *Acts* (Plate 75) acquired from Würzburg in 1636, which is still the most important biblical text in the Bodleian, a manuscript probably used by the Venerable Bede himself. Also from Würzburg came two of the few printed books among Laud's gifts, both on vellum, one a magnificent Würzburg Missal, the other a copy of a rare Breviary (Plate 79) printed for that diocese by the city's first printer. Alas, the manuscripts imported from Germany were almost all stripped of their covers (no doubt to facilitate packing) and irrecoverable details of provenance were thereby lost. It has to be remembered that interest in the historical and evidential value of early bindings is a growth only of the present century. As it was, before their presentation the bulk of all Laudian manuscripts had been rebound, through the agency of Richard Badger the London printer, in plain dark calf with the Archbishop's arms (Plate 74) stamped in gilt on both covers. This uniform livery was applied not only to manuscripts shipped from abroad but also to acquisitions from nearer home, so that little is discoverable today, even about the immediate sources of the manuscripts which Laud acquired in England, beyond the names of some owners who were his contemporaries, mostly antiquaries, churchmen and merchants. For example, the exceedingly important version of the Anglo-Saxon Chronicle (Plate 76) which had been continued up to the year 1154 at the Abbey of Peterborough, and is one of Laud's most outstanding gifts, came from the Anglo-Saxon manuscripts of William Lisle.

Besides the early mediaeval codices from German religious foundations which formed the major part of Laud's third and largest donation in 1639, there was a group of Hebrew manuscripts, further contributing towards the ultimate total of almost fifty such manuscripts which Laud collected for the Bodleian. Outstanding among these was the Laudian *Mahzor* (Plate 80) one of the finest surviving examples of an early Hebrew community prayerbook lavishly illuminated. This was written in south Germany about the year 1290 and was acquired by Laud in 1636, so is no doubt another trophy rescued from the spoils of the Thirty Years War. Laud's fourth and last donation was sent in November 1640, when the 'shades of the prison house' were about to close round him. His accompanying letter refers to the uncertainties of the times, and expresses his wish to place in safe custody in the Bodleian further manuscripts of like quality and interest to his former gifts, though fewer in number. There were in all forty-six volumes, many of them oriental; among them an album containing some collector's assemblage of various Indian miniature paintings (Plate 81), one of the earliest of such collections ever to reach the West. A further fifteen manuscripts reached the Bodleian at some date after the Archbishop had resigned the Oxford Chancellorship, which he did in a letter written from the Tower of London, to which Parliament had sent him on 1 March 1641, four years before he was beheaded there.

Whereas Bodley and Thomas James had sensibly concentrated on building up the Library's stock of printed books, and though a considerable number of western manuscripts, chiefly from England's mediaeval past, had also been gathered in from various sources, there were in their two lifetimes few manuscripts in the Bodleian in Greek or oriental languages. Laud had set himself to remedy this shortcoming. To the Greek manuscripts of the Roe and Barocci collections so recently secured for Oxford, Laud himself now added nearly 100 others of his own; even more impressive, for here he was breaking new ground, was the grand total of 145 Arabic manuscripts he gathered, which together with the Laudian Professorship helped Oxford to establish itself as a home of oriental studies famed throughout Europe and beyond, and initiated a tradition of benefactions of Near and Far East materials which has continued ever since. Lack of information once again obscures the picture of how in detail Laud's oriental purchases were realized. We do know that in 1634 by a royal edict, which Laud doubtless prompted, the Turkey Company was obliged to serve the interests of scholarship as well as of trade by importing, on each voyage home of every one of its ships, one Arabic or Persian manuscript to be delivered to the Archbishop; only copies of the Koran were excepted 'because', in the words of the edict, 'there is great choice of them here already'. Not all Laud's collecting initiatives met with success. John Greaves, Professor of Mathematics at Gresham College, London, visited Alexandria and Constantinople in 1638 on Laud's behalf in quest of oriental manuscripts, but his high hopes were frustrated by one of those sudden twists which were even then a feature of Middle Eastern politics: Laud's (and Roe's) eighty-year-old friend the Orthodox Patriarch Cyril Lucar was strangled as a traitor by his Turkish masters and so the treasures of Mount Athos, from among which the Patriarch had intended to present Laud, through Greaves, with unedited Greek texts, remained undespoiled. Greaves himself, on a warning from Greek friends, was obliged to restore surrept-

82. **Bronze bust of Charles I, by Le Sueur**

In 1631, about the time when the sculptor Hubert Le Sueur was executing his standing bronze statue of the Earl of Pembroke (Plate 71), he made and signed a marble bust of King Charles which was to be the prototype of a number of bronze busts ordered over the next few years, many of which still survive. The earliest among these is the one here illustrated, given to the Bodleian by Laud in 1636 and set in its present plaster niche in 1641, facing the Founder's bust (Plate 46) across the great archway at the entrance to Duke Humfrey's Library. Modelled on earlier examples by Le Sueur's French predecessors and masters, this formal portrait largely created the royal image for the King's contemporaries and for posterity. Stylistically it also bears witness to the current vogue for those portrait busts from Imperial Rome which the age of the Renaissance had rediscovered and eagerly collected. Charles I was himself one of the leading art collectors in Europe, and besides paintings he also bought sculptures, even including Graeco-Roman ones; indeed a writer in 1634 commented on his 'Royal liking of ancient statues'.

Laud wrote that he wanted this bust to be so placed with his gift of manuscripts that under its royal gaze no one might dare to desecrate the volumes in any way.

83. Loggan's view of Selden End in 1675
This is the lower of the two engravings which were printed together as one plate of Loggan's *Oxonia illustrata*, 1675; the pair to it, Arts End, is reproduced here as Plate 43. These two engravings were dedicated by the artist to Thomas Barlow, to whom, as Bodley's then Librarian, had fallen the task of filling this new wing with Selden's great library, which gave it the name it still bears. This, the later of the two wings to be built, has more elaborate galleries but a plainer ceiling than Arts End, and like the other it, too, preserves its appearance virtually unchanged from that which Loggan recorded more than 300 years ago. This picture of it gains in dignity from the absence of clutter on the floor space, now occupied by bookcases and tables for readers, clutter which would have prevented such leisurely strolls of elegant Restoration visitors as Loggan depicts. Its amplitude made this a fine setting for University hospitality, as when in 1663 Charles II, his Queen and the Duke and Duchess of York were first subjected to a speech (delivered on his knees by Nathaniel Crewe, the Senior Proctor) at the far end of Duke Humfrey from here, but were then 'conducted to Selden's Library, and there entertained with a very sumptuous banquet'. In 1687 the Duke of York, now King James II, was again entertained here to a breakfast. The King asked no one to join him at the table, so that when he rose to go there was a wild scramble of courtiers and academics for the untouched remains of the 111 dishes provided, which had cost the University £160.

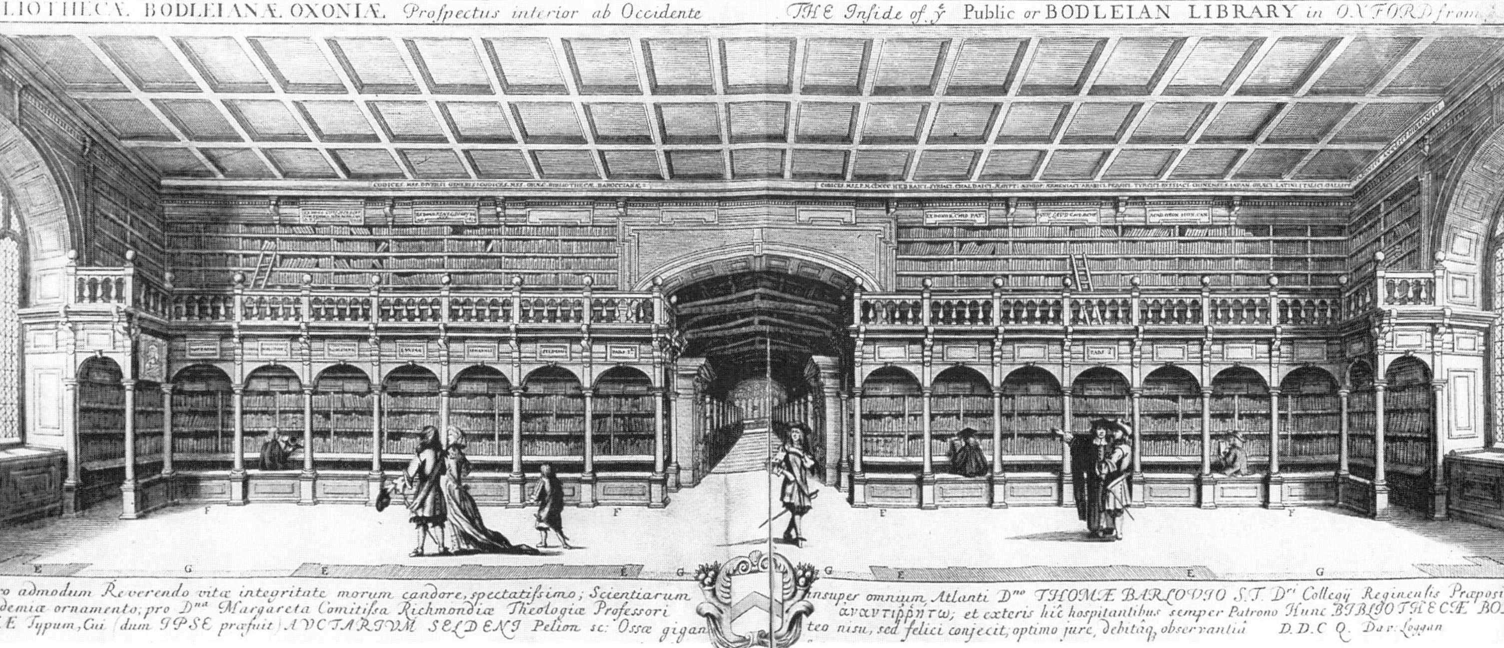

itiously fourteen manuscripts he had actually bought from another monastery, and to forefeit his purchase money 'for feare of a worse inconvenience' as he wrote home to a friend in England, with typically Anglo-Saxon understatement. But despite the distance, difficulties and even perils of collecting in what was already becoming an internationally competitive field, Laud was able to enrich Oxford with almost 200 oriental manuscripts.

Unlike those many who, before and since, have formed collections of different sorts and sizes and have subsequently given, bequeathed or sold them to the Bodleian, Laud bought, and that on a grand scale, not to gratify any personal tastes but directly to equip the newly re-founded Library of his University with texts (especially unpublished ones) which would benefit the learned world. Indeed he actually stipulated that any of his manuscripts might be allowed outside the Library if used as copy for printing by the University Press, for which he obtained from the Crown extensive new privileges. In 1629 when his benefactions began there were around 1,000 manuscripts in the Bodleian, and with the addition of those of Roe, Barocci and Digby which came to Oxford via Laud's London residence, this number had risen, by the year 1634, to about 1,650. In the next five years Laud's own gifts had totalled no fewer than 1,250, thereby almost doubling the previous number of Bodleian manuscripts and so vastly extending their range as to provoke envy, admiration and keen interest among European scholars.

The perennial logistic problem of librarians, that of finding space to house sudden accessions on this princely scale, was solved initially by housing manuscripts in the Tower (Plate 49) and the Gallery of the newly completed Schools Quadrangle. Further relief was at hand. Part of the generous funds bequeathed in his will was intended by Bodley for 'some beautiful enlargement at the west end' and this new wing, built along the west wall of the Divinity School and of the Library above it, was begun in 1634 and completed in 1640. Designed in a somewhat newer and more classical style, for all its Gothic fan-vaulting, the ground floor provided a much-needed Convocation House for the meetings of the University's own parliament, and later even occasionally for sessions of the nation's Parliament. Above the Convocation House, after the old turret staircases had been swept away which originally gave access to Duke Humfrey's Library, a long, spacious room was created, soon to be termed Selden End, onto the ample shelves of which these huge new accessions could gradually be moved. Its dignified, well-lit interior, which can be enjoyed in the fine detail of David Loggan's 1675 engraving (Plate 83), has been a resort beloved by generations of scholars down the centuries, while from time to time it also served a not strictly library purpose by providing a noble setting for the University to entertain to a banquet a visiting Head of State, were he Parliamentary general or Stuart King.

CHAPTER IV

Survivals and Arrivals

1640–1665

Early in 1620, when Thomas James decided to retire from the post of Bodley's Librarian because of increasing ill-health, the Curators, whose duty it was by statute to find a successor within three days, elected in his place John Rous, a Fellow of Oriel College since 1600. Rous was then aged about forty-six, almost the same age as the man he succeeded, yet he was destined to hold office for more than thirty years, dying at the ripe age of seventy-eight after a tenure which was to see the Library continue, intact, through extreme changes of fortune. During his first two decades he carried out the onerous but thankful task of incorporating enormous manuscript accessions, among them those of the Barocci, Roe, Digby and Laud gifts which were described in Chapter III. He also supervised the construction between 1634 and 1640 of the (future) Selden End, into which he was able to gather, not only those great collections but also the Library's hitherto physically scattered manuscripts, including those which, after Sir Thomas Bodley's death, Thomas James had been able to sort out from among the foundation collections of printed books. Unlike his predecessor, Rous published comparatively little, but in 1631 he is found writing the preface to a small pamphlet, perhaps compiled on his initiative, in which eight young Oxford graduates, all of whom later achieved some distinction for their writings, paid tribute in Latin verses thanking a citizen of Danzig, Johann Cirenberg, who had presented a valuable manuscript concerning the Council of Basel to Sir Thomas Roe, who promptly added it to the large gift he had made to the Bodleian in the previous year.

Expressing the Library's gratitude to its benefactors and entertaining its visitors, both the scholars and the sightseers – these sides of a librarian's life were (and are) far from unimportant additions to the daily routine. Among Rous's first duties, in the earliest weeks of his long tenure of office, had been to make that 'verie prettie speech' at the solemn reception of the presentation copy of King James's *Works* (Plate 59). The speech effectively expressed the kind of adulation the monarch expected and enjoyed; it was not, however, printed until Thomas Hearne, with his passion for gathering up even the uncollected leavings of history, disinterred it many years later. It contained an allusion to a visit Rous had paid seven years before to the Palatine Library, then still at Heidelberg, thus revealing a small but significant personal detail about a Librarian whose private career is rather sparsely documented.

In print, Rous's principal monument was the supplement he published in 1635 to James's 1620 Bodleian *Catalogue*. That *Catalogue* had included a thirty-six-page Appendix, and Rous modestly called his own anonymous supplement a second edition of that Jamesian Appendix, though adding on his titlepage the claim that it had been enlarged by the names of some 3,000 authors, a measure of the Library's continued

84. **A unique '1602' *Venus and Adonis* from Robert Burton's library**
Originally published in 1593, *Venus and Adonis* marks Shakespeare's first appearance in print and rapidly became his favourite work among readers; the next forty-three years saw the issue of at least fifteen further editions of which copies (or fragments) still survive. Under the law which governs survival (correlating mass popularity with mass destruction of copies through sheer wear and tear), it is likely that other editions, for which we have no tangible evidence today, were also in fact actually printed during that period. As it is, eleven of the fifteen surviving editions are now known in a single copy each, and out of these eleven unique surviving copies the Bodleian possesses no fewer than six. The present edition was the earliest of our six to arrive, being picked by the Librarian, John Rous, from among the books left by Robert Burton at his death in 1640. Rous also selected Burton's copy of an edition of Shakespeare's other 'best seller', *The Rape of Lucrece*, though he could only describe it in his autograph catalogue of Burton's books as 'imperfect', since it lacked the title and the final leaf. Later, a perfect copy, which came to us with Malone's collection in 1821, revealed that Burton's *Lucrece* belonged to a 1600 edition, which today is known only from these two Bodleian copies.

Detective work on printers' types and ornaments has shown that this present edition was really printed about 1607–8 and is a forgery of a genuine edition of 1602, of which, again, the Bodleian has the only copy known today. This piracy cunningly used the genuine device of the publisher William Leake, the then owner of the poem's copyright; for making this piracy, Robert Raworth, who repeatedly got into trouble for printing unlicensed editions, was sentenced by the Stationers' Company to forfeit his printing-press.

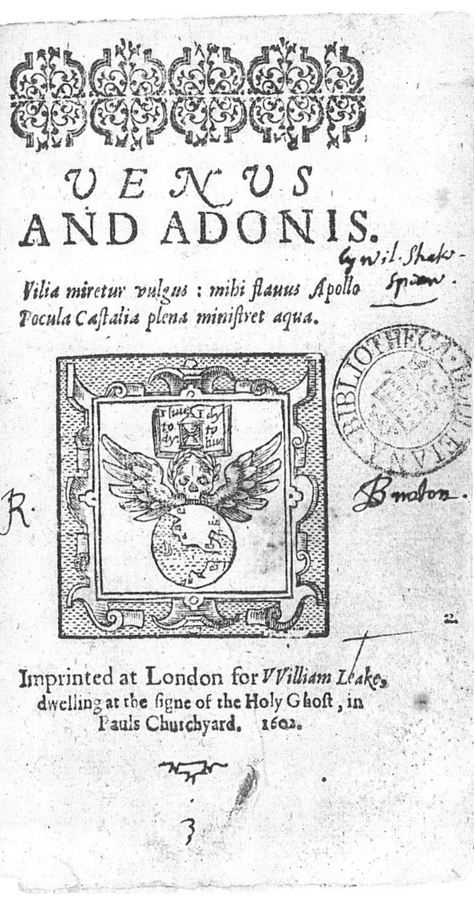

VENUS AND ADONIS.

Vilia miretur vulgus : mihi flauus Apollo
Pocula Castalia plena ministret aqua.

Imprinted at London for *VVilliam Leake*, dwelling at the signe of the Holy Ghost, in Pauls Churchyard. 1602.

In addition to his autograph or initials, Robert Burton frequently wrote in his books at the foot of the titlepage a mark of ownership (shown here and in Plate 86) consisting of three linked 'r's.

growth during the previous fifteen years; manuscripts and printed books were still, however, described in a single series. That same year the University printer also issued a revised and much enlarged edition of the 'Catalogue of writers on the books of the Bible', one of those subject listings which Thomas James had included in his original 1605 *Catalogue* for the assistance of readers. This revision was an anonymous work by Jean Verneuil, a French Protestant refugee, who was Sub-Librarian from 1618 until his death in 1647. From the year 1635, therefore, readers and outside scholars could purchase, for the total sum of only five shillings, the 1620 *Catalogue*, plus these two supplements. So, when the distinguished historian Sir Henry Spelman presented a copy of his pioneering *Glossary* of obsolete law terms, the Library paid for a copy of its 'new catalogue' (that of 1620, with the 1635 Appendix) to be bound in vellum and sent to him in return. But it was to be almost another forty years before a new printed Bodleian *Catalogue* would be available.

An even more revealing indication of Rous's real quality as a librarian is to be found in his treatment of the legacy made to the Bodleian by Robert Burton, the author of *The Anatomy of Melancholy* who died early in 1640. In his will, drawn up six months before his death, besides bequeathing £100 to form a fund for book purchases in avowed imitation of the bequest of Margaret Brooke (Plate 67), Burton had stated 'If I have any bookes the Universitye Library hath not, lett them take them'. Even if the grammar of the sentence conferring the gift can be faulted, this proved a most generous bequest. Though (in his own estimate) a man of only moderate means, Burton, a member of Christ Church, had been an assiduous book buyer ever since his undergraduate days, as can be seen from the annotations he wrote in many of his books. By the time of his death in his sixty-third year he had amassed over 1,700 books. For that period it was a large private library and has been the subject of a comprehensive study recently published by Nicolas Kiessling. Today more than 1,500 of those 1,700 books are still in Oxford, divided almost equally between the Bodleian and Christ Church, to which he also left a similarly worded right of selection.

The list of what Rous chose for the Bodleian is preserved, written in his own hand, and it shows him – for there is no evidence that anyone but Bodley's Librarian himself made the choice of books – exercising a real independence of judgment. Knowing as well as evidently he did, after twenty years in office, the strengths and weaknesses of Bodley's then holdings, he took the opportunity presented by Burton's wide-ranging and idiosyncratic tastes to fill gaps in those holdings which were partly the result of deliberate choice by Sir Thomas and his first Librarian, and partly had occurred through the negligence of the Stationers' Company to fulfil its deposit undertakings to the University. Early concentration on standard editions of important texts

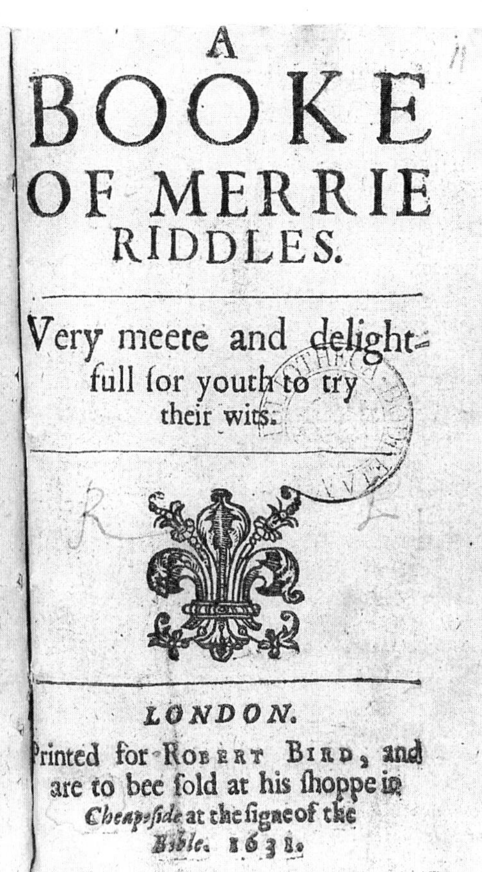

A
BOOKE
OF MERRIE
RIDDLES.

Very meete and delightfull for youth to try their wits.

LONDON.
Printed for ROBERT BIRD, and are to bee ſold at his ſhoppe in *Cheapſide* at the ſigne of the *Bible*. 1631.

85. ***A Booke of Merrie Riddles*, 1631**
Like the proverb, the riddle belongs to every age and every culture. It runs through all folk literatures and fairy tales and at times has even taken elaborate literary forms, as witness in our own country the Latin metrical riddles of St Aldhelm in the seventh century, and the Anglo-Saxon riddles in the Exeter Book. Its attraction lies in the concealment of the familiar by describing it in unfamiliar and mystifying ways, akin to metaphor. Sometimes a reward or forfeit was attached to its solution. In Greek mythology the Theban Sphinx, who fed on those who failed to guess her riddle, destroyed herself after Oedipus had guessed it correctly. In the Old Testament Samson set a riddle to the thirty Philistines and when they guessed it he angrily abandoned the wife who had wormed the answer out of him on her countrymen's behalf. The Queen of Sheba tested the wisdom of Solomon with 'hard questions', which would have been cast in riddle form.

Since the era of printing, it may be said that, although little of all that was put into print has come through to the present, enough of the literature of riddles can be pieced together to prove its wide and long-continuing appeal. Literary allusions confirm that popularity; it was a *Book of Riddles* which Master Slender in *The Merry Wives of Windsor* forgot that he had lent to Alice Shortcake. These popular collections manifest strong family connections. Indeed riddles, and also jokes, are still current in the child's playground that have pedigrees which can be traced back through several centuries. A single leaf in the Bodleian, with another at Edinburgh which is from the same binding, belong to a vanished edition of a *Book of a Hundred Riddles* printed about 1530 by William Rastell, whose father had earlier published *A Hundred Mery Talys*. The contents of those two leaves are sufficient to reveal that a collection which amused the subjects of King Kenry VIII is related to others printed a century or more later for Jacobean and Caroline wits, 'useful', as the publisher claims on one titlepage, 'for any yong man or child to know if he be quick-witted or no'.

Among Robert Burton's books chosen for the Bodleian are two English riddle books; one, *The Booke of Meery Riddles*, dated 1629, is one of only three copies now known, while the other, a similar compilation from a rival publisher two years later, entitled *A Booke of Merrie Riddles*, here illustrated, is unique.

Tom Thumbe,
His Life and Death:
Wherein is declared many Maruailous Acts of Manhood, full of wonder, and ſtrange merriments:
Which little Knight liued in King *Arthurs* time, and famous in the Court of *Great-Brittaine*.

London Printed for *John Wright*. 1630.

86. ***Tom Thumbe, His Life and Death*, 1630**
Stories about Tom Thumb, a tiny fellow no taller than his father's thumb, exploit the enduring appeal of whatever is miniature. Many absurd adventures were told of this diminutive hero, who undoubtedly was familiar in folk legend long before he appears in any literature which found its way into print. This is shown, for example, by Reginald Scot's *Discoverie of Witchcraft*, published in 1584, in which Tom Thumb is mentioned in company with Puck, Robin Goodfellow and 'such other bugs' (bugbears) – imaginary characters used to thrill and scare children and ignorant people. His long-lasting popularity is also alluded to in the final lines of the earliest surviving edition, dated 1630, of a poem on his Life and Death, of which only this copy is known, which bears Robert Burton's manuscript cipher written under the imprint. These lines celebrate a character

Whose fame still lives in England here,
  amongst the Countrey sort,
Of whom our Wives and Children small
  tell tales of pleasant sport.

One of the tales, about Tom accidentally baked by his mother inside a pudding, is alluded to in verses prefixed to Coryate's *Crudities* in 1611, and also in 1624 by Ben Jonson in his masque *The Fortunate Isles.* A London author, Richard Johnson, (two of whose rare works came to the Bodleian in Burton's bequest) scored many popular successes and is probably responsible for a prose *History of Tom Thumbe, the little* which appeared in 1621. Johnson's immensely popular account of the *Seven Champions of Christendome*, first published in 1596 and many times reprinted, had recounted legends of seven national patron saints described in the unexpected setting of Arthurian romances of chivalry. And so, at the comic level, even Tom Thumb is made into a knight at King Arthur's court and is pictured here on the poem's titlepage as a minute warrior armed cap-à-pie and mounted on a full-sized charger. This very same woodcut is found in a damaged state (perhaps through much intermediate use), in a page-for-page reprint, in the next edition to have survived which appeared about twenty-five years later. Of that later edition a copy is also in the Bodleian, among Anthony Wood's books, and it, too, is unique.

There were also numerous subsequent editions, and indeed in various forms the Thumb Cycle has continued to delight at least a nursery audience right up to the present day.

had by now well equipped the Bodleian in theology, law, medicine and philosophy. But Burton who, as an Oxford scholar, had (as he remarked) enjoyed the use of its splendid libraries, had himself also tucked away on his own shelves a rich assemblage of books of a kind which no serious contemporary librarian but Rous might have thought worthy of attention. The contrast is pointed by Rous's decision to record in the Benefactors' Register only the Latin books he had selected from Burton's library; the rest, though listed by him in his manuscript inventory, he omitted from the Register with the excuse that they were too many to enumerate (and doubtless also too lightweight to mention in its grave, Latin pages). Though many other libraries, then and since, could, and do, duplicate the more serious books Rous chose, yet among his choices of English-printed books, for example in the fields of plays, poetry, marvels and murders, news- and jest-books, more than fifty remain to this day unique, that is, unknown in any other library. The three examples here illustrated from among Burton's unique English books are a pocket edition of Shakespeare's most popular poem (Plate 84), a mock-heroic *Tom Thumbe* (Plate 86), and a book of riddles (Plate 85).

Still further light on the true stature of Rous as Librarian is afforded by his relations with the poet Milton. A friendship between the two men, bred of a shared Puritan outlook, has been inferred, but indications of any such relationship actually survive only in the wording chosen by Milton when sending presentation copies of his works to the Bodleian. Nevertheless it is a fact that Milton visited Oxford in 1635, while he was living with his old father near Windsor, and that he then incorporated M.A., which a Cambridge graduate was, and is, entitled to do. It is most probable that one reason for his visit was to find his way into what he himself later termed 'that most ancient and famous Library' and to make himself known to Rous. The Librarian was a man already more than twice Milton's age but one to whom the classical learning and scholarly tastes of the younger man would have been very congenial. By that year, 1635, at the age of twenty-seven, Milton had published nothing of all that he had so far written except the brief epitaph prefixed, anonymously, in 1632 to the Second Folio of Shakespeare. By 1645, however, only ten years later, Milton had become a well-known public figure through his major part in published controversies and it is not surprising to find that in a surviving list of twenty-four recent publications which Rous purchased for the Library in June 1645, two of Milton's most famous tracts on divorce and on liberty of the press are included.

The fact that two such revolutionary works were bought, and from an Oxford bookseller too, during the time the royal court was still in residence in the city, certainly testifies to the Librarian's independence of mind. It also shows how the operation of the deposit agreement with the Stationers' Company, which Laud as Chancellor had reinforced in 1637, had collapsed with the abolition of Star Chamber in 1640 and the subsequent outbreak of the Civil War, which interrupted normal communications between London and Oxford. Yet any deduction from the presence of those two Milton tracts among Rous's choice of books should not be pressed too far; the rest of the list shows him making sure, as a good librarian should, that both sides of current controversies were represented on the Library's shelves. Thus, for example, Sir Thomas Browne's *Religio medici* is matched by Sir Kenelm Digby's critical *Observations* on it, and also by Alexander Ross's reply to Digby; similarly, seven of Prynne's pamphlets are there, but so also are several answers to them.

It could well be that the presentation of a volume of his prose tracts which Milton made to Rous's friend the learned Patrick Young, the royal librarian, had come to the knowledge of Rous, who let it be known to Milton that a similar gift for the Bodleian would be welcome. It duly arrived, in the shape of a stout quarto volume containing all eleven of the English tracts Milton had published up to that time, bound in chronological order. Prefixed is a page of Latin entirely in Milton's hand, saluting Rous as 'that most learned man and honest judge of books', who had said that he would be glad to admit these works into this 'shrine of everlasting remembrance' there to remain as it were beyond reach, so Milton hoped, of envy and slander. Milton's own manuscript list of the contents, prefixed to this gift-volume, adds a copy of his *Poems* in Latin and English, bound and 'sent separately', obviously because of its smaller size. This, the first collected edition of Milton's poems, is a modest octavo, which is dated 1645 but actually appeared in January 1646. Somehow this little volume miscarried and, in response to a request from Rous, Milton sent a replacement copy in which, be it noted, he had in his own autograph corrected misprints in two of the English poems; for one of these corrections no other manuscript authority is known. But the chief glory of this replacement copy is that it contains a Latin manuscript poem specially composed by Milton, in the form of a mock-heroic Ode to Rous (Plate 88). Milton did not afterwards forget the Bodleian; in 1651, when he had already been for two years secretary for foreign tongues to the Council of State of the new Commonwealth, he sent the Library a presentation copy of the revised edition in folio of his famous *Pro populo anglicano defensio*, which he had written against Claude de Saumaise's defence of King Charles.

As guardian of what was already establishing itself as a nationally, indeed an internationally, important institution Rous naturally had dealings with many influential men of his time. The best-remembered incident in his career involved him in a minor confrontation with the reigning monarch. Rous was no stranger to royalty. As Bodley's

87. **The Bodley Medal, 1646**
The Library accounts for 1646 record a payment of two shillings 'to Mr Warren that made his [i.e. Sir Thomas Bodley's] medale'. Besides the profile of the Founder, the medal bears on its reverse the standing figure of a woman who holds in her hands busts of the sun and the moon. Around her is the Latin inscription: AETERNITAS R[EI] P[UBLICAE] LITERARIAE – the everlastingness of the republic of letters. This evocation of the permanence of the things of the spirit may represent the reaction of someone connected with the Library to the momentous and threatening events which were going on around him, for 1646 was the year that saw the surrender of Oxford at the end of June to the Parliamentary army under Sir Thomas Fairfax, the King having slipped out of the city in

disguise at the end of April. There is indeed no obvious direct connection between the medal and these events, but we may also note that in 1647 someone (perhaps Gerard Langbaine) published at Oxford for the first time the autobiography which Bodley had written in 1609, a valuable document in which the Founder explains his own motives in undertaking his great enterprise. That, too, may have been a re-assertion of the national importance of the Bodleian and of its safe custody; the victorious General Fairfax (later to be a notable benefactor of the Library), as soon as he entered the city showed his understanding of its supreme value by placing a guard of soldiers to preserve the Bodleian and its treasures from vandalism.

The Bodley Medal is seemingly made of lead brazed over and the name 'Warin' is engraved on it. There were two medallic artists of this name (Warin or Varin) working at that time, Jean, who spent much of his life in France, and Claude, possibly a brother, who appears to have spent some years in England, and who died in Lyons in 1654. It is Claude, with a style more heavy-handed than that of Jean, who is believed to have been almost certainly the artist of this Bodley Medal. There are several medals in the British Museum attributed to these artists (including an unbrazed copy of that of Bodley) but of these only one other is attributed to Claude, being a medal struck in 1638 in honour of John Prideaux, the Regius Professor of Divinity at Oxford from 1615 to 1641, who later became Bishop of Worcester. An engraving of both sides of the Bodley Medal appears as a vignette on page 1 of Francis Wise's catalogue of Bodleian coins, 1750, but there it is described as being of silver. Both sides appear also, stamped in gold, on the front cover of the Bodleian Tercentenary volume, *Pietas Oxoniensis*, 1902, but for this the British Museum medal was used.

Librarian he had, of course, to be in attendance when royal visitors were to be shown round. It was in August 1629 that King Charles I with his Queen first visited the Library. At that date even the 'Vice-Deus', as the Public Orator termed him on that occasion, still had to climb the narrow spiral staircase at the west end of Duke Humfrey to gain access to the Library. But seven years later when the King on his second visit arrived to inspect the new west wing (now Selden End), the Library's eastern staircases had recently been carried up another flight to give access directly into Arts End. Here the King sat, in front of the great east window, looking at manuscripts brought out of the grilled cupboards for him to admire. These would surely have included some of the treasures newly bestowed by the Chancellor, Laud, the host to this royal visit, who will no doubt also have shown the King, who was very conscious of his public image, the monarch's bust in bronze by Le Sueur (Plate 82) which Laud had just presented to stand in a niche where it could keep a royal eye on the safety of the manuscripts, and on the good behaviour of the readers, below it.

The next occasion, however, when the Bodleian became involved with the King took place in a very different atmosphere. Even before Charles raised his standard at Nottingham on 22 August 1642, letters from the King at York were read in Convocation on 11 July asking for loans of money. Although Oxford town was at heart Parliamentarian, the University threw itself behind the royal cause; a 'loan' of £860 from the University Chest was accompanied by £500 from the Bodleian Chest. Not long before, the balance in the Bodleian Chest had been sufficient to allow the University – temporarily embarrassed by the expenses of the royal visit in 1636 and by the cost of building the Convocation House and the Selden End above it – to borrow out of it a sum of no less than £640, which was paid back in 1638. But the £500 now lent to the King was never repaid, though the debt was carried forward hopefully from year to year; librarians, like elephants, have long memories and it was not until 1782, one hundred and forty years later, that the royal debt was finally written off.

In September 1642 a short occupation of Oxford by Parliamentary troops caused alarm and some damage; troopers forced their way into the Schools building, thinking it was a college, 'and there lay, searching and tumbling to and fro of the Library books'; but on 29 October King Charles led his forces into the city, which became the royal head-quarters for almost the next four years. University buildings, including the rooms round the Schools Quadrangle, were now put to unfamiliar uses, civil or military, connected with the Court, the Government, and the Judiciary, or for the storage of munitions and grain. The city was fortified and all men aged between sixteen and sixty had to work one day a week on the defences or pay twelve pence for a substitute. At a time of great financial stringency, therefore, Rous was forced to find

88. Milton's manuscript Ode to Bodley's Librarian

It is admirably fitting that the earliest entrance of Milton's poetry onto the shelves of the Bodleian should be in the form of its author's first appearance before the general reader as a poet and under his own name, and that this pioneering volume should have been received from Milton's own hand.

After his return from Italy in 1636, current developments in church and state had led Milton, with regret, for some years to lay aside his preferred role of poet and his ambition to compose an epic in English, and instead 'to embark' (in his own words) 'in a troubled sea of noises and hoarse disputes' by writing his celebrated and formidable cluster of prose polemics. But in 1645 a lull in these controversies and his reconciliation with his wife gave him leisure to gather together the poems he had written from his undergraduate days onwards, and to let Humphrey Mosely, a keen publisher of English literature, print them for him. The result was a small volume, registered for publication in October 1645 and certainly in print by 2 January 1646, with the title *Poems . . . both English and Latin*. In this collection are reprinted *Comus*, which had been published in 1637 without the poet's name, and *Lycidas*, which had been tucked away at the end of a Cambridge volume of obituary verses printed in 1638. And here also are printed for the first time some of his best-loved shorter poems, including *L'Allegro*, *Il Penseroso* and *On the Morning of Christ's Nativity* and also his finest Latin poem, the *Epitaphium Damonis*, a pastoral elegy on his dearest friend, who died during Milton's journey to Italy.

It is no surprise, therefore, when in

Ad Joannem Rousium, Oxoniensis Academiæ
Bibliothecarium.
De libro poëmatum amisso quem ille sibi denuò
mitti postulabat, ut cum aliis nostris in Bibliotheca
publica reponeret. Ode Joannis Miltonj.

Strophe

Gemelle cultu simplici gaudens liber,
Fronde licet geminâ,
Munditieque nitens non operosâ,
Quam manus attulit

this sum for thirty-one weeks to hire a man 'to worke at the bullworks' in place of the Library Porter, Thomas Roche. It was not only labour that the Royalist cause needed but money also. Colleges were called upon to yield up their silver plate and their Fellows to pay for the maintenance of foot soldiers at four shillings a week. Rous, who had lived in Oriel since his election to a Fellowship in 1600 and who was to die there, still unmarried, subscribed £50. Even if not unsolicited, it was a generous amount, for it was considerably more than the £40 which he received each year as Bodley's Librarian. Other indications suggest he had private means besides his salary; he lent his own College £60 when it was in distress through the war, and in his will he bequeathed £20 to the Bodleian and £50 to the Oriel building fund.

The last and best-known incident which involved Rous personally with the King shows him as a faithful custodian of the Library entrusted to his care. It was an encounter which does credit to both parties and occurred just after Christmas 1645, a few months before Charles left Oxford in secret, never to return there. A note was sent from the King ordering Rous or his deputy to 'Deliver unto the bearer hereof, for the present use of His Majesty, a book entitled *Histoire*

1646 at the request of the Librarian, John Rous, Milton presented to the Bodleian a collection of his recent prose writings for preservation in that 'shrine of everlasting remembrance', he should have added to the gift a copy of his newly published *Poems*. Because of its smaller size it could not be bound up in the same quarto volume as the prose tracts, so it was sent separately, but as we learn from Milton's own account, it somehow got lost and never arrived. In response to a request from Rous, Milton sent another copy and with it a manuscript Ode to John Rous in Latin, specially composed for the occasion, of which the opening lines are here reproduced. The handwriting is not Milton's own; when the Ode was first put into print by the poet in the second edition of his poems the year before his death in 1674, it bore the exact date of its composition, 23 January 1646/47, and by that time his poor eyesight, which had begun to fail some five years earlier, may explain why the Ode was written out for him by another hand. This has been claimed as that of his younger nephew John Phillips, who, with his brother Edward, had been brought up and educated in his uncle's house since 1640. That Milton himself supervised the copy is proved by a manuscript correction which is unmistakably in the poet's own hand.

The poem is mock heroic and assumes the shape of a Greek chorus consisting of three strophes each followed by an antistrophe and is rounded off with an epodos. In classic language replete with learned allusions, it reveals the facts of the original's loss and replacement at Rous's request, for all of which it is our only source, and bids the new copy of his youthful verses look forward to a peaceful future in Oxford under the protection of the learned Rous.

universelle du Sieur D'Aubigné and 'this shall be your warrant'. The strongly royalist Samuel Fell, Dean of Christ Church, where the King had his lodgings, added his authority as Vice-Chancellor to this demand. But Rous was unmoved. He went directly into the royal presence armed with the Library Statutes which he showed the King, who cancelled his book-order after reading the Founder's prohibition against lending, and expressed his approval that Bodley's ordinance should be 'religiously observed'.

Either just before or just after the King's final departure from Oxford, Rous is found, from the Library accounts, making small payments (surely no more than gratuities) 'to the painter that drew Sir Thomas Bodley's picture and to Mr Warren that made his medale to each of them 2s'. The portrait of Bodley, the medal (Plate 87) struck in his honour, and the publication in 1647 by the University Printer of the Founder's autobiography, made from a Bodleian transcript of the lost autograph, may together represent some assertion of the enduring importance and identity of the Library at a time of uncertainty and peril. The anonymous editor of Bodley's *Life* was probably Gerard Langbaine the elder, who had become Keeper of the University Archives in 1644 and later D.D. and Provost of Queen's College. In 1642-3 the Library accounts show Rous paying £1 'to buy a French standish (inkstand) to present Mr Langbane for his paines about' the Barocci Greek manuscripts, and three years afterwards Rous spent 6s 8d on a pair of gloves (a very popular ceremonial token of gratitude) for Langbaine for his further help in cataloguing and arranging Greek manuscripts. As a cataloguer of manuscripts Langbaine was far ahead of other men of his time and though his descriptions remained unprinted, after his death in 1658 the Library did buy and preserve his notebooks, in which the results of his scholarly labour can still be studied and admired.

Part of the first Bodleian Account Book, recently published with admirable annotations, covers more than three-quarters of Rous's long term as Librarian and affords glimpses of the routine of his library administration at many different levels, ranging from the payment of £1,000 to the contractor who by 1640 had panelled and shelved the new west wing (Selden End, Plate 83) down to tenpence paid for 'a bell roape' to sound Sir Thomas Bodley's bell (Plate 44). As is to be expected there are in these accounts substantial amounts recorded for book purchases, including quite large sums paid to London booksellers, initially for purchases from the spring and autumn Frankfurt Book Fairs, for which the agent was generally that same Henry Featherstone whose enterprise secured the Barocci collection for England. He presented to the Library in 1630 a collection of Hebrew books and in 1632 Rous made a special journey to London 'to end and perfect all accompts with Mr Fetherston, having given over trading'. Later, when

62

the Thirty Years War disrupted the Frankfurt Fairs, books continued to be bought from Italy and France, at least up until the outbreak of the Civil War. Consignments of foreign purchases were sometimes sent by London booksellers on approval, books found to be already in the Library being returnable. The carriage of books (which in bulk are among the weightier human artefacts) is a frequent Library expense. Large loads came by barge up the Thames to Burcot, some six miles from Oxford, and thence by road; smaller ones could be entrusted to the University Carrier, who also delivered letters.

Most of Bodley's own large fortune of over £12,000 had been earmarked in his will for his three further great building projects: the third storey of the Schools Quadrangle for book storage, the new western wing (Selden End) and the staircases giving access into the Library from the Schools. But in his lifetime he had given (Plate 45) estates from which his Library derived, in the form of rents, its main annual income, amounting at this time to just under £140. To this were added each year any sums of money donated or bequeathed by benefactors, which were placed in the Chest and spent on the purchase of books. There were also occasional credits accruing from the sale of the Library's printed *Catalogues* and from the sale of books out of the Library. These books were not at this date actual duplicates, but editions which were considered to have become obsolete; the prevailing policy was to hold only the most recent (and therefore, it was ingenuously assumed, necessarily the best) editions of scholarly texts, so that even volumes which had been given by the earliest benefactors

89. Presentation binding on Hevelius's *Selenographia*, 1647

Like another earlier astronomer, Tycho Brahe (Plate 61), Johann Hevelius also built and equipped on the shores of the Baltic his own private observatory, where he made the discoveries which he described and published at his own cost in a series of important books. Of a list of seventeen separate titles of his own published works, which Hevelius added at the end of a book of his printed in 1679, the Library possesses all but two (which were acquired otherwise) in copies with presentation inscriptions from the author himself to the Bodleian. These came in a series of five gifts spread over almost forty years and began with the first and most important of his books, *Selenographia sive Lunae descriptio*, published in his native town of Danzig in 1647 and presented in 1649. In 1668, four years after his eminence as an astronomer had led to his election as a Fellow of the Royal Society of London, he sent to the Bodleian through the hands of Henry Oldenburg, the Secretary of the Royal Society, a group of nine further works, for which the Vice-Chancellor, John Fell, wrote him a letter of thanks in the University's name. In one of the works sent in this batch Hevelius printed the unpublished observations of the self-taught astronomical genius Jeremiah Horrocks, a Lancashire curate who in 1639 was the first man to predict and then observe a transit of Venus.

Author's presentation copies from Hevelius cannot be described as uncommon. He inherited in 1649 his father's brewery in Danzig, which he had helped to run, and he could therefore afford to publish his own books and to be generous in giving away copies. A selection published in 1683 from the correspondence addressed to him contains many letters from astronomers and other men of learning in various countries thanking him for copies of his works which he had sent them. Among his English correspondents are found the famous names of Ussher, Halley and Flamsteed and also Dr John Wallis, to whom besides many letters Hevelius sent inscribed presentation copies of several of his books. Wallis, who in his turn dedicated to Hevelius a little booklet published in 1656 describing an eclipse of the sun of which Wallis himself had taken observations at Oxford two years before, was Savilian Professor of Geometry for more than fifty years. He bequeathed his presentation copies of Hevelius to the special Library which Sir Henry Savile had founded for the use of the Savilian Professors; this Savilian Library, which was originally housed in the first-floor room over the archway in the Tower of the Five Orders (Plate 49), was finally handed over to the Bodleian in 1884. By this transfer were added to the Bodleian's already fine collection of Hevelius the copies of his works presented by Hevelius to Wallis, and also seven further copies contained in two volumes presented to the Savilian Library by Sir Christopher Wren in 1673, the year the latter resigned the Professorship of Astronomy (Plate 118).

Pride of place among all these many Hevelius presentation copies now on the Bodleian shelves must be given to this splendid copy of *Selenographia* which he gave in 1649. Obviously this, his first book, deserved a special binding, and the result is a notable example of a type of design which is still little known in Western Europe.

Dictae Illustrissimae Bibliothecae Bodleianae, cum officiosa bene
merendi voluntate, atque diuturnitatis longaevae votis, dono offe
roque; non dubitans, ut ut minusculum hocce sit tenue et
exiguum, quin nobilissimi animum exhibentis propensum optime
sint interpretaturi omnes. Scribebam Gedani, Anno Salu
tis 1649, die 18 Novemb. St. Greg.

Johannes Hevelius

90. Inscription by Hevelius presenting *Selenographia* to the Bodleian

It is known that Hevelius visited London in 1631, and although he seems to have spent a good deal of time in England over the years, his command of the language was very imperfect. That mattered little when it came to his large European correspondence; letters, treatises and presentation inscriptions were written, like this one, in the author's own clear handwriting and in stylish and idiomatic Latin, the international language of educated men. The present inscription, lengthier than most as befits so sumptuous a gift, reveals that Hevelius himself had formerly visited the Bodleian, and expresses the hope that its Curators will not, even with their profusion of treasures, disdain this small gift and his accompanying good wishes.

and still wore on their covers the livery of their noble donors, were packed off to the marketplace under this rule. From time to time sums were also received for the admission of undergraduates – at £2 apiece – as Bodleian readers.

The Library's yearly outgoings were recorded in the accounts as either 'ordinary', i.e. recurrent within each financial year, or 'extraordinary'. The 'ordinary' expenses were the salaries, paid half-yearly, of the three members of the Staff (Keeper, Under-Keeper, and Porter) amounting at this time to a little more than £50. There were also two small payments to the Crown as quitrents for the five houses in Distaff Lane, London, which formed part of Bodley's endowment of his Library. The other item of ordinary expenditure, which heads each year's account, was the substantial and unvarying sum of £17 8s 4d spent on the occasion of a dinner given to the Vice-Chancellor, the Proctors, and the other Curators at their annual Visitation of the Library, which was, and still is, made each year on 8 November, the anniversary of the opening day in 1602. Besides being dined and being presented with gloves all round (according to a carefully-graded scale of importance), the Vice-Chancellor received under Bodley's provision a 'fee' of £6 13s 4d and the two Proctors £2 apiece. These fees and the cost of the gloves made up the bulk of the Visitation expenses, for the dinner itself cost no more than £2.

The 'extraordinary' expenses of running the Library naturally varied from year to year. Book purchases from abroad were made, as they still are, when funds allowed and opportunities offered. Books received from English sources at no cost under the deposit agreement (Plate 40) came in sheets, unbound, and throughout the accounts there is a constant sprinkle of entries for payments made to more than a score of different local Oxford bookbinders for the books sent out to their workshops for binding and checked in on return (Plate 64). Historians of bookbinding have been able to identify the handiwork of

91. **An engraved moon map from *Selenographia***
This was the book which earned Hevelius the title of 'Father of lunar cartography'. Its many beautiful copperplate illustrations were engraved by the author himself and record, with careful exactitude of time and place and circumstance, the observations he had made of the moon, its surface and movements, from his own private observatory at Danzig. By a skilful use of linear shading only, Hevelius has contrived to give his plates not only the impression of height and depth, but even of variations of colour.

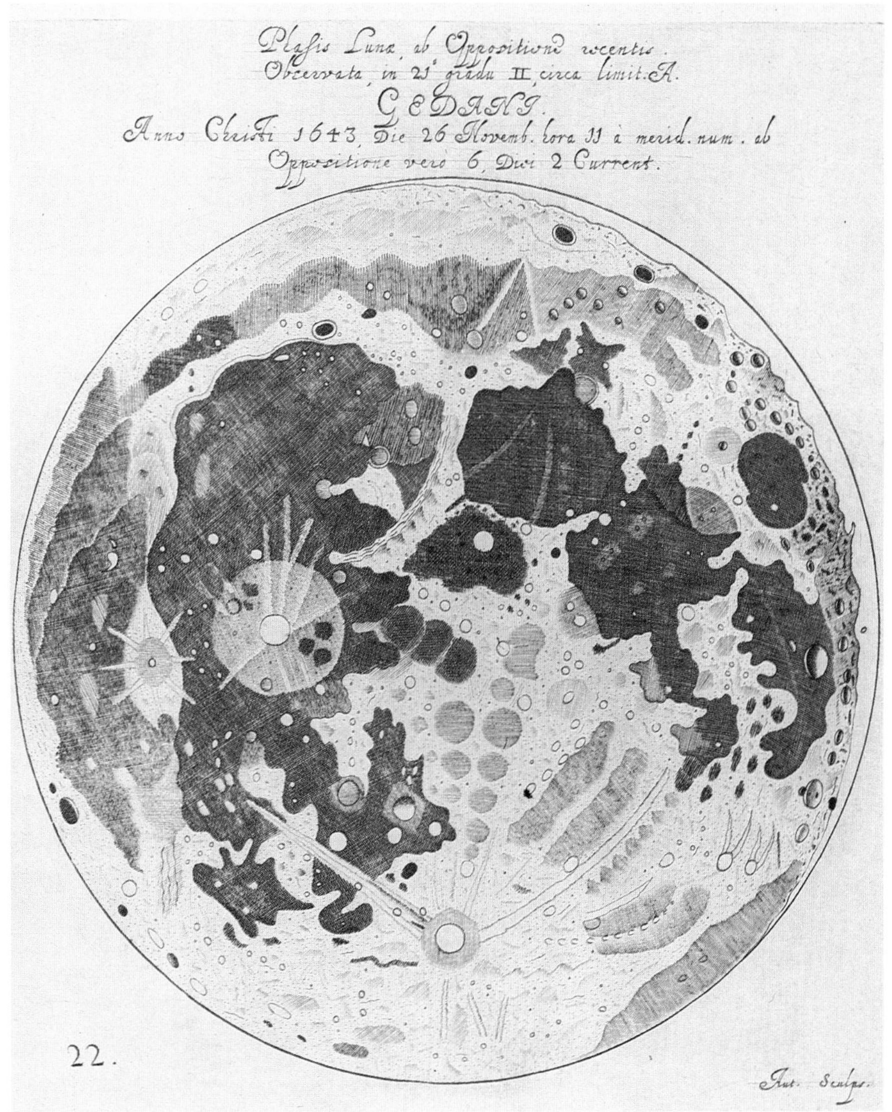

many of these named individual craftsmen, who were also employed, of course, by College libraries. Payments were likewise made for the 'clippes', chains and swivels for the folio volumes shelved in Duke Humfrey's Library. 'Strings', or ties of linen tape, had to be provided and readers were expected to refasten the ties after using the books. But readers, then as now, were apt to grow careless and eventually the Library had all the ties trimmed away. On several occasions one shilling was paid to 'certeyne poore schollers for helping the Porter to tye books against the Visitation of the Library', a sign that the Curators kept watch on the good appearance of the shelves, as well as checking their contents, which they did by means of the original handlists, which still survive.

The fabric of the Library building and its upkeep required the services of specialist workmen such as masons, plumbers, carpenters, glaziers and blacksmiths. Most of these were recruited as the needs arose, though some were regular employees; for example, the plumber and his son were paid a fixed sum half-yearly for cleaning the lead roofs and shovelling away snow. Goodman Norton, who kept the Quadrangle clean, was paid quarterly, and a poor woman and her two daughters also received a quarterly wage for helping the Porter with sweeping indoors and dusting the books; doubtless they would have used that 'long cane to reache the cobwebbs in the Librarie' for which eighteen pence had once been expended.

Within the walls there were many other recurrent jobs to be paid for: a goldsmith was repeatedly called in to repair the clasps of the Benefactors' Register (Plate 18) which must have been constantly handled. It also needed to be written up to date, for which a professional scribe was employed, together with a herald-painter to add the arms of specially important donors and also to paint inscriptions over the shelves and cupboards where notable collections, such as those of Laud and Digby, were housed. The absence of any separate printed catalogues of the manuscripts, once these had been sorted out from among the printed books, explains the payments made from time to time to scholars and scribes who were called upon to make manuscript copies and transcripts, at the Library's expense and for the use of readers, of such various lists and special catalogues as did already exist. The hopes of Langbaine and others for a comprehensive catalogue of the Library's exceedingly rich manuscript collections were not, however, destined to be fulfilled until the end of the century.

Even before hostilities interrupted the flow of books, including deposit copies, between London and Oxford, the Library was experiencing difficulties with the Stationers' Company in operating the agreement satisfactorily. The yearly payments to the Beadle of the Company for his part in collecting the books seem regularly to have been paid in arrears, probably an indication of fluctuating success in the results of his endeavours. The expenses incurred for various journeys to London on the part of the Librarian or Under-Librarian are also likely to reflect efforts as much to keep this important source operative as to undertake any positive search by the Library officers for donations of books, manuscripts, and gifts of money.

At least until the eve of the Civil War donations continued to reach the Library from lesser benefactors in addition to the major gifts already described in Chapter III. Individual benefactors included a number of merchants trading to the Middle and Far East, whose gifts helped to swell the Bodleian's oriental collections, and pointed forward to the wonderful influx of oriental materials which was to be a feature of the Library's development in the second half of the seventeenth century. The accounts supplement the Benefactors' Register in charting the arrival and treatment of various donations. For instance, a thank-offering, similar to that made to Spelman in 1637/38, had been made three years earlier in the form of 'a catalogue complete bound in vellam filleted with silke riband strings sent to William Burton Esquire that gave us the Lelande'. If John Leland, 'King's antiquary' of Henry VIII, may be called the father of English monastic history and bibliography, then in some measure William Burton might be termed the progenitor of the Bodleian's accumulated riches in local and topographical materials, initially through the gift just mentioned, which he made to the Library in 1632, of the seven quarto volumes containing the original manuscripts of Leland's *Itinerary*, and the four folio volumes of his *Collectanea*. The gift of these seminal works to the Bodleian was a presage of future growth there and of that rich harvest of materials which succeeding centuries were to lay beside them and which generations of scholars were to enjoy up to the present day. William, the elder brother of Robert Burton, that notable Bodleian benefactor, was himself one of the pioneers of county history, publishing a valuable *Description of Leicestershire* in 1622. He was also the friend and patron of the young William Dugdale, whose important *Antiquities of Warwickshire* William Burton helped to plan. Dugdale, whose indefatigable energies embraced royalism and mediaeval studies with equal fervour, came to Oxford with the King and was among the few scholars who used the Bodleian during the lean years of the Civil War. The researches of Dugdale, which were to culminate in the *Monasticon Anglicanum*, were based on the huge manuscript collections of a Yorkshire antiquary, Roger Dodsworth, which afterwards came to the Bodleian by bequest of Sir Thomas Fairfax. They remain today beside those many manuscripts made by Dugdale himself, which came eventually into the Library via the Ashmolean Museum. Leland's own writings continued to inspire and challenge the emulation of learned men. In the next century they first reached publication through the labours of Thomas Hearne, while Bishop Tanner's great *Bibliotheca* was designed to re-edit and extensively supplement Leland's account of British writers; the Bodleian houses the papers of both these eminent scholars. Tanner's bequest included an important early transcript of Leland's *Itinerary* made by the Elizabethan antiquary John Stow, and later still two more copies, one of them made by Burton himself in 1628, came to the Library in the vast topographical collections of Richard Gough.

The first foreign reader had been admitted to the Bodleian only three months after it opened in 1602; thereafter foreign students, mostly from Northern Europe, came in increasing numbers, especially after the impressive resources of this new repository had been advertised to the learned public through the printed *Catalogues* of 1605 and 1620. In particular, the mounting numbers of Greek and oriental manuscripts drew distinguished scholars to Oxford, despite irksome conditions which the Curators insisted upon for any readers of manuscripts who were not members of the University. But one young foreigner who certainly remembered with gratitude his visit to the Bodleian was the twenty-year-old son of a prosperous brewer in Danzig. This was Johann Hevelius, who travelled in England during 1631 and later devoted his inherited wealth to astronomy. An autograph inscription in the copy of his first and most famous book (Plates 89, 90, 91), which he sent to the Library in 1649, describes the pleasure and admiration the Bodleian had evoked in him. It was no passing mood. During almost forty years a further fourteen inscribed copies of his writings were sent to the Bodleian by this renowned astronomer, who felt it an honour to have his works placed on its shelves among its great store of treasures.

By the year 1644, in which Rous reached the age of seventy, the harmful effects of wartime conditions on the Library must have begun to cause him great anxiety; the loan to the King had deprived the Bodleian Chest of most of its ready cash, and the rents actually received that year brought in less than half the normal yearly income. During the next two years no rents at all came in, and by November 1646 the cash balance had sunk to £23. For three quarters of the year ending June 1647, Rous drew only £5 of salary.

Finance was not his only worry. The physical safety of the Library was indeed assured by the victorious besieger, General Fairfax, who set a guard of soldiers over it as soon as Oxford surrendered to the Parliamentary forces on 29 June 1646. Among the Articles of Surrender it was ordered that the Great Seal of England (the very palladium of royal sovereignty) was to be locked in a chest and placed in the Bodleian; from there it was taken to the Speaker of the House of Commons and was broken up a few weeks later.

Once having captured Oxford, that stronghold of church and crown, the Parliament lost no time in setting about (as other Parliaments before and since have striven to do) to remould the University nearer to the heart's desire. On 1 May 1647 an Ordinance of Parliament appointed twenty-four Visitors to carry out the reformation of the University. These were to report to a Standing Committee of seventy-eight members of both Houses, among whom was John Selden who, since the death of Sir Thomas Roe, was Oxford's only M.P. A letter was printed about a year later appealing to him to protect the University, which had struggled under its Vice-Chancellor Dr Samuel Fell to defend its ancient privileges. But Fell, with the Heads of Houses and other Fellows who proved recalcitrant, was expelled, and the University settled down to a grudging acceptance of the new regime.

Cromwell and General Fairfax came to Oxford in May 1649 to observe the new reforms and were duly made Doctors of Civil Law and given a banquet in the Bodleian. But Royalist discontent continued to seethe; an often reprinted satirical broadside, partly in macaronic Latin verse, painted a picture of Oxford desolated by the Parliamentary Visitors, the Bodleian empty but for the Janitor, with many books lying about in disarray because 'There's few could understandum'.

Rous, like most of the other Fellows of his college, Oriel, refused submission to the Visitors but managed to retain his Fellowship. A suggestion that he be replaced as Librarian by one of the new men Parliament had introduced into Oxford, fortunately came to nothing and he ended his life in April 1652, the only Bodley's Librarian to die in office in over a hundred years.

His successor was Thomas Barlow, then in his forty-sixth year, Fellow of Queen's since 1633 and destined to become its Provost in

92. **Portrait of John Selden**
The only authenticated portrait of John Selden is a half-length painted early in the 1650s showing him much as John Aubrey described him – 'sharp oval face, head not very big, long nose inclining to one side, full popping eie (gray)'. Sir Peter Lely may have painted the original, and one of the several surviving copies was bequeathed to the Ashmolean by its founder in 1692.

The portrait here reproduced also traditionally represents John Selden. Although it shows a younger man with a milder countenance, the features are not irreconcilable with the authenticated portrait, since the style of dress is said to indicate the mid-1640s. Moreover it is probably this portrait which Thomas Hearne mentions in the Bodleian in 1708 – 'T'was lately removed into the Gallery [the Picture Gallery, now the Upper Reading Room] out of that part of the Library where his books are plac'd'. That the Bodleian should already have commemorated its great benefactor by hanging this image in Selden End argues strongly in favour of the identification, and an additional copy of it is also in the Library's possession.

However, the history of a third 'Selden' portrait in the Library exemplifies the caution needed in accepting old assertions. The removal referred to by Hearne in 1708 resulted from the University's purchase in that year ('for the great price of £21 10s') of 'an excellent picture of Mr Selden'. The painting's excellence as an example of Lely's early style is unquestioned, but in spite of its arrival here little more than fifty years after the supposed sitter's death, it has recently been proved to portray Sir George Booth, later Lord Delamere, a man nearly forty years Selden's junior.

192

Heigh in the hevynnis figure circulere
The rody sterres twynklyng as the fyre
And in Aquary Citherea the clere
Rynsid hir tressis like the goldin wyre
That late tofore in fair and fresche atyre
Through capricorn heved hir hornis bright
North northward approchit the myd nyght

Quhen as I lay in bed allone waking
New partit out of slepe a lyte tofore
Fell me to mynd of many diverse thing
Off this and that, can I noght say quharfore
Bot slepe for craft in erth myght I no more
For quhich as tho coude I no better wyle
Bot toke a boke to rede apon a quhile

Off quhich the name is clepit properly
Boece, eftir him that was the compiloure
Schewing counsele of philosophye
Compilit by that noble senatoure
Off rome, quhilom that was the warldis floure
And from estate by fortune a quhile
Forjugit was to povert in exile

And there to here this worthy lord and clerk
His metir suete full of moralitee
His flourit pen so fair he set awerk
Discriving first of his prosperitee
And out of that his infelicitee
And than how he in his poetly report
In philosophy can him to confort

For quhich thogh I in purpose at my boke
To borowe a slepe at thilke tyme began
Or ever I stent my best was more to loke
Upon the writing of this noble man
That in him self the full recover wan
Off his infortune poverti and distresse
And in tham set his verray sekernesse

93. ***The Kingis Quair* by King James I of Scotland**

That the first 'Scottish Chaucerian' should be the King himself seems too good to be true. The 'quire'-sized poem, a courtly work of considerable merit, purports to celebrate, in the voice of King James I of Scotland, his happy but arranged marriage, during the brief honeymoon period between his romantic imprisonment and bloody murder. From the King's personal experience of life's reverses, the poet draws out a moral allegory on the nature of Fortune and the divine order, and on the power of love in man's acceptance of his fate. Present opinion in the fluctuating critical battle perhaps favours its royal authorship.

In 1406, the twelve-year-old Prince James had been sent by ship to further his education in France, but was captured by English pirates; the event hastened his father's death and his own absentee accession to the throne. His English education, during his imprisonment from 1406 to 1424, proved a good substitute, to judge by his poetry and his later governmental policy. Towards the end, Henry V trusted his prisoner sufficiently to make him co-commander with Humfrey, Duke of Gloucester (Plate 3), three years his senior, at the successful Siege of Dreux in 1421; his marriage to the English noblewoman Joan Beaufort in 1424 was a condition of his final release. Dialectologists still argue whether the English of the poem – a mixture of Northern and Midland forms – can be reconciled with the life history of a person who spent his childhood in Scotland, his adolescence and young manhood in England (though with Scottish attendants) and his maturity back in Scotland. If the attribution is accepted, the poem's date of composition would perhaps be c. 1435. The King's assassination at Perth in 1437 took place in Queen Joan's presence.

The poet names his dear masters Chaucer and Gower as 'superlative as poetis laureate'; with Lydgate, they are the prime influences on his work. Appropriately, this, the only surviving copy of *The Kingis Quair*, appears in a Scottish manuscript alongside Chaucer's *Troilus and Criseyde*, *The Parlement of Foules*, and *The Legend of Good Women*; and there are also in it other minor English and Scots poems by Lydgate, Hoccleve, perhaps even William Dunbar, and one, also unique to this manuscript, the anonymous *Quare of Jelusy*. Through comparison with other manuscripts, the main scribe can probably be identified as James Gray, secretary to successive Archbishops of St Andrews. This scribe names King James IV, the poet's great-grandson, as the reigning monarch, so the manuscript must have been written during his reign, 1488–1513. Script and decoration, rather amateurish in quality, show modified French influence in contrast to English manuscripts of this date. An *ex libris*, scribbled almost as a pen-trial, reads: 'liber Henrici domini Sincla[i]r'. Henry, Lord Sinclair, great-great-nephew of James I, and an important book-collector (Gavin Douglas dedicated to him the first English translation of Virgil's *Aeneid*), held his barony from 1489 to 1513 and died with his King at the battle of Flodden. Gray perhaps wrote out the manuscript directly for Sinclair. Sinclair's royal connections (his great-grandfather had been the admiral responsible for the young prince on the fateful voyage of 1406) add credence to the manuscript's two attributions of *The Kingis Quair* to James I, one at the end in the hand of the second original scribe and the other at the beginning in a near-contemporary addition.

After a succession of Sinclairs and other owners, the manuscript finally reached the Bodleian with the library of John Selden. *The Kingis Quair* was apparently first noticed by Thomas Tanner who entered 'Jacobus Stuartus i rex Scotiae' in his posthumously published *Bibliotheca Britannico-Hibernica*, 1748. Tanner's description was noticed by a Scottish historian, William Tytler, who procured a transcript and issued the first published text of the poem in 1783.

1657. He was known for his own wide learning and patronage of learned men, and as a controversialist and master of casuistry, which enabled him during the political upheavals which occurred throughout his public life, to justify to himself, if not to others, his own changes of front. Like Rous, Barlow had refused in 1648 to submit to the Visitors and had been expelled, but thanks probably in part to Selden, he did not lose his Fellowship. He allowed himself the secret satisfaction of publishing anonymously a somewhat heavy-handed skit (of which he only admitted authorship years later to Anthony Wood) mocking the 'Proceedings of the Visitours and other Bedlamites'.

From the time he took office he showed himself unsympathetic to the ambitious schemes for a universal subject catalogue of the Library which various members of the 'Experimental Philosophy Club', recently founded in Oxford, and later to become the Royal Society, had mooted among themselves. A Calvinist himself, he even attempted to tarnish the 'New Philosophy' as inspired by Papistry, to which he was a lifelong foe. The schemes foundered and the would-be cataloguers, a

continued on page 122

94. **The Agincourt Song**

The word 'carrel' is still used in the Bodleian, as in various churches which have preserved their ancient monastic cloisters, to describe one in a series of small enclosed studies each open on one side and lit by its own window, fitted with a seat, a desk and shelves for the books of the occupying reader or scribe. The dictionary describes the word as an obsolete spelling of 'carol' which had the original meaning of a ring – as defining an enclosed space, especially a ring-dance accompanied by a song; it then came to be used of the joyous song itself which accompanied the dance. The mark of a carol, as a distinctive song form of the late Middle Ages, is that it was a popular song the poem of which was written in stanzas, and had prefixed lines of a 'burden' or chorus which were repeated after each stanza.

Today the word is mainly used in association with Christmas which is, of course, the pre-eminent season for expressing Christian joy by song, but formerly there were also carols for many other festive occasions in the year. One of the most celebrated English mediaeval carols on a non-Christmas theme is the Agincourt Song, which celebrates the victory won at Agincourt on 25 October 1415 by the army of King Henry V over a much larger French force. This carol, which is written in English for two voices with a Latin chorus for three voices, is known today only from two manuscripts, the present one, which is generally assigned to the mid-fifteenth century, and a slightly shorter version found on a vellum roll in the Library of Trinity College, Cambridge, also written in the same century. The date of its original composition must certainly be contemporary with the initial wave of national rejoicing, since it alludes to the arrival of the French prisoners who accompanied the King's triumphal entry into London on 23 November 1415, but makes no reference to later events in the King's reign.

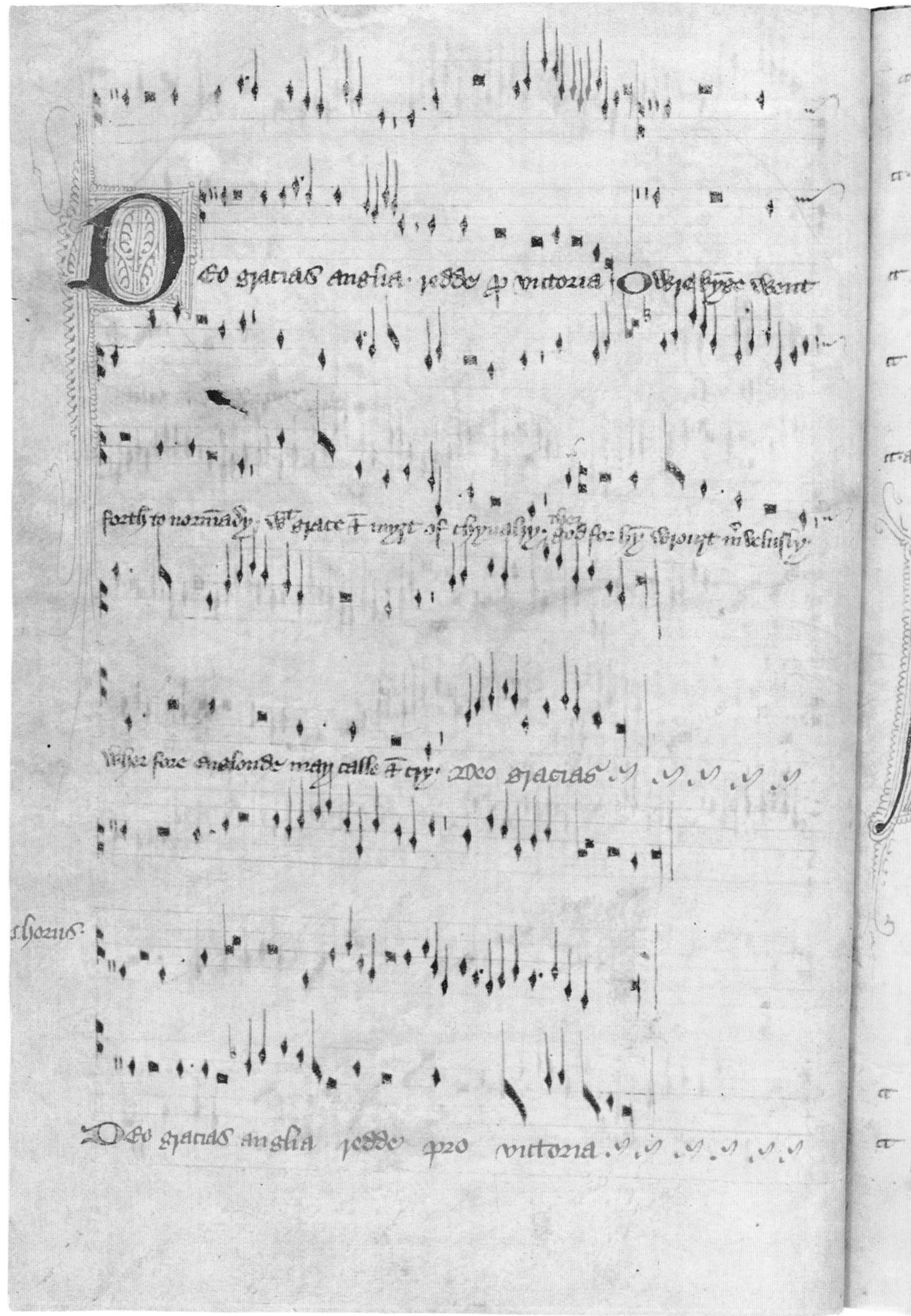

The Bodleian copy of the Agincourt Song occurs in a small manuscript originating almost certainly from Worcester, which gives both the words and the musical settings of a very precious group of English mediaeval carols. The presence of this manuscript in a volume now containing a miscellaneous collection of unrelated items seems to indicate that when it arrived in the Library among John Selden's huge collections it was at that time unbound.

95. **Two Caxtons from Selden's library**

Because from its earliest origins the Library's collections have to a large extent been assembled by scholars for scholars, its own funds and those of its benefactors have seldom been used to adorn the covers of books and manuscripts with those costly bindings in which wealthy book-collectors down the centuries have been prone to reclothe their specially-favoured treasures. Hence, in the Bodleian a higher proportion of books remain to this day in their original condition than in other great libraries formed more recently out of books which had already passed through the ordeal of rebinding. This is especially true of the Bodleian's holdings of mediaeval manuscripts and early printed books, though happily it also applies to much material dating from more recent centuries. Considered as an historical object as well as a text, a book has more to tell us about its origins and status if the physical evidence has not been stripped away or even disturbed.

Understandably, though regrettably, the tendency to isolate a special treasure by plucking it out of the meaner context in which it survived, has played havoc with the majority of existing examples of the works which were issued from the press set up in Westminster in 1476 by England's first printer, William Caxton. Yet there still remains some scattered evidence of how his products were first marketed and what customers bought them and when. From this it seems clear that at least some Caxtons were acquired in chronological groups by purchasers from his own shop and were bound for them by the bindery which worked in close co-operation with his printing-house.

Selden has the distinction of having been one of the earliest book-buyers to collect Caxtons for what they were – monuments of English typography. The thirteen examples that came from his library were among the first Caxtons to enter the Bodleian and they included the first book printed in the English language and Caxton's earliest illustrated book. Together, Selden's Caxtons form the largest group received from a single owner before those which Francis Douce bequeathed a century and a half later. It was a noble beginning to the Bodleian's present great assemblage of Caxtons.

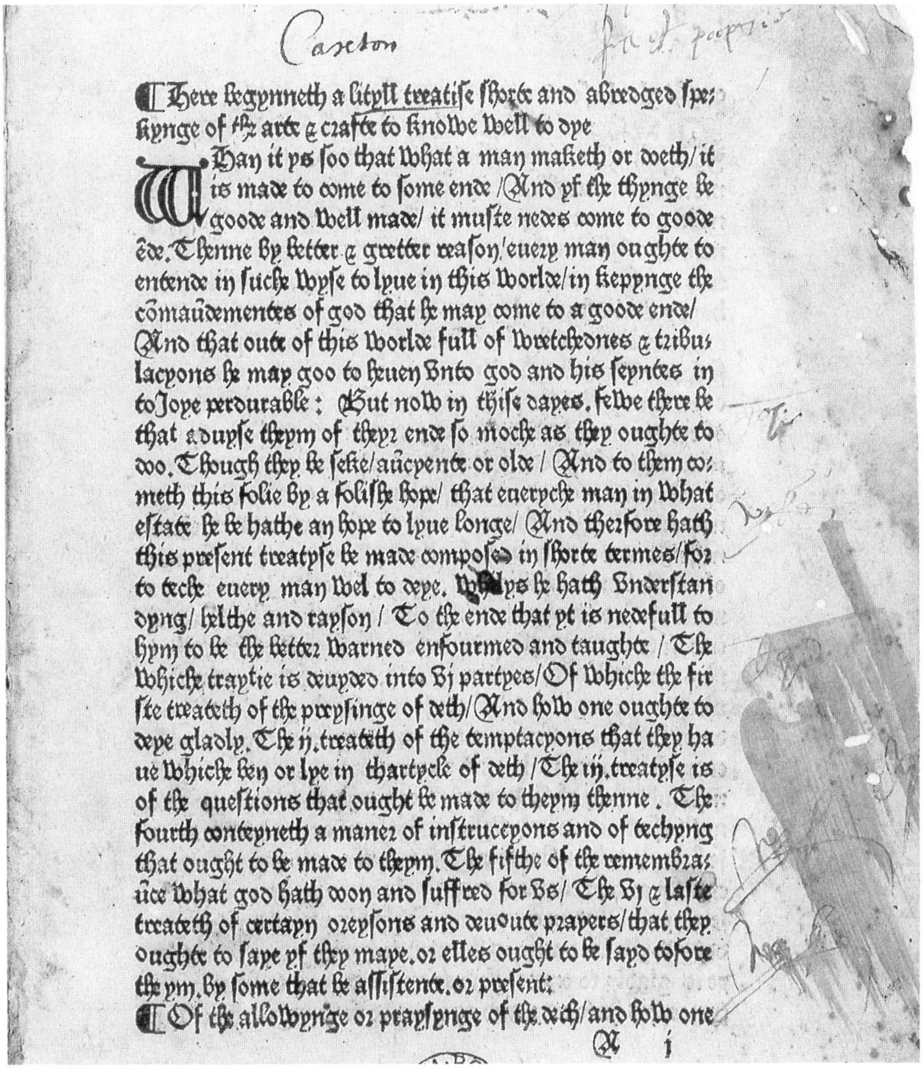

Among Selden's thirteen there are two examples of those Caxton books which still often survive, as did his copies, in the same associated pairs, indicating that they were originally printed and sold together. Another two of his Caxtons form a single volume and the closeness of their printing dates suggests that they were bought together in the fifteenth century, even though their present binding is from a century or more later. The earlier of the two items in this volume is Caxton's second edition of the *Directorium*, a popular handbook for priests; it dates from 1489 and no other copy survives, apart from three fragments. The other item is the short tract here illustrated, which Caxton himself finished translating (from an anonymous French original) on 15 June 1490, the year before he died. Only three copies of this first edition are recorded besides this one.

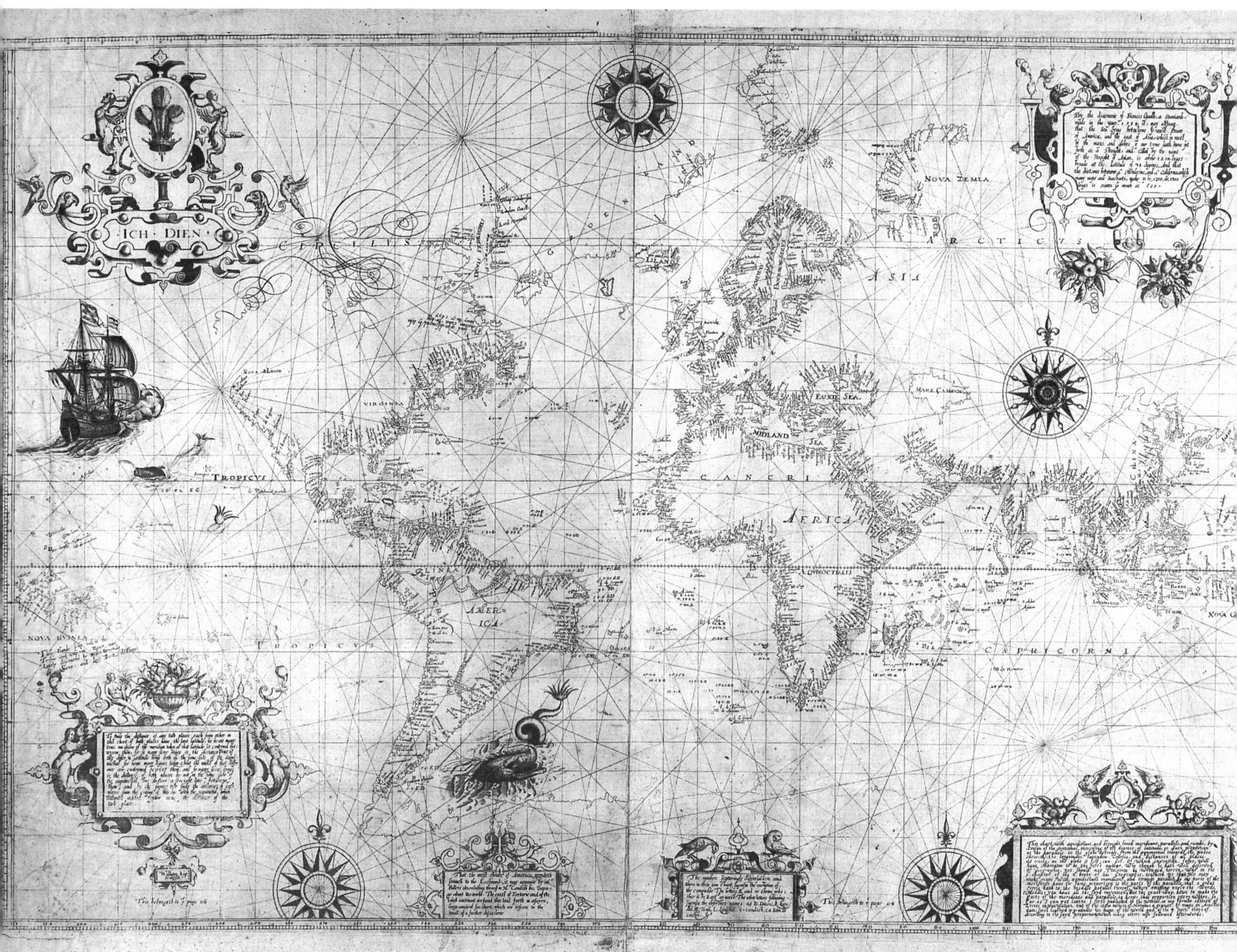

most distinguished group of scholars, dispersed, while Barlow occupied himself with more practical matters. Attempts are recorded in the accounts to collect rents and arrears of rents from Bodley's London properties, and to ascertain what books had been published by the Stationers' Company over the previous ten years, so that the Library's right to free copies of them could be asserted and pursued. Cromwell, who had been elected Chancellor of the University in 1651, wrote in 1654 to the Vice-Chancellor asking for the loan of a Bodleian manuscript on behalf of the Portuguese Ambassador, but Barlow stood firm as Rous had done, and sent only a copy of the Founder's Statute forbidding loans. Cromwell, like King Charles before him, accepted the refusal with a good grace, and in the same year he even

96. Edward Wright's second sea-chart of the world, c. 1610
Although this fine engraved chart includes (twice) the words 'This belongeth to ye page 116', it is a surprising fact that no copy of the revised second edition of Edward Wright's *Certaine Errors of Navigation*, published in 1610, is known with this plate included, although it was undeniably prepared for insertion into that book. Perhaps it should be remembered that printing from an engraved copperplate was an entirely separate operation which required a different kind of press from that used for the letterpress of the book concerned.

The chart here illustrated was actually found inserted into Selden's copy of Ortelius's *Theatrum orbis terrarum*, Antwerp, 1574; it represents the perfected state of the engraving and was formerly thought to be unique, until a second copy came to light in a New York library. One copy in an earlier proof state is known, and later modifications were made when the copperplate was re-used in 1655.

Signed by its engraver William Kip, this is a later and larger version of Wright's earlier chart (Plate 65) and includes observations of magnetic variations and revisions based on more recent explorations and discoveries. Like its predecessor, it, too, is drawn on the Mercator Projection. In the top left-hand corner is displayed the crest and motto of Prince Henry, who had just been created Prince of Wales. This pictorial dedication to him is a fitting one, for Wright had been the Prince's mathematics tutor and later his librarian. As such he had in a few years put together for his young pupil a large library designed for the all-round education of a future king; the collection (still largely preserved within the old Royal Library) is, as is to be expected, notably strong in all branches of scientific learning, that sphere in which Wright was himself so conspicuous an ornament.

bought and presented more than twenty Greek manuscripts which had remained in the library of the Earls of Pembroke, and these are still kept in the Bodleian under Cromwell's name, so earning a place (next after Laud!) on the tablet recording Bodley's greatest benefactors.

John Evelyn visited the Library in 1654 and figures as a benefactor in the following year and subsequently; among his gifts were some additions to the collection of engravings presented in 1659 and named from its donor the 'Scroope Album'. In his diary he records some of the 'treasures' he was shown on his visit: a Turkish vestment of linen on which the whole Koran was written in Arabic; one of Esther Inglis's calligraphic manuscripts; Sir Thomas Roe's Arabic manuscript of the early Church Councils (Plate 72) and 'a hieroglyphical table or carte, folded up like a map; I suppose it painted on asses' hide; extremely rare' – obviously a description of Archbishop Laud's Mexican Codex (Plate 78).

In the late summer of 1654 Convocation had passed a grace allowing Selden to borrow three manuscripts at a time for a year from certain named collections in return for a bond of £100 on each. This proposed loan gave rise to a well-argued memorandum by Barlow strongly opposing any relaxation of the Founder's total ban on lending Bodleian books. The loan scheme never took effect, since only three months later John Selden was dead.

The Bodleian portrait of him (Plate 92), which formerly hung over the gallery in Selden End where his library first came to rest in Oxford, shows (if the portrait is of him, as is traditionally claimed) a man of serious, refined and scholarly countenance. He came to be widely recognised as one of the most learned men of his time in more than one field, and his immense legal and historical knowledge was put to good use in his public and private life, and through his books which served to forward the general progress of learning. In many legal, historical and constitutional controversies in which he played a part he arrived at his own positions with a notable independence of judgment which justifies the motto written in his own hand in Greek on most of the books in his library: 'Freedom above all' (Plate 69). He might have held important office in the State 'had he not', as a contemporary wrote of him, 'undervalued all other employments in respect of his studies'. He is now remembered chiefly for the many books he wrote, for his *Table Talk*, published after his death by his secretary, and above all for the incomparable library he formed.

Unlike those of Laud, whose purchases were made directly to equip his University's Library with a wide-ranging diversity of scholarly texts, Selden's acquisitions were those of a scholar buying for his own study and pleasure. There is no evidence that he actually contemplated giving or bequeathing his entire library to the Bodleian. Indeed, what his will and codicil show is that he meant the Bodleian to have his

Greek manuscripts, most of his oriental manuscripts, and whatever of his Talmudical and Rabbinical printed books the Library did not already possess. But somehow, in the text of the will as it now survives, there is no mention of either the University or the Bodleian. Despite this, his four executors were in no doubt of his true intentions. Two days after Selden's death, they summoned Gerard Langbaine, the Grecian scholar, and Edward Pococke, the orientalist, to Carmelite House where Selden had lived, armed with an up-to-date Bodleian *Catalogue*, to sort out what was to go to Oxford. The rest of the library, except some Arabic manuscripts bequeathed to the College of Physicians, Selden left to his executors, instructing them either to divide the books amongst themselves or to give them to some institution, but not to 'put them to any common sale'. They first approached Selden's own Inner Temple, but the sheer size of the library was more than that body could find space for, and eventually, nearly two years later, Selden's old University, to which he was always devoted, though he had left Hart Hall without taking a degree, wrote to the executors asking them to present the library to Oxford, where the Bodleian's new west end was ready to receive it, as a memorial to Selden.

Barlow will certainly have been an active supporter, if not the initiator of this request. A prolonged period of consideration ensued and it was eventually two and a half years later that Selden's four executors, among whom the prime mover appears to have been Judge Matthew Hale, later to become Lord Chief Justice of the King's Bench, signified their assent to the gift, while laying down specific conditions including that his books be 'for ever hereafter kept together in one distinct pile and body under the name of Mr Selden's Library' – a precedent which the Bodleian Library has since continued to follow on suitable occasions.

A table carefully compiled about the middle of the century gave a total for the whole Bodleian of just under 16,000 volumes of which more than 3,000 were manuscripts, a figure which hardly differs from that optimistically claimed by Thomas James in the preface to his 1620 *Catalogue*. To this new, well-substantiated total, were now added by Selden's bequest and the gift of his executors, about 8,000 more. Within this massive increase in the Bodleian's holding are to be found a variety of manuscripts, totalling 368 in number, not only of Western

97. **A binding made for Francis Bacon**
In 1617, the year in which Francis Bacon became Lord Keeper, Selden had written and presented to him 'A brief Discourse touching the office of Lord Chancellor of England', and the presence of a copy of the 1622 edition of *The Historie of . . . Henry the Seventh* in Selden's library, inscribed by him with a note that it was a gift from the author, Bacon, is further testimony of personal and literary links between the two men as authors, in addition to the status both shared as great lawyers involved in public affairs. Bacon's gift was bound in plain calf, without the punning crest which is found on the binding here illustrated, as well as on a book given by Bacon to the Bodleian in 1620 (described under Plate 62).

The present binding covers a copy of Garcilaso de la Vega, *Primera parte de los commentarios reales* printed at Lisbon in 1619. As Bacon left no heir, this binding must date from some time in the seven years before his death in 1626. It has been suggested that this was also a present from Bacon to Selden, but besides the crest it bears no other evidence to confirm the conjecture, and since Selden owned two other books bearing Bacon's crest, it seems most likely that all three were acquired by Selden after Bacon's library was dispersed following his death. Among books recorded as bearing the boar crest, several others besides this one are likewise bound in limp vellum without strengthening boards but with silk ties to hold the covers together. Vellum was used in England for the binding of manuscript account books and the like from the fourteenth, and for printed books from the sixteenth, century; it became fashionable among the literate, leisured classes in the reigns of James I and Charles I. John Earle, in his *Microcosmographie* of 1628, describes 'A young gentleman of the University' with his books in 'neate silke strings, which he is loth to untye or take downe for feare of misplacing', and this seems to imply limp vellum. The present overall design of small floral tools anticipates those used in England after the Restoration, especially the daisy-like ones in the inner border.

origin, but including many in Hebrew, Arabic, Persian and other oriental languages. The executors also presented, along with maps (Plates 65, 96), Selden's valuable collection of antique statues and inscriptions.

Selden's own output as author and editor amounts to nearly thirty works, yet these would not have brought him any great income, for there was, for many years after his death, still no author's copyright and no royalties. The source of Selden's wealth which gave him economic freedom and enabled him to buy books in such great numbers and to act as a literary patron, came from his legal practice and from his association with the Earl of Kent and his Countess, who was a rich heiress. To them he acted as steward and close friend, eventually becoming a major beneficiary under the Countess's will.

Although the sources from which Selden assembled his very large and extremely varied collection of books and manuscripts remain for the most part unknown today, such clues as can be gathered out of the books themselves are of great interest and help to illustrate his enormous range of interests and his wide circle of friends.

A general survey enables four elements of the library to be distinguished: books presented by Continental scholars; gifts from English friends and admirers; books acquired secondhand, after the deaths of earlier collectors; books both English and foreign purchased new from the bookselling trade. Because Selden's library was, with that of Richard Holdsworth, one of the two greatest single collections formed in England in the seventeenth century, and still survives intact, each of these four constituent elements offers material worthy of attention.

It is clear that his own published books quickly spread his name and reputation for learning throughout Europe, so that though he himself never travelled out of England, he yet enjoyed contacts with many foreign scholars, and these are reflected in books still to be found in the Selden collection. For example, the senior in a group of three famous Leiden professors with whom he was in touch, was Daniel Heinsius, the Flemish poet and historian to whom in 1617 Selden had dedicated his first, pioneering, oriental study, *De diis Syris*. Heinsius responded by causing Selden's book to be reprinted at Leiden in 1629, and also by sending two of his own books to Selden with presentation inscriptions. A second Leiden admirer was J.F. Gronovius, who had been admitted as a Bodleian reader in 1629. Selden possessed three of his books which this Professor of Classics had sent him as a tribute to the English scholar who had published *Marmorea Arundelliana*.

In that work, published in 1628,Selden had described the collections of ancient art formed by Thomas, the connoisseur Earl of Arundel. The Arundel marbles were presented to the University in 1667 by Lord Henry Howard at the suggestion of John Evelyn, where they joined

Selden's own collection, and were later on display in the Bodleian Picture Gallery. They are now in the Ashmolean Museum. In 1653 came a presentation copy of his *Lexicon* from yet another Leiden luminary, Jacobus Golius, the Professor of Arabic. It is pleasant to recall that after the death of Golius almost three-quarters of his large collection of oriental manuscripts were bought at auction in Holland in 1696 by Edward Bernard on behalf of Narcissus Marsh, who bequeathed them to the Bodleian in 1713.

English scholars and men of letters were no less eager than their Continental counterparts to pay tribute to John Selden; among authors from whom inscribed copies are to be found in his library are the historians Camden and Spelman, the classical scholar Thomas Farnaby, and the philosophers and scientists Bacon (Plate 97), Lord Herbert of Cherbury, and Robert Fludd. Selden also had friends among the poets and literary men of his day; many sent him complimentary copies of their works and despite his own massive output of original writing and editing he found time to contribute prefatory and other material for ten books published by friends. These include two by Michael Drayton and the collected *Workes* of Ben Jonson, with whom he was on specially intimate terms. He also received from, and exchanged tributes with, other writers in widely different fields such as the Welsh lexicographer John Davies, Augustine Vincent the herald, and Samuel Purchas, the author of *Purchas his Pilgrimes*, from whose library Selden later acquired its principal treasure, the 'Codex Mendoza' (Plate 98).

Little evidence survives from the seventeenth century of the working of what today would be called the secondhand book trade, though the distinction between new and used copies is a relatively modern one. It is obvious enough that any bookseller would have retailed whatever he thought he could sell, and his stock might come from many sources; the presence in Selden's library of several quite extensive groups of books, each group formerly owned by a different collector, seems to indicate that the family of some deceased collector would have asked a bookseller to quote for all the dead man's books not specifically bequeathed, leaving him to market them as best he might. This sort of procedure could explain how it is that of Selden's forty printed books from the library of Sir Robert Cotton, only one bears an inscription showing that it was actually given by Cotton to Selden. Similarly, of four books formerly Francis Bacon's, only one was a gift (Plate 97). Even more strikingly, not one gift inscription is to be found among no fewer than eighteen books from the library of John Donne, most of them still in those limp vellum bindings in which the poet had had them clothed. Thirty-three volumes came from the shelves of Charles Blount, Lord Mountjoy, who had died when Selden was only twenty-two, and another group bears the armorial stamps of George

continued on page 130

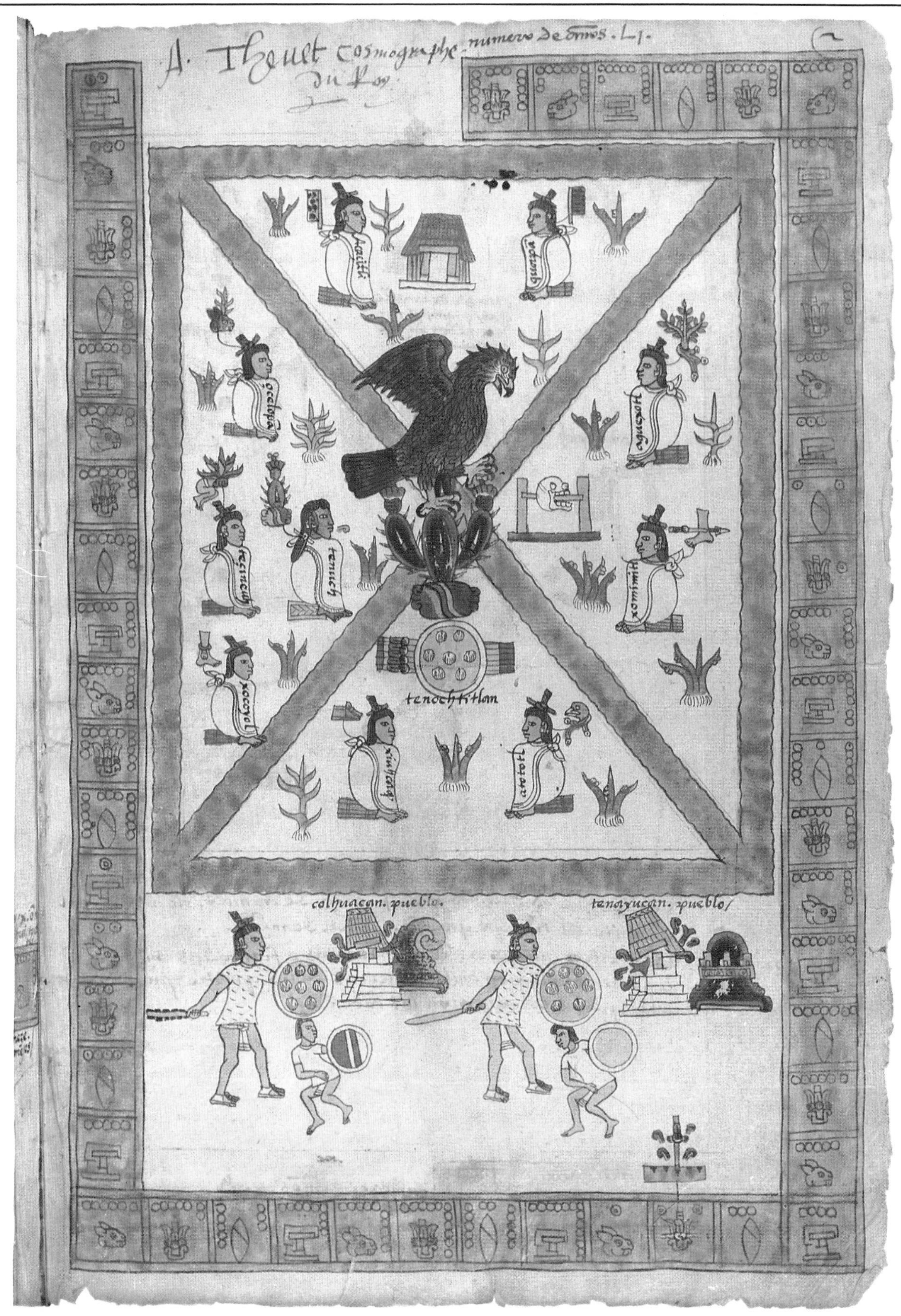
A. Thevet cosmographe du Roy
numero de años .LI.
tenochtitlan
colhuacan. pueblo.
tenayucan. pueblo.

98. The Mexican 'Codex Mendoza'

Three of the Bodleian's five precious early Mexican manuscripts came with Selden's collection. Of these, one, now called the 'Codex Selden' is, like 'Codex Bodley' and 'Codex Laud' (Plate 78), a 'screenfold'; the 'Selden Roll' which details the adventurous journey of four Heroes, is painted on a scroll of native paper made from the bark of the fig tree. Selden's third Mexican manuscript differs from the others in being a volume in standard European format, on paper imported from Spain. It takes its name from Antonio de Mendoza, Conde de Tendilla, who was the first Viceroy of Mexico, occupying that post from 1535 to 1550. He was an enlightened ruler, who established a mint, introduced printing, and sent out explorers to California, Peru and the Philippines. He also founded a College for the children of Mexican nobles and petitioned the Crown for a University, which was established only after his death.

Mendoza commissioned this Codex for presentation to his master the Emperor Charles V, to inform that monarch concerning this new and valuable portion of his vast empire. The contents consist of three parts: (1) a copy of a lost chronicle (1325–1521) of the Aztec lords of Tenochtitlan who eventually came to dominate the whole area; (2) a copy of the ancient Tribute Roll, listing 400 towns paying annual dues (fully described) to the last native Emperor, Montezuma II; (3) an original account by the artist himself describing Aztec life 'from year to year'.

All this was then annotated in Spanish by a Nahuatl-speaking Spanish priest who established the meaning of the pictographs by questioning native speakers, and who also provided an introduction and notes. The manuscript therefore provides what has been happily termed another 'Rosetta stone' for the elucidation of the language and symbolism of Aztec culture.

Within its green border, which gives the chronology (according to the Aztec cycle of fifty-two years), the opening page of the Chronicle, here reproduced, depicts the foundation story of what was to become Mexico City, on a site where, in the middle of a lake of clear water (represented here by the blue diagonal cross and square) stood a rocky islet on which grew a great prickly-pear tree where a red-tailed eagle had built its eyrie. Around this centrepiece are pictured the first ruler and his warriors, while below are represented the defeat and destruction of the first two towns conquered by the successful Mixtec tribe.

In an early example of facsimile reproduction this same page was copied, life-size, in a woodcut as one of the illustrations for the account of Mexico drawn from the 'Codex Mendoza' and printed in a large collection of travels entitled *Hakluytus posthumus or Purchas his Pilgrimes* published in 1625 by a London clergyman Samuel Purchas, himself at that time the proud possessor of the 'Codex Mendoza', which he described as 'the choisest of my Iewels'. The manuscript, Purchas tells us in his account of its earlier history, had been bequeathed to him in 1616 by Richard Hakluyt, the friend to whose famous *Principall Navigations* Purchas regarded his own *Pilgrimes* as a sequel. Hakluyt, like Purchas, was a clergyman and in 1583 had gone to Paris to be chaplain to the English Ambassador there and during his stay in Paris he met the French King's Geographer, André Thevet, who then owned the 'Codex Mendoza', which Hakluyt subsequently acquired from him for the sum of twenty gold crowns.

While in Hakluyt's possession a translation of it had been made at the instigation of Sir Walter Raleigh (Plate 20) by Michael Lok, the merchant adventurer who had backed the voyages of Martin Frobisher (Plate 104). This translation was still unpublished when it passed, along with the Codex, into the hands of Purchas, who incorporated it into his *Pilgrimes* in 1625.

Exactly how Thevet himself had come into possession of the Codex is not known, but he wrote his name repeatedly in it, twice adding the date 1553, and on the page here reproduced he adds to his name the proud title 'Cosmographe du Roy'. But it is doubtless from Thevet that information derives about the still earlier adventures of the Codex. The original Spanish annotator tells us that his native informants took so long to agree about the meaning of some of the 'glyphs' (pictographs) that he was (quite literally) in danger of 'missing the boat'; he had only ten days left to finish his work before the ship which was to carry it left for Hispaniola (Santo Domingo) to join the fleet there assembled for the voyage back to Spain. The Codex caught the boat, but it never reached the Emperor for whom it was prepared; the ship and its precious burden were captured at sea by French men-of-war and carried off to France. So began more than a century of wandering, ending with Selden's acquisition of the Codex at some date after the death of Purchas in 1626, and its eventual transfer to the Bodleian. There it was later to inspire Edward King, Viscount Kingsborough, to devote his life, and eventually to ruin his whole fortune, in the study and publication of his pioneering *Antiquities of Mexico*, a magnificent though uncompleted work in nine imperial folio volumes issued in 1830–48, in which a reproduction of 'Codex Mendoza' had pride of place in the first volume.

Carew, Earl of Totnes. Among other former owners represented each by a group of his books are the internationally well-known mathematical writer and astrologer John Dee, along with others whose names are hardly remembered today – Sir Daniel Dun (a fellow lawyer and M.P. for Oxford), Thomas Crashawe (another lawyer), Abraham Hartwell the younger and Edward Gwynne.

Outside the three categories of acquisitions just described, lies the fourth and by far the largest part of the library, namely those thousands of volumes acquired (it can safely be assumed) mostly through the book trade, though on occasion by private purchase from individual owners. During the early years of the reign of Charles I several enterprising London booksellers travelled abroad and brought back large stocks of new and secondhand books. From such stocks Selden, an assiduous book-buyer living, as he did, and working in London, was well placed to be able to take his pick, and also to obtain through them those many new foreign books he must personally have asked them to procure for him.

The wealth of Greek, Hebrew and oriental manuscripts and printed books in his collection is highlighted by Selden himself in the terms of his will. Much of the rest of the library, which came by gift of his executors, consisted of a huge range of materials, chiefly in Latin and foreign languages, but embracing also the language, laws and history of his own country. Though clearly he never set out to form a collection of English literature, yet he manifested a remarkable instinct for acquiring items of special value and importance. For example, his manuscript of *The Kingis Quair* (Plate 93) is the sole witness to the text of Scotland's first Chaucerian poet, and the same volume contains other mediaeval English and Scots poems, one of them also unique. The words and music of the famous polyphonic secular carol known as the Agincourt Song (Plate 94), written in English with a Latin chorus, is part of a Selden manuscript which preserves various mediaeval carols. Among his printed books, one single volume comprises twenty-six popular pieces printed in black-letter between 1509 and 1605, embracing all kinds of romances, jests and ballads – the folk and street literature, always of legendary rarity, which over the centuries has become something of a Bodleian speciality. Of eighteen out of the twenty-six pieces, Selden's copy is unique, while six of the rest are known by only one other copy apiece, and only two by two other copies.

It would be anachronistic to think of Selden as a collector of incunables as such, with one very notable exception. To a man as learned in English history as Selden, the significance of England's first printer, William Caxton (Plate 95), with his astonishingly large output of texts, both courtly and popular, must have made a special appeal. In his long years as a book buyer Selden managed to amass (there is no

99. **The first book printed in Japan from moveable types, 1591**

The earliest European entered Japan in 1542, and only seven years later the great missionary St Francis Xavier landed there and founded a Jesuit mission which grew rapidly. Only a little more than thirty years later, three Japanese Christian princes despatched an embassy to Europe, whose members were present at the coronation of Pope Sixtus V in Rome in 1585. When they set out from Nagasaki early in 1582 the ambassadors had been accompanied by Alessandro Valignano, an Italian priest long since appointed the official Visitor for all the Jesuit missions in the Far East. But at Goa on their journey westwards Valignano received orders to remain in India as Jesuit Provincial, and it was not until 1587 that the returning envoys rejoined him there, bringing with them the printing-press and matrices for Roman type which he had ordered from Portugal for use in the Japanese mission field. It was soon put to use, to print a Latin speech delivered by one of the envoys, thanking Valignano and the Society of Jesus for their help in arranging their embassy. This speech, printed at Goa by a Japanese Christian and dated 1588, was the first of all the many pieces which this Japanese mission press was to print during its subsequent wanderings from place to place.

Valignano himself had meanwhile been appointed Ambassador from the Portuguese Viceroy of India to the court of the Japanese ruler Hideyoshi, with the aim of persuading him to withdraw or mitigate the edict which he had issued in 1587 against the Christians. The party left Goa and sailed as far as Macao, the Portuguese settlement on the China coast near Canton. While he waited there for news that his own embassy would be acceptable to Hideyoshi, Valignano employed his new press on two books in Latin, both destined specifically for students in the Jesuit colleges he had other word for it) no fewer than thirteen examples, and that in an age when few even among scholars were aware of Caxton's importance. Aside from this group, his fifteenth-century books, some one hundred and thirty in number, are found in all the many fields in which his collection is so rich – history, law, medicine, philosophy and theology. Particularly welcome to the Bodleian was a perfect copy of that 1479 Latin translation of Aristotle's *Nicomachean Ethics* which was the second book, and the first university text-book, ever printed at Oxford.

Polymath and polyglot though he himself was, Selden also collected books in languages of which he cannot have understood a single word. Yet, like Sir Thomas Bodley, he foresaw their future significance. Such were the Chinese map, which had been on display in his London house, and the six Chinese books which his library added to the Bodleian's Chinese collection; such was his copy of the first book ever printed in Japan with moveable types and in Western characters (Plate 99) though there was no one then to decipher and document for him its historical importance and virtual uniqueness. Such, too, were the printed books and three painted codices which helped to raise the Bodleian to pre-

SANCTOS
NOGOSAGVEONO
VCHINVQIGAQI
quan dai ichi.

FIIENNOCVNITACACVNOGVN
IESVSNOCOMPANHIANOCOLLEGIO
Cazzusa ni voite Superiores no von yuruxi uo cŏ
muri core uo fan to nasu mono nari. Goxuxxe izai
MDLXXXXI.

already founded in Japan. The first, a work on the Christian education of youth, is dated 1588, the other, an account of the journey and experiences of the four envoys to Europe, written up from their diaries by Valignano himself, is dated 1589/90. Both books bear the imprint of the Jesuit House at Macao.

At length the party was able to proceed and arrived back at Nagasaki on 7 July 1590, more than eight years after it had set out from there. The press was set up in the Jesuit College at Katsusa and there was published the first book ever printed with moveable types on Japanese soil, and the press's first in the Japanese language. Its text, a *Compendium of the Acts of the Saints* taken from the *Flos sanctorum* and other sources, was firstly translated by two Japanese catechists, who had joined the Society of Jesus in 1580; it had then to be transliterated into Western syllables and finally set up in the Roman type by native craftsmen. The titlepage cut, here reproduced, engraved on copperplate (a technique also introduced by the missionaries), was executed in imitation of a European original, by one of the Japanese artists trained in the College at Katsusa, where the book, printed on locally-made paper, was issued in 1591. By the time that Spanish Franciscans from the Philippines settled at Kyoto in 1593 the Jesuits were already able to offer them a printed grammar and a dictionary to help them learn Japanese, and it is recorded that this 1591 *Compendium* was used as a textbook in the kindergarten school attached to the Franciscan hospice there.

It was long believed that the Bodleian copy, which reached the Library in 1659 among Selden's books, was the unique survivor from this edition, but recently a second copy has been found, in the Marciana Library at Venice. Of the two dozen or so different products of this mission press which are known to exist today – and there are an equal number of other titles recorded by contemporary sources as printed, of which no copies have yet been found – most are, quite understandably, of similarly outstanding rarity. Fortunately, in its long history the Bodleian has acquired no fewer than four others, two printed at Amakusa, to which by the year 1592 the press had been moved for greater safety, and two printed at Nagasaki, after the College at Amakusa had been forced by persecution to close in 1597. One of these four, a Japanese translation of Luis de Granada's Spanish version of the *Imitatio Christi*, represents, as does the *Compendium*, the spiritual element in the output from the press; it survives in only one other copy besides that in the Bodleian. The remaining three books which the Bodleian owns are of great importance linguistically, comprising the first printed Japanese dictionary (1595) which was compiled in three languages, a comprehensive Japanese-Portuguese lexicon (1603) and the *Arte da lingoa de Japam* (1604–08), the first scientific study of the language, also surviving in only one other copy.

100. **Drake's Chair**
For two centuries the most famous objects in the Picture Gallery were Guy Fawkes's Lantern, Joseph's Coat of Many Colours, and Drake's Chair. Of the hundreds of curiosities, natural and artificial, which had accumulated in the Library, the chair alone remains here, following successive dispersals to other University institutions.

A fellow-Devonian and exact contemporary of Sir Thomas Bodley, Francis Drake embarked in 1577 on a great voyage which made him the first Englishman to circumnavigate the world. After three years his ship the Golden Hind arrived back at Plymouth, and by the Queen's order was taken to Deptford, where on 4 April 1581 she knighted Drake on board the ship and was entertained to a banquet. A special dry-dock was constructed, but the much-buffeted ship quickly decayed and by 1618 the Venetian ambassador's secretary mentions its 'relics, which looked exactly like the bleached ribs and bare skull of a dead horse'.

It fell to John Davies, Storekeeper at Deptford Dockyard, to arrange for her final breaking-up. Pepys (Plate 117) describes Davies as 'a very pretty man', and when he spent a night at

eminence as a repository of early Mexican records (Plates 78, 98).

His last year as Librarian Barlow spent unpacking, sorting and placing the Selden books, which came from London by water. Anthony Wood, who helped in these operations, records that several pairs of spectacles were found in volumes where Selden had left them and forgotten to take them out again, and one pair the Librarian gave to Wood who 'kept it in memorie of Selden to his last day'. So great were the costs of the carriage, installation and binding of this 'unparalleled gift', (the phrase is Barlow's own) that to meet them Convocation imposed a graded levy on all members of the University. Even undergraduates had to pay one shilling each. The levy raised £143 13s.

Gerard Langbaine, whose learning and wise council had for so many years been at the service of the Bodleian, died in 1658, and was succeeded as Provost of Queen's by Bodley's Librarian. A most valuable manuscript, *Fasciculi zizaniorum* ('Little bundles of tares'), the contemporary account from which the history of Wyclif and his followers

Davies's house, he wrote of being 'so princelike lodged, with so much respect and honour that I was almost at a loss how to behave myself'; he noted that the study was 'filled with good books'. From the ship's timbers Davies caused an armchair to be made and this he presented to the Bodleian in 1662. A fellow-official at the Dockyard was the brother of Abraham Cowley and the poet agreed to provide verses in Latin and English which are engraved on metal plates attached to the chair. He was also moved to write an 'Ode, sitting and drinking in the chair, made out of the reliques of Sir Francis Drake's ship'. Cowley had already given the Bodleian in 1656 a copy of his collected *Poems* with an additional ode in his own handwriting which speaks of the Library as 'Learning's Pantheon', and so on, for five stanzas.

Two other similar chairs are recorded, one of them now at Drake's old home, Buckland Abbey, but these may be early copies of the Library's original. In Cowley's words

> Let not the Pope's itself with this compare,
> This is the only Universal Chair.

Drake's Chair is normally on view in the Divinity School.

is chiefly known, came to the Bodleian by Langbaine's bequest. A gift of a very different kind was made in the same year by a brother-in-law of Cromwell: a crocodile from Jamaica, now, alas, no longer on view. Still much admired by visitors is another gift made about the same time, Drake's Chair (Plate 100), fashioned from the timbers of the first English ship to circumnavigate the globe.

In 1660 the monarchy was restored and many who had been displaced returned to Oxford; the ensuing politico-religious 'musical chairs' displaced some occupants and replaced others. Henry Stubbe, a writer of wide learning who had been made Under-Librarian of the Bodleian by John Owen, the Independent who became Vice-Chancellor after being Cromwell's chaplain, lost his post after only two years for publishing anonymously a book criticising the universities and the clergy. He was succeeded as Under-Librarian by Thomas Hyde, the future Bodley's Librarian.

In the Library as elsewhere the royalists set about effacing as far as was practicable the traces of the preceding regime, as the Parliamentarians had done after their capture of Oxford. Thus, an entry in the Benefactors' Register recording two books given in 1657 by Hugh Peters, the noted Independent divine who in October 1660 had paid the forfeit of his life for abetting the execution of Charles I, was carefully pasted over to conceal his no longer acceptable name. Another leaf following this has been cut out entirely; possibly it recorded the Greek manuscripts given by Cromwell, whose name does not figure at all in the Register. The contemporary rumour that the set of his own controversial tracts presented by Milton had been thrown out or even burnt is belied by the fact that they are there in the Library today (Plate 88). The simplest explanation of their presence is not that they were later rescued and returned but that in the fervour of the royalist reaction they were no longer exhibited but were discreetly hidden away, perhaps in the Librarian's study, so effectively indeed as to escape mention in the 1674 printed Bodleian *Catalogue*.

Another sign of the times is apparent in an entry in the accounts for 1661 'for polishing the rust from the King's picture and setting it up againe in the Librarie £1 12s 6d'. This can only refer to the bronze bust of Charles I given by Laud (Plate 82) now restored to its niche after a presumed period in hiding during the Commonwealth.

In September 1660 Barlow resigned as Bodley's Librarian to take the Lady Margaret Professorship of Divinity. Possibly, as Wood hints, he may have recoiled from the immense task of listing the Selden collections. That burden fell to his successor Thomas Lockey, B.D., of Christ Church, who had been ejected by the Parliamentary Visitors and had returned to Oxford only after the Restoration. Lockey was a noted tutor, a man of a retired and studious character, and a connoisseur and collector of statues and pictures. His inventory includes books valued at £200, and after his death in 1679 the Bodleian bought £16 15s-worth of his books from an Oxford bookseller.

Three years after his restoration Charles II revisited Oxford and stayed a week at Christ Church, where, in his early teens, he had lived with his father during the Civil War. The University entertained him and his court to 'a very sumptuous banquett' in Selden End (Plate 83). While the new Chancellor Edward Hyde, recently created Earl of Clarendon, showed his royal guests round, Lockey must have been in attendance, but he was not required to make a speech. That duty was performed by the Senior Proctor, Nathaniel Crewe the elder, one who, like Lockey himself and twenty-two other Oxford men, had contributed verses to the University's formal volume addressed to Cromwell in 1654, and then in 1660 had done an about turn and joined in a similar official collection in honour of the Restoration. Crewe's speech was delivered on his knees 'neer the globes', that is, at the entrance to Duke Humfrey's Library where the two globes formerly stood, as can be seen in Loggan's engraving (Plate 43).

Wood, who was notably sharp in some of his judgments, did not find Lockey a very efficient Librarian. Nevertheless, in a letter to Archbishop Sheldon Lockey stated that despite the size of Selden's library, 'an accession of about 30,000 authors', 'I have by mine owne payns disposed of [it] in a Catalogue to be inserted in the General'. This claim is borne out by the existence of a listing in Lockey's hand of Selden's collections. However, Lockey grossly underestimated the time required for the complex task of integrating the Selden and the Bodleian holdings into a new general catalogue for publication. The endeavour, which was to be carried through by his successor Thomas Hyde, proved to be manifestly beyond Lockey's powers, and a year later he resigned his post and took a canonry at Christ Church.

CHAPTER V

Two Great Catalogues

1665–1700

Thomas Hyde, who took over after Lockey's retirement in November 1665, had been his predecessor's Under-Librarian for the last six years. His election was unanimous, suggesting that the electors considered that his library experience put him in a better position than any other possible candidate to understand the nature and urgency of certain problems which would confront him in his new office. It is satisfactory to record that just over thirty-five years later, when he himself came to retire in 1701 at the age of nearly sixty-five, each of two extensive and longstanding needs had in fact at last been met. The first of these was for a full and up-to-date *Catalogue* of the Library's printed books, and the second, and no less pressing, was for a comprehensive listing of the accumulated riches of the Bodleian manuscripts, which already formed an exceptionally high proportion of all the volumes held. Apart from the six years he had spent helping to run the Library, what other qualifications did Hyde bring to the tasks which faced him?

He began his academic life and continued to the end as principally an orientalist. His earliest beginnings in that way were made under his father in the Shropshire vicarage where he was born in 1636. Entering King's College, Cambridge, at the age of sixteen, he studied under Abraham Wheelock, the Professor of Arabic and University Librarian, and it was Wheelock who recommended Hyde to Bryan Walton, who in 1652 had begun to invite subscriptions for the Polyglot Bible he proposed to edit.

The Bible, issued between 1654 and 1657, involved the co-operation of many scholars including the young Hyde, whose principal contribution to that massive enterprise was his transliteration from Hebrew characters of a Persian translation of the Pentateuch. Already in an Oxford speech put into print in 1657, its author had saluted Hyde as 'that most learned young man, the careful restorer of the Persian Pentateuch,' in reference to his part in the Polyglot. Thus his reputation had preceded him to Oxford, for in 1658 he moved to Queen's College and became Reader in Hebrew, and a year later was made Under-Librarian to Barlow. It must have given him pleasure in his Library post to see put on the shelves in 1661 the copy of the Polyglot presented to the Bodleian by Walton himself, who had resided in Oxford for some years, studying oriental languages, until ejected by the Parliamentary Visitors in 1647.

Throughout his long Oxford career Hyde continued to publish important oriental texts, many of them in Persian, but including also a treatise on Chinese weights and measures. Robert Boyle, who settled in Oxford in 1654, in addition to his eminence as a 'natural philosopher' and founder-member of the Royal Society, deserves also to be remembered for putting his fortune behind a number of publications aimed at making the Scriptures and other Christian writings available in native vernacular versions for missionary purposes. Among these

101. **A presentation copy of John Eliot's Massachusetts Bible, 1663**

This was not only the first complete Bible printed in North America, it was also the first in a language spoken by natives of that continent, and the first anywhere put into print in a new language solely for missionary purposes. Its translator was John Eliot, a graduate of Jesus College, Cambridge, who embraced Puritan opinions and migrated to New England, where his manifold labours earned him the title of 'Apostle of the Indians'. The printing of this translation was sponsored by the local Commissioners of the 'New England Company', which had been founded in London by Act of Parliament in 1649. This body, the earliest British missionary society, undertook to pay for the book's production and sent out Marmaduke Johnson in 1660 as assistant to share the work with Samuel Green, already established at Cambridge, Massachusetts. In 1640 Green had published the 'Bay Psalm Book', of which the same John Eliot had been one of the three compilers, and of that book the Bodleian possesses the only copy outside the New World. The London Society also sent out a new printing-press and supplies of paper. The New Testament was printed and issued by the two partners in 1661 and copies of it were bound with the Old Testament, which is dated 1663, to make a complete edition of the Bible in the language of the Massachusetts Indians.

In 1667, Harvard University, founded in the daughter-town of Cambridge, New England, as the earliest institution for higher learning in North America, sent this copy of the Massachusetts Bible, just recently printed on its premises, to Ralph Freke, Esquire, a retired lawyer living in England and a 'Nobl benefactor of the abovesayd Colledg' as its manuscript inscription (here reproduced) proclaims him. When this thank-offering from 'Haverd Colleg' reached him, Freke was already in his seventies and may well have felt himself too old to set about mastering the Massachusetts language, which it had taken even the exceedingly industrious Eliot several years to learn. Considering also how few there must have been among the Bible readers in his own Wiltshire village of Hannington who could appreciate the language of that distant Indian people, it is easy to understand why, in the following year, 1668, the old squire decided – no doubt with pride and probably also with some relief – to hand over his trophy for safekeeping to the Library of his own University (he had graduated M.A. from Hart Hall, Oxford, in 1619), that very Library to which he had already given in 1657 a valuable collection of gold and silver coins. And there his Bible has remained ever since, still at its original shelfmark. Sadly, the Massachusetts people and its language have long since become extinct.

The Freke copy is entirely in the Massachusetts language, though it also has, prefixed to the New Testament, the additional English titlepage and the dedicatory letter to King Charles II. A finely-bound copy of the other issue, which has an English titlepage to the Old Testament, was given to the Bodleian early in the eighteenth century by Sir Henry Ashurst Bt of Waterstock in Oxfordshire. These extra English leaves were printed for insertion into copies of the Bible sent back to the mother country. One such copy was presented to King Charles II by Robert Boyle, the great experimental philosopher, who had become the first 'Governor' of the New England Company; the dedicatory letter was intended to persuade the monarch to renew the missionary society's charter, and in this Boyle was successful.

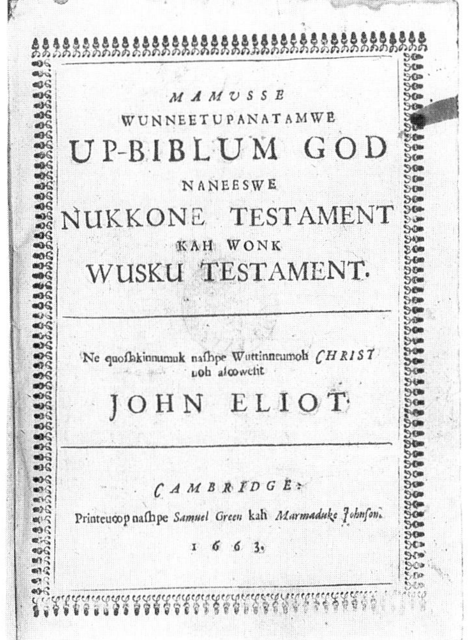

MAMUSSE
WUNNEETUPANATAMWE
UP-BIBLUM GOD
NANEESWE
NUKKONE TESTAMENT
KAH WONK
WUSKU TESTAMENT.

Ne quoshkinnumuk nashpe Wuttinneumoh CHRIST
noh asoowesit
JOHN ELIOT.

CAMBRIDGE:
Printeuoop nashpe Samuel Green kah Marmaduke Johnson.
1663.

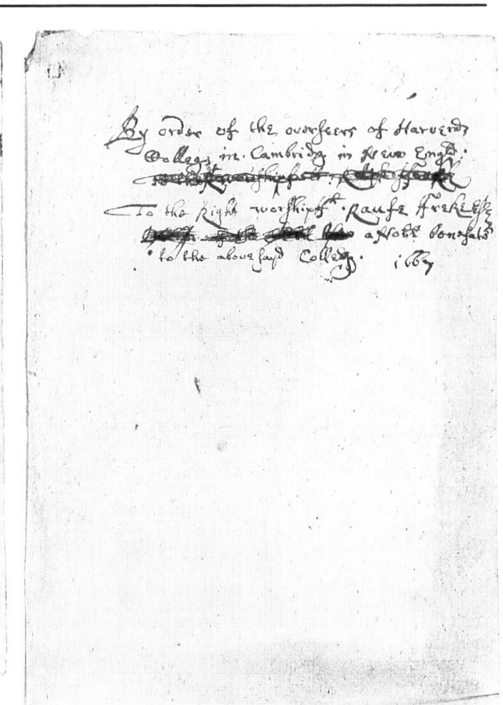

By order of the overseers of Harverd
Collegg in Cambridg in New Engld:
To the Right worshipfll Raufe Freke Esq
[illegible] benefactor
to the abovesayd Colledg. 1667

were the *Massachusetts Bible* of 1663 (Plate 101), a Turkish New Testament in 1666 (the earliest Oxford New Testament) and in 1677 an Oxford reprint of a Malayan translation of the Gospels and Acts. This contains a learned preface by Dr Thomas Marshall, a future benefactor of the Bodleian, and a dedication by Hyde to Boyle, who paid the entire cost of the edition.

Hyde's own ultimate publication, and the one which carried his reputation still further to fellow orientalists throughout Europe, was a pioneering history of the religion of the ancient Persians. It was published in Oxford in 1700, a little before he put into effect his long-considered decision to resign as Bodley's Librarian. Six years earlier Anthony Wood had listed thirty-one as yet unpublished works on all of which Hyde had already made some progress. Yet despite his well-deserved contemporary fame for his oriental learning, time was eventually to show that Hyde's most enduring monument must unquestionably be held to be his new *Catalogue* of the Bodleian's printed books.

When he took office it was forty-five years since the last general *Catalogue*, that of Thomas James, had been issued in 1620; Rous's supplement to it had been added in 1635. Since that time nothing had been put into print to tell the outside world the extent of the Bodleian's ever-growing holdings. It was not only the world at large that needed to be told. University readers and those who came to Oxford from outside to use the Library would still have to consult, or ask one of the librarians to consult for them, one of those thick, squat little volumes in which copies of the 1620 *Catalogue* and its supplement had been bound with interleaving onto which new accessions were entered by the staff. Several of these still survive, and the minutely written entries with their abbreviated titles and shelfmarks must have made consultation difficult at all times, especially in a reading-room where any form of artificial light had been specifically forbidden by the Founder's statutes. And there had, of course, during those years been growth, not always steady and predictable, but always sufficient to keep up the pressure, lest the *Catalogue* should fall seriously into arrears. To what might be termed the routine year-by-year intake arising from the somewhat intermittent operation of the copyright agreement, supplemented so far as fluctuating resources permitted by a fairly cumbrous routine for purchasing selected foreign publications, there had also been during those years a small but constant trickle of gifts presented by well-wishers from many different walks of life.

The transfer to the Bodleian in 1860 of books and manuscripts which had accrued to the Ashmolean Museum since its foundation, was part of a wider process of re-organization which the University undertook of the many different types of objects which it had come to possess during the long centuries of its existence. This went hand in hand with the widening and increasing specialization of its academic disciplines. The smallness of the beautiful original Ashmolean Museum precluded any great expansion there, and it remained basically the collection given by its founder as well as being the centre for science teaching. It was therefore the more ample spaces afforded by the adjacent Bodleian Picture Gallery which continued then and long afterwards to receive and exhibit gifts of all kinds, of which the most important were coins, prints and portraits. Among the latter were paintings of national heroes as different as the Elizabethan explorer Sir Martin Frobisher (Plate 104) given in 1674, and the Venetian theologian Paolo Sarpi (Plate 105) presented the following year. Naturally enough there were also portraits of benefactors and men of learning, including Archbishop Laud (Plate 68), Selden (Plate 92), Junius (Plate 106) and the great mathematician John Wallis, whose likeness was given by Samuel Pepys. Many of these now hang on the walls of different reading-rooms in the Old Library, where they may literally be looked up to by those toiling at the desks below, who may well be using the fruits of their labours.

Any imagined picture of Bodley's Librarian sitting down to work on his *Catalogue* with suspended over his head the stuffed crocodile presented in 1658 must reluctantly be abandoned, for in the accounts for 1671 is recorded an outlay of twelve shillings 'For a case for the great Crocodile'; evidently for public exhibition in the Picture Gallery. But once safely encased the great crocodile was not left alone with his glory: in 1678 the same Library accounts show that fifteen shillings was spent for the carriage from Lechlade of a whale which had been caught in the Severn, presented by William Jordan, an apothecary at

102. ***The Rule of St Benedict***
The oldest manuscript of *The Rule of St Benedict* to survive anywhere is also probably the oldest book of English origin in the Bodleian's collections. Written around the year 700 its early history is unknown, but its monumental formality of presentation, usually reserved for copies of the Gospels, implies in its first owner (prelate or community) a deep veneration for the *Rule*. Most significant is the fact that the scribe who copied it also corrected the text himself from another manuscript containing a different version of the text, demonstrating that only a century and a half after the death of St Benedict in Southern Italy, texts of his *Rule* were circulating in far-away Britain already modified by variations and revisions. Even on the Continent the Benedictine formula did not become established as the enduring norm for the religious life until the later eighth century.

The script itself is a symbol of the union between the Celtic and Roman churches. Scribes who had inherited the calligraphic traditions of Irish foundations in Northumbria and elsewhere were much influenced by the uncial scripts of imported codices such as the Laudian *Acts* (Plate 75). The resulting imitation, 'English uncial', has its own unique quality: a noble stateliness, but also a ponderous artificiality, in contrast to the fluid grace of fifth-century uncial manuscripts. The blackness and thickness of the strokes, the almost abstract spirit of formal calligraphy, must be inherited from the Celtic past. Like its near contemporaries, the Books of Lindisfarne and Kells, the Hatton *Rule* is a masterpiece of calligraphy, a happy blend of native and imported influences. The lavish illumination of those Gospel books would have been out of place in a non-biblical text, so the decorated initials echo the Doric simplicity of the script; nevertheless the vermilion letters in their black outlines are expertly shaped, and the red dots which surround them are characteristic of Insular book-decoration from the earliest times.

A covering of later mediaeval tawed leather obscures a binding structure of great antiquity and interest. The sewing and cords have even been considered eighth century, while the wooden boards are replacements which were probably added at the same time as the back flyleaf. The latter is a fragment from a late eleventh-century manuscript written at Worcester Cathedral Priory (Benedictine), and thus provides the first precise location for the manuscript. Since the leaf contains a gross error of transcription, it is probably a cancelled leaf from the Worcester scriptorium rather than a relic from a book which had reached the end of its working life; this dates the binding repair on the *Rule* to only shortly after the date when the flyleaf was written. The *Rule* remained at Worcester until the seventeenth century.

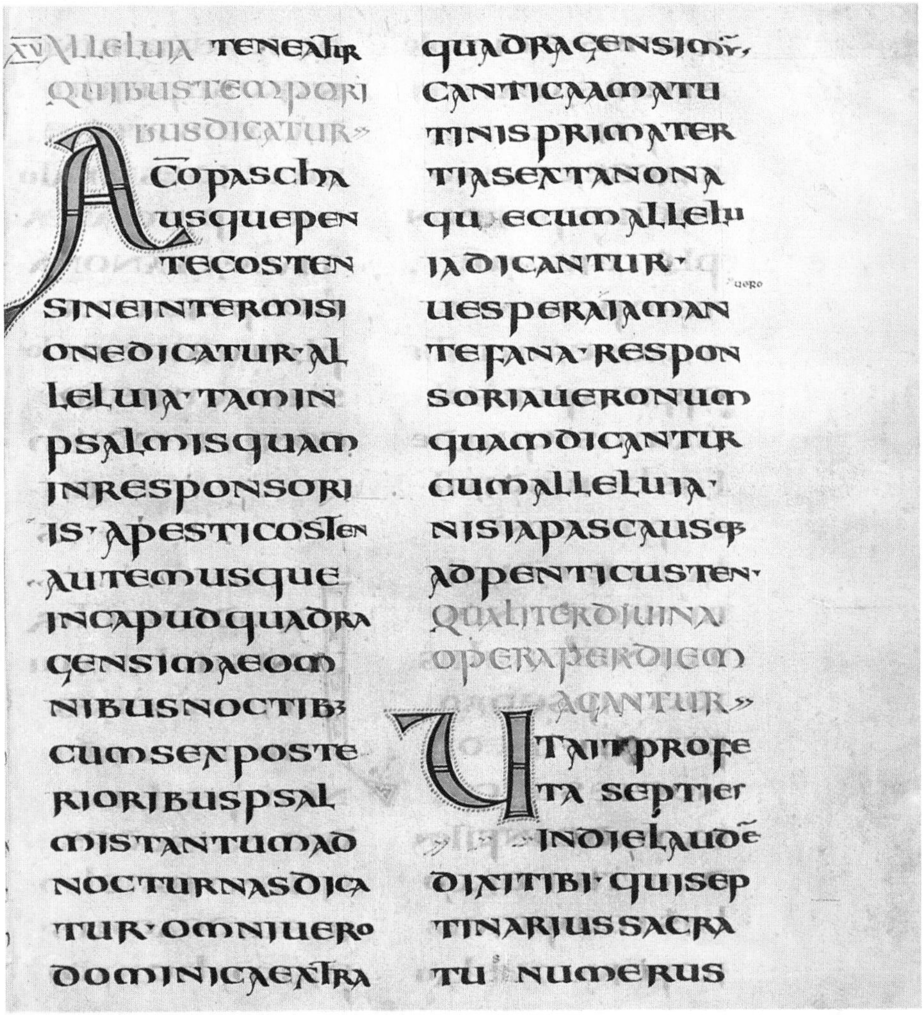

Gloucester. More important to Hyde as compiler of the *Catalogue*, but more taxing too, were sudden large accessions such as the eight hundred books which came from Robert Burton's library (Plates 84, 86). Such benefactions must have aroused the interest and expectations of readers who got to hear of them but could not soon sample their contents, since the same small staff which had to maintain continuous service in the reading-room had also to cope with the extra burden of arranging among themselves for the new intake to be catalogued, shelfmarked, handlisted, possibly also repaired, and then chained, before new entries could be added or interpolated into the increasingly inadequate copies of the current *Catalogue*. The very year that Hyde himself had become a member of the staff as Under-Librarian saw the arrival of 'Mr Selden's Library'. This massive increase, still among the largest ever made to the Bodleian, meant that the Library had suddenly grown by approximately half its previous size or that (put another way) of all the copies which Hyde had to register for his proposed new *Catalogue* one in every three came from Selden's collection.

Inevitably there was much duplication between such a collection and the Library into which it was now being incorporated. Selden's executors had foreseen this as most probable, and the two-and-a-half years between the University's original letter requesting the gift and the actual arrival of the collection in Oxford were doubtless in part spent weeding out at least some of the duplicates. Even after its delivery more were found and a list in Lockey's hand, but preserved among Barlow's papers, records books sent on to Gloucester Cathedral Library by order of the executors, a choice explained no doubt by the leading presence among them of Matthew Hale, whose home was at Alderley in Gloucestershire.

The elimination of 'duplicates', including in that term books which were held to be superseded by newer editions, had been official policy since the Founder's day, partly to make room on the shelves and partly to raise money for further book purchases, though the latter result was often not commensurate with the time and labour it involved for the staff. At some date before the publication of Hyde's *Catalogue*, the original chained copy of the Shakespeare First Folio (Plate 64), much tattered after forty years of constant handling by readers (tangible proof of the poet's popularity), was replaced by a copy of the Third Folio dated 1664, received, it is to be hoped, from the publishers direct, under the new statutory obligation imposed by law for the first time in 1662. The publication of the new *Catalogue* with its clearly printed shelfmarks will have made it easier and quicker to check for multiple copies, and the process of elimination still continued after the *Catalogue* was in print; in 1676 what was evidently a very considerable sale must have taken place. Several books are known bearing inscriptions that they were bought out of the Bodleian in that year; two of these have recently found their way back, one of them with its original chain still attached after three hundred years.

Hyde's *Catalogus impressorum librorum bibliothecae Bodleianae in academia Oxoniensi* was published in 1674 and bears the imprint of the newly-founded University Press, housed since 1669 in the splendid theatre which Christopher Wren had designed and Archbishop Gilbert Sheldon had presented, wholly at his own expense, to his old University, on a site between the Divinity School and the city wall. The double doors, which form the main entrance to Wren's grand semi-circular amphitheatre, face directly (and only an academic cap-throw away) the north side of the Divinity School, and Wren daringly inserted an ogival doorway into its Perpendicular flank so that on special occasions processions could walk through the School and wheel right into the Theatre for the final ceremony, as indeed they still do today.

In his preface to the reader Hyde reveals the stages through which his work on the *Catalogue* had gone: how he began the task immediately

103. **A presentation copy of King Alfred's translation of St Gregory's *Pastoral Care***

The brilliant promise of English eighth-century scholarship scarcely survived the troubles, sackings and invasion of the ninth – in great contrast to the Carolingian renaissance on the Continent. The reign of King Alfred (871–899) inspired a brave but faltering revival. A major feature of Alfred's educational reforms consisted of the translations into Old English of important Latin texts – St Augustine's *Soliloquia*, Bede's *Historia ecclesiastica*, the Psalms, Boethius's *De consolatione philosophiae*, Gregory the Great's *Regula pastoralis* and Orosius's *Historia* – inspired by or even personally undertaken by the King himself. Alfred sent a copy of the *Pastoral Care* in his own translation to each of his bishops – an appropriate text for such a presentation.

What makes this manuscript one of England's greatest historic treasures is that it is the only surviving book which can actually be linked with King Alfred himself. It is the very copy sent by the King to Waerferth, Bishop of Worcester (died 915), between 890 and 897. The evidence for this claim is that the preface, which consists of a letter from Alfred addressed to the Bishop by name, is clearly an addition to the rest of the manuscript, presumably in the handwriting of one of Alfred's clerks. The letter also mentions an accompanying aestel, a pointer used for following the lines of writing; it has been suggested that Oxford's other great treasure of this period, the 'Alfred Jewel' at the Ashmolean Museum, is the pommel of such a pointer, which Alfred would have sent to one of his bishops to stimulate more attentive reading of the translated *Pastoral Care*. The metalwork of the Jewel is a technical masterpiece, but the scripts of the Worcester *Pastoral Care* and its general appearance show a great deterioration in the quality of the book arts. The scripts are plainly derived from the earlier English manuscript tradition, but the scribes – presumably from the royal Chancery – must have been more used to writing documents than books. The manuscript's uneven quality is itself mute testimony to the decline which Alfred strove so courageously to remedy.

Later annotations in a Worcester script are perhaps by the hand of Wulfstan, Bishop of Worcester from 1003 to 1016. The manuscript remained at Worcester Cathedral throughout the Middle Ages.

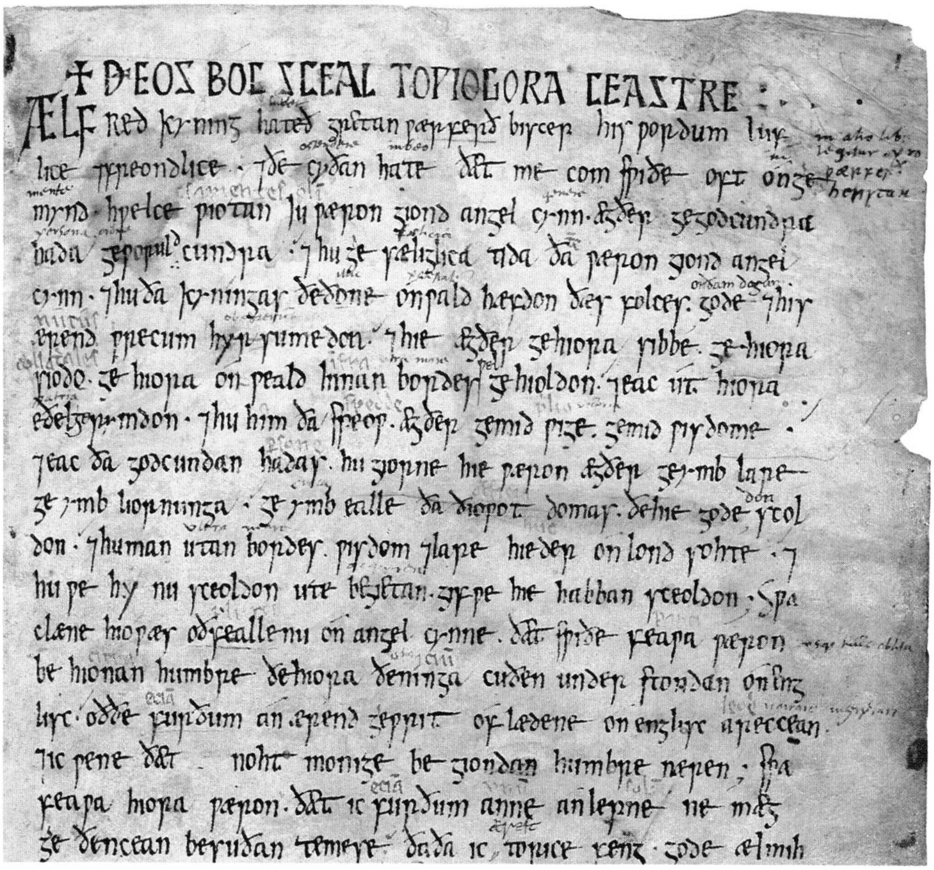

upon his election as Librarian, thinking that single-handed he could accomplish it in two, or at most three, years. Against all such expectations, it took him six years to compile his *Catalogue* and make a fair copy of it, then another year was spent on the revision, inserting and adding new accessions, and finally while the book was at the press two further years were occupied in the daily grind of checking and proof-correcting. Hyde does not minimize the tedious and physically exhausting labours in which this had involved him, or the difficulties, of which the ordinary reader was quite unaware, of making a consistent and intelligible presentation of such a formidable quantity of disparate materials as the Bodleian then contained. His illuminating preface strongly suggests that he evolved his own rules and principles as his work progressed; he had no comparable catalogue to guide him and very few reference books to help him, for example, to detect hidden authorships and identify and differentiate writers who, in days before nomenclature began to be standardized, might themselves use various forms and spellings even of their own names.

His entries went far beyond those of the two earlier printed Bodleian *Catalogues* in fullness and accuracy: he would quote the wording on a titlepage rather than describe or paraphrase it as his predecessors had often done, and this must have necessitated weeks and months of checking existing entries by personal scrutiny of the volumes on the shelves. He was alive to the peril to such a checking procedure posed by 'coupling' (the Founder's own word for the binding together of different works into a single volume) and he introduced multicolouring of the fore-edges of such volumes to mark the constituent parts. He made very generous use of cross-references from variant forms to his chosen headings, and was at pains to include individually works which were to be found incorporated within larger collections such as, for example, those of legal commentaries. A scholar and editor of renown himself, his intention was to smooth the pathways which would lead other scholars to the objects of their search. This concern for the needs of his readers put him far ahead of his time and set standards which were afterwards adopted widely elsewhere in imitation of him. Even today, when the design of catalogues is in some danger of becoming an involved taxonomic exercise performed by specialists who are not themselves users of books, Hyde's volume still retains much of its value as a quick guide to a large number of books, mainly in Latin, produced during the first two centuries of printing, being especially serviceable among the byways of scholarship traced out by a quantity of less well-known writers.

By its dignified folio format, its legibility and the amplitude of its coverage of learned, if not so much of popular, literature (there are only three entries under Shakespeare, plus a cross-reference to Fletcher for *The Two Noble Kinsmen*) Hyde's *Catalogue* provided what Bodleian readers needed and also something which scholars could buy for themselves. A copy cost nineteen shillings and those who were admitted to the Library as readers were expected to purchase one from the Janitor, Emmanuel Pritchard. He, for his assistance to Hyde, was rewarded with £5 and a hundred copies of the *Catalogue* at a discount of one shilling to sell; Hyde himself received £160 for completing the *Catalogue*. The Vice-Chancellor paid Dr Fell and his three partners at the University Press £725 for printing one thousand copies. How they were disposed for sale is uncertain, but the London bookseller and publisher Moses Pitt, who with three others bought the right to print bibles for the University in the Sheldonian Theatre in 1678, included the *Catalogue* in the first recorded 'trade sale' (an auction, restricted to booksellers only, of multiple copies of books) in the following year. It would be surprising if the presentation by Pitt to the Bodleian in 1680 of a volume containing four separate works printed by Caxton were not a token of the gratitude he felt for the publishing rights he had just obtained from Oxford. This was an especially appropriate gift, increasing as it did the fine collection of Caxtons which the Library had already by this time begun to build up (Plate 95). Whatever were the other arrangements for its disposal, the *Catalogue* sold very well, and in 1692 Edward Bernard recommended to the Library's Curators 'That no person be any longer obliged to take off one *Catalogue* of the

104. **Portrait of Sir Martin Frobisher by Cornelius Ketel**
Raleigh (Plate 20), Drake (Plate 100), Gilbert and Hawkins were all fellow-Devonians with Sir Thomas Bodley, whereas Martin Frobisher was born far from the sea, near Wakefield. On his father's early death he was sent to London, and already at the age of fifteen, is heard of on an expedition to Guinea. His prowess and enterprise eventually brought him to the notice of Queen Elizabeth, and this culminated in his voyage of 1576, on board the Gabriel, in search of a North-West passage to China and India. He was away for four months, returning in the belief that the present-day Frobisher's Bay, an extensive creek in Baffin Island, was the opening of the mythical passage. He brought back an Eskimo, and a piece of pyrites which alchemists declared to contain gold. In

consequence the Queen herself invested in an expedition which repeated the journey in 1577, and loaded 200 tons of minerals, as well as a family of Eskimos. The gold remained elusive, so a yet larger expedition returned in 1578, only to confirm that the gold was an illusion. Fortunately, Frobisher retained the Queen's confidence, and he played an important part in the defeat of the Spanish Armada, after which he was knighted. He died in 1594, at the age of perhaps fifty-five, of wounds received at the Siege of Brest.

Cornelius Ketel's portrait is dated 1577 and appropriately includes a terrestrial globe displaying the area between Europe and the Arctic regions from which Frobisher had just returned. In an easy stance, and wearing everyday clothes, one hand reposing on the guard of a very large sword and the other holding a formidable pistol ready to fire, Frobisher studies the spectator with an undeceived stare. This is the only full-length portrait among the few identifiable paintings of the many which Ketel is known to have produced in England. Ketel (1548–1616) was a Dutchman, and had worked at Fontainebleau before reaching London in 1573. He came to the notice of the Court with an allegorical painting, but his employment seems to have been entirely on portraits, and by 1581 he had returned to Amsterdam.

The accounts of the Cathay Company, which financed Frobisher's second voyage, reveal the kind of commissions which Ketel may have found irksome, although handsomely paid. The Company wished to record the appearance of the Eskimo captured by Frobisher, and Ketel provided three paintings, at £5 each, of the 'strange man' in native and in English apparel, while for a 'small picture' and 'for his picture naked' he was paid £1 apiece. Further, he received £6 for 'a great picture of the ship Gabriel', and £5 for a 'great picture of Captayne Furbusher'.

The 'Captayne Furbusher' is not heard of again until 1674 when it was received at the Bodleian, accompanied by a portrait of Grotius, as the gift of Dr Walter Charleton, a physician to the King and an Oxford graduate. It remains one of the best-known portraits in the Bodleian Picture Gallery, and although at some distant period it has been cut down at the right side, the most recent cleaning, in 1960, has revealed it to be far from 'ruined', as was sometimes stated.

105. **Portrait of Paolo Sarpi**

When in 1604 the Library's benefactor Sir Henry Wotton was sent as ambassador to the Venetian Republic the success of England's policies and of his own aspirations partly depended on his relations with a Servite friar, Father Paolo Sarpi, 'the most deep and general scholar of the world'. Sarpi was at the centre of a circle of influential Venetians whose independence of thought and determination to defend their liberties led Wotton to believe they would be favourable to Protestant ideas in religion. The demands of the new Pope, Paul V, having provoked Venetian defiance, on 17 April 1606 the Republic was put under an interdict; Sarpi was then designated by the Venetians 'Theological Counsellor to the State'. After a year the interdict was lifted, and Sarpi became the personification of successful resistance to papal encroachment.

In September of that year Wotton writes that he has sent off a likeness painted by stealth, together with a collection of the friar's writings, to be shown to James I, but at Milan all was confiscated. The same week an attempt was made to stab Sarpi to death, but he survived, one blow being deflected by a cheekbone. However, on 21 December Wotton could report that he was dispatching a newly-taken portrait, now showing a black patch over the facial wound. The portrait arrived safely and several copies are recorded. Wotton had also brought Sarpi's highly-critical *History* of the Council of Trent to the King's attention, and it was in England, in 1619, that it was first published, in Italian and in English; the next year a Latin version was also printed in London but with a disguised imprint for circulation in Europe, where it became the standard Protestant history of the Council. Hence the inscription which, as we learn from a letter accompanying a copy of the portrait, Wotton himself had composed; it runs: PAULUS SARPIUS VENETUS CONCILII TRIDENTINI EVISCERATOR – Paolo Sarpi the Venetian, who tore the guts out of the Council of Trent.

The present painting only came to the Library in 1675, as the gift of Dr John Lamphire, the Camden Professor of Ancient History. Although the Benefactor's Register specifically claims it to be an original ('talem quam originalem seu archetypon vocamus') its history prior to 1675 is unfortunately not recorded.

printed books at his admission to the library: seeing but few exemplars are left of that impression & such as the University may have occasion to use for presents or otherwise'. Four years later, when the Press's Warehouse-Keeper made the first inventory of stock, the cupboard was bare of *Catalogues*.

That copies were used for presentation is evidenced by the dispatch of one in 1675 to Cosmo de' Medici, Grand Duke of Tuscany, who had visited Oxford in 1669 and been shown the Library 'and all its rarityes' by Hyde, together with two other handsome Sheldonian imprints: Wood's *Historia et antiquitates Universitatis Oxoniensis* and Loggan's *Oxonia illustrata*. Individual scholars, such as John Locke, annotated their personal copies with their own collections of books. But it was institutional usage which must have absorbed most copies; as the largest catalogue of printed books ever published to that date it became the standard against which other libraries measured their own holdings: interleaved and marked up 'Hydes' became the working catalogues of many such: the Ashmolean Museum, for example, which used Wood's copy, and Oxford and Cambridge colleges. Abroad, Mabillon, in his *Traité des études monastiques* (1692), recommends among the principal catalogues which were required by an ecclesiastical library 'celle d'Oxfort', and the Bibliothèque Mazarine in Paris relied upon a copy until 1760.

During Hyde's first decade as Librarian the Bodleian had very little money of its own to dispose of. For a variety of reasons its financial resources regularly proved insufficient for the desirable growth of its book collections; the royal debt of £500 was not yet repaid, and the Great Fire of London had destroyed the houses in Distaff Lane which Bodley himself had given as a means of revenue. It was the Library's good fortune that on several occasions during the last third of the seventeenth century the University showed itself willing to provide surprisingly large sums for the purchase of special collections. The first of these was that of over one hundred mediaeval manuscripts put together by Christopher, first Baron Hatton.

Antiquary and collector, Lord Hatton was a scholar himself and, through his library, a mid-wife to the scholarship of others such as Dugdale, Junius and Marshall. Like his relation, Lord Chancellor Sir Christopher Hatton, Elizabeth's favourite, he was an ardent loyalist, and was Controller of the Royal Household while Charles I's court was in Oxford from 1643 to 1646. It was during these years that he borrowed, and Dugdale worked on, a number of manuscripts of outstanding importance from Worcester Cathedral, including the earliest known manuscript of *The Rule of St Benedict* (Plate 102), King Alfred's translation into Old English of St Gregory's *Pastoral Care* (Plate 103), and two manuscripts which had belonged to St Dunstan (Plate 23) at Glastonbury. Other manuscripts also had an English monastic

106. **Portrait of Francis Junius by Van Dyck**
The Flemish-born Anthony Van Dyck, knighted in 1632 by his patron Charles I, became the leading portraitist of his age. For years he had been projecting the publication of a set of engravings from portrait studies of famous men made by him on his travels. He died in 1641 aged only forty-two, and the volume appeared posthumously in 1646, containing one hundred heads of illustrious persons, some etched by Van Dyck himself, the rest the work of other notable engravers of the time. This vivid portrait of Junius, painted on a small panel in monochrome, much resembles in size and style those – many still exist – which were used for that volume, though Junius, who was only later to gain a European reputation, was not included therein. According to the first of two versions of the portrait etched by Wenceslas Hollar, who was a fellow-member of the Arundel household, it represents Junius at the age of forty-nine, and was therefore painted about 1638. The panel evidently remained in the sitter's possession, for it came to Oxford from Windsor, where Junius had died aged eighty-eight in the house of his nephew Dr Isaac Vossius, along with the dead scholar's papers and his

types, sent from Eton by barge.

Even before this painting was executed, Junius was already known to the artist, for in a letter written in August 1636 Van Dyck congratulated Junius on his 'most learned composition', a reference to his treatise *De pictura veterum*, which also earned praise from Rubens; the book is dated 1637 so Junius had evidently let Van Dyck see it prior to publication. In the same letter Van Dyck asked Junius for a motto to be placed under the engraving of Sir Kenelm Digby which did find its place in Van Dyck's *Centum icones* of 1646. After this portrait came to the Bodleian another version of it was engraved by Michael Burghers, who had been appointed 'Engraver to the University' in 1692; it was used as the frontispiece for an Anglo-Saxon text published at Oxford in 1698, 'printed with the Junian types'.

provenance or were acquired from the collections of earlier scholars, and of especial interest is one which Duke Humfrey had presented to the old University Library in 1444. These and other of Lord Hatton's books were, after his death in 1670, sold to the bookseller Robert Scot, then the Bodleian's principal London agent. Most of these were bought by the University in the following year, a transaction probably referred to in the Library accounts as costing £156.

In that same year the former Parliamentary general, Thomas Fairfax, the third Baron, who had protected the Bodleian when he received the surrender of Oxford in 1646, became a second time its benefactor after his death. He then brought to the Library by his bequest two valuable additions. The smaller part was his personal and family collection of interesting mediaeval manuscripts, covering British literature and history, some with north of England and Scottish provenances, and many of them acquired by the antiquary Charles Fairfax, who was his uncle. The other part of the Fairfax gift was the collections which had come into his possession on the death of Roger Dodsworth, the Yorkshire-born historian to whom he had paid an annual sum to support him in his researches. Now preserved in just over one hundred and sixty volumes, they constitute the largest single body of research materials surviving from – and surely the largest ever compiled during – the seventeeth century in England. They were the life's work of a tireless scholar who for more than thirty-five years had written notes and extracts derived from public records and private muniments, from church monuments, wills, and the cartularies, manuscripts, papers and other evidences gathered by innumerable land-owners and fellow antiquaries. His collections formed the origin, and most of the matter, for the first two volumes of the justly renowned *Monasticon Anglicanum*, which is generally known as the work of his collaborator William Dugdale. After the compiler's death in 1654 their new owner Fairfax lent eighteen volumes of Dodsworth's notes to Dugdale when the latter was preparing his *Baronage*. Once again the younger scholar built on the secure foundation laid by the older man without (as some other scholars have asserted) sufficient acknowledgement. Although the joint efforts of these two men resulted in two publications which re-directed and guided the subsequent course of English historical studies, they did not by any means exhaust the potential of Dodsworth's materials. Perhaps it is their complexity and vast total bulk which has meant that they have always been difficult to survey and to use, but researchers will long continue to quarry therein and not seldom to find documents quoted which have otherwise disappeared. In Oxford Dodsworth's own manuscripts were in peril of deteriorating through damp, but Anthony Wood saw the danger and with the permission of the Vice-Chancellor spent a whole month drying them out in the sun by spreading them on the lead roofs

107. **The 'Caedmon Manuscript'**

According to the Venerable Bede, Caedmon, the earliest known English poet, was a labourer and subsequently a monk at the monastery of Whitby, having received his poetic gift through a miraculous vision. He died around the year 680. Caedmon's name does not appear in the manuscript but has been associated with it since the first printed edition was published in 1655 by Francis Junius, to whom this manuscript had been given by Archbishop Ussher. The attribution rests solely on the similarity between Bede's description of Caedmon's subject-matter and the contents of the Junius manuscript, which contains Anglo-Saxon paraphrases in alliterative verse of parts of the Old Testament. Even if some germ of Caedmon's inspiration lingers in these poems, they must have undergone innumerable interpolations and unimaginable linguistic changes during the three centuries which separate his time from the date of this manuscript. Nevertheless, the surprising tenacity of Insular culture through the Viking devastations of the ninth century shows itself in Anglo-Saxon script, which still uses the letter-forms of Bede's time. The argument that the poems are too literary for an ex-labourer overlooks the undoubted fact that Caedmon the visionary was no ordinary labourer.

The cycle of drawings illustrating Genesis is by two hands. The first is relatively crude; the second, using coloured inks, has a sketchy, impressionistic style, as in this picture of Noah ploughing. The scribe left spaces for further drawings, at the end of Genesis and in the following texts, which were never filled in. Iconographically, the existing drawings are of enormous interest: they seem to have been composed directly for this manuscript, and a range of influences is apparent, from late antiquity to the direct inspiration of the Old English text. The drawings may well have provided the inspiration for Lewis Carroll's phrase 'Anglo-Saxon attitudes' – he would have been able to see the manuscript on display in a show-case in Duke Humfrey's Library in the 1860s.

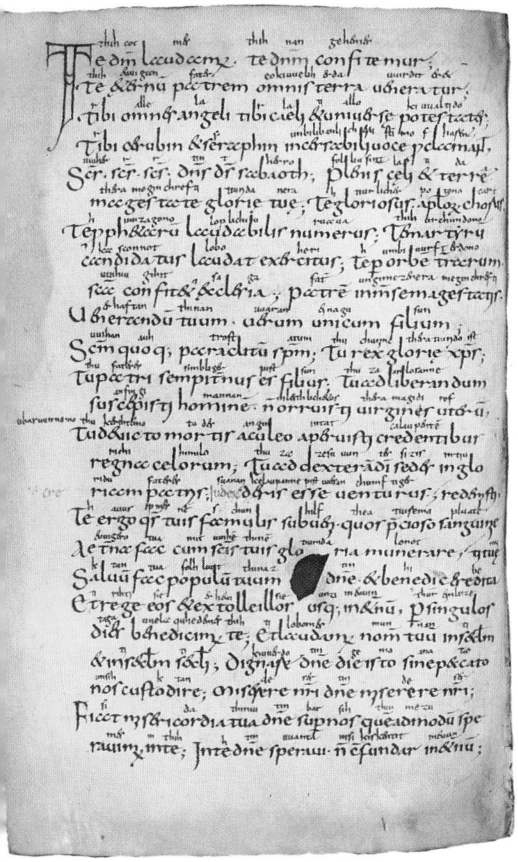

of the Schools Quadrangle (see the endpapers of this book). Though he did this to honour Dodsworth's memory, this act of conservation is not the least of Wood's own services to learning.

A much smaller but notable benefaction came in 1675 when a secretary to Louis XIV named Henri Justel (whose Protestant faith led him some years later, before the revocation of the Edict of Nantes, to flee to England, where he later became librarian of the King's library at St James's) sent over from France to the Bodleian, through his friend the scholar George Hickes, a group of his father's manuscripts. These included three late sixth-century canon law texts which Justel had used (with Gulielmus Voellus) in editing and publishing his father's work as *Bibliotheca juris canonici veteris* in 1661. This precious gift was recorded in the Benefactors' Register (Plates 18, 19) and the University honoured the donor with a Doctorate of Civil Law. By contrast, some mystery surrounds two other gifts made to the Library at about this time. Each gift was of a single manuscript and each has since been known by its donor's name. The mystery is chiefly how to account for the remarkable fact that the Benefactors' Register contains no record of either gift, though both were of outstanding importance in content and in appearance. The 'Vernon Manuscript' was given by Col. Edward Vernon, an Oxford graduate, and since a man so-named was

108. **Old High German interlinear gloss in the Hymnal from Murbach Abbey**

The Bodleian's most important monument to the German language is a complex assemblage of nine Carolingian 'booklets', including the 'Murbach hymns', the three glossaries known by the name of their last owner, Francis Junius, grammatical texts, commentaries on the Creed and the Lord's Prayer, and material by one of the prime movers of the Carolingian renaissance, Alcuin. The texts were all written in the late eighth or ninth centuries and the volume was restored in 1461 at Murbach Abbey, an eighth-century Benedictine foundation near Colmar, on the French side of the present day frontier where France, Germany and Switzerland converge, at the direction of its Abbot Bartholomaus von Andlau, whose zealous care for the Abbey's library is attested in many other Murbach manuscripts.

The booklet which contains the Murbach Hymnal is itself composite, in two distinct script-styles. The collection, which comprises nearly thirty well-known Latin hymns, including the *Te Deum* here shown, represents the more elaborate version of the Old Hymnal, and is duplicated in five other northern Continental manuscripts of the eighth and ninth centuries. What gives this copy its unique importance is the Old High German translation written, possibly in the Murbach scriptorium, over each line of the Latin text. This booklet also contains one of the three glossaries, 'Junius C'. 'Junius A' shows glossary making at its most primitive stage, where lists of difficult Latin words with explanations in Latin or Old High German are left in the order of the texts in which the compiler encountered them: *Genesis*, *Exodus*, etc., and some non-biblical works as well. The next step towards a full-scale dictionary is alphabetization: in 'Junius B' and 'Junius C' the words are grouped under their initial letters, A, B, C, D, etc., but not in strict alphabetical order within each letter. All three glossaries seem to date from the early ninth century.

In the seventeenth century the volume belonged successively to three scholars who did much to develop the history of linguistics into a serious discipline: Marcus Z. Boxhorn, Isaac Vossius and Francis Junius.

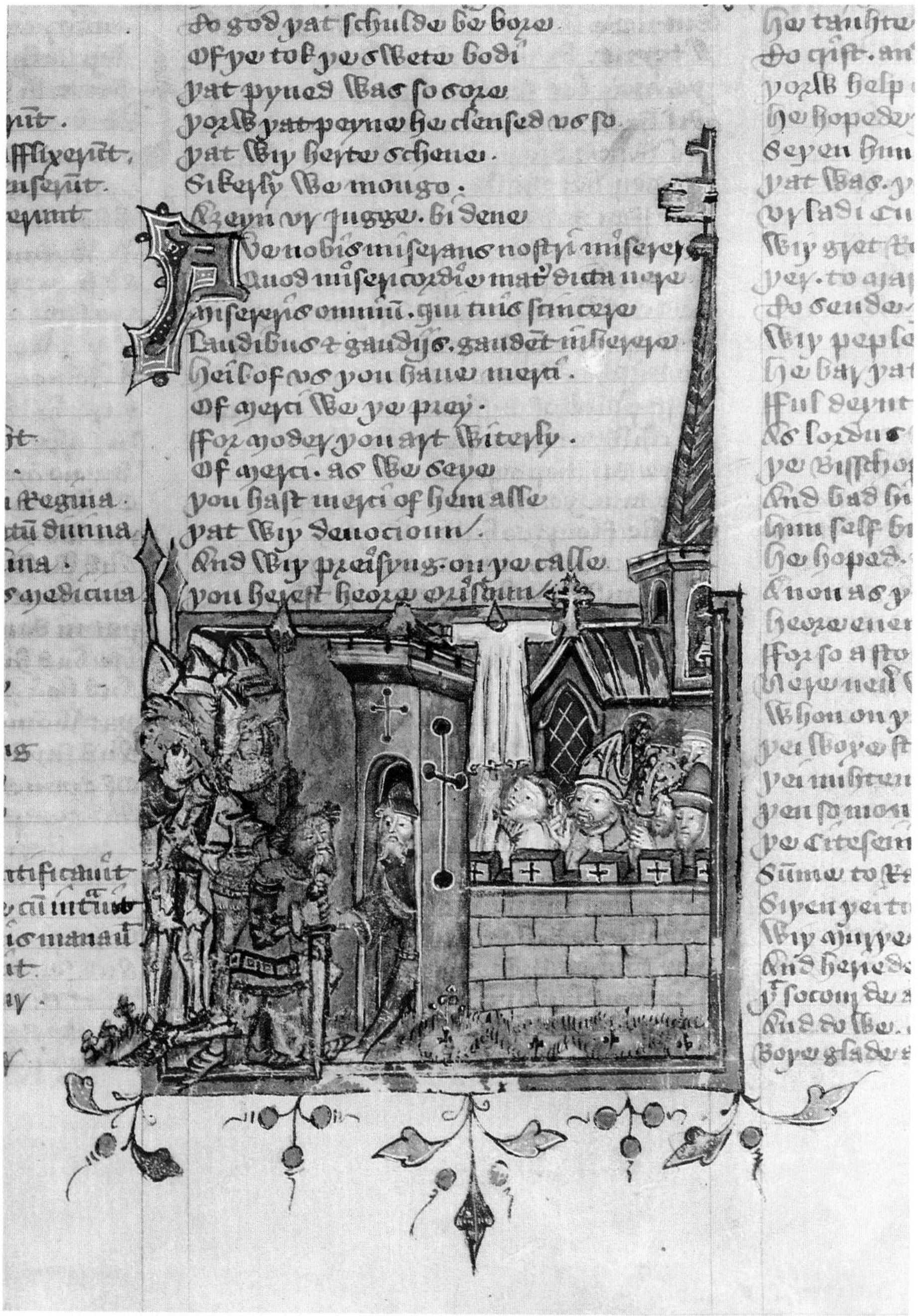

109. **A battle scene from the 'Vernon Manuscript'**

Even after the loss of seventy or eighty leaves this manuscript, which dates from the end of the fourteenth century, is the largest surviving anthology of Middle-English literature, weighing almost fifty pounds. The 350 remaining leaves (representing 175 calf-skins) contain over 400 items of a mainly religious character, mostly in Middle-English poetry and prose but with a little Latin and Anglo-Norman; a library, in fact, comprising a considerable proportion of all known literature in Middle-English up to the time of Chaucer.

Analysis of the dialects represented in the various works reveals the Vernon's chronological and geographical range: compositions and exemplars from many parts of the country were used by the manuscript's two scribes, though the originals were regularized, modernized and even radically altered. There is a distinctive version of the thirteenth-century *Ancrene Riwle*, instructions for anchoresses, one of the most important survivals of earlier Middle-English prose; copies of famous and wide-spread fourteenth-century texts such as Langland's *Piers Plowman*, an interestingly late survival of the 'A-text', and the *Pricke of Conscience* ascribed to Richard Rolle; recent texts by contemporary authors such as Walter Hilton's *Scale of Perfection*; and a profusion of shorter lyrics, some only known from this manuscript. Other important unique texts are the *Vernon Miracles*, part of a cycle of miracles of the Blessed Virgin Mary in Middle-English short couplets (it is sad to record that the table of contents lists forty-two miracles, but only eight-and-a-half now survive; the first, shown here, being 'The relief of Crotey [i.e. Chartres] besieged by Rollo'); *Lives* of nine saints in translations into Middle-English verse from the *Legenda aurea* (including Ambrose, Augustine, and perhaps significantly the Cistercians' St Bernard); an Arthurian Grail romance, *Joseph of Arimathia*, and a prose narrative of the Legend of Adam and Eve.

This 'vast massy manuscript', as Bernard described it, is so dauntingly huge that its main use continues to be as a quarry for the editors of individual texts (a quarry available around the world since the publication in 1986 of an excellent facsimile introduced by A.I. Doyle). Nevertheless, the study of anthologies themselves is coming to be recognized as throwing useful light on the interests of mediaeval readers, on their attitudes to individual texts as revealed by the union of originally independent material, and on the changes which compilers may have introduced to mesh the different pieces together.

The Vernon's compilers express their intention as being 'in latyn tonge Salus anime, and in englyhs [*sic*] tonge Sowlehele' [i.e. salvation], both for the public audiences to whom the earlier saints' lives and homilies were originally to be recited, or for the individual readers of the later prose compositions and personal lyrics.

A compilation on this scale must have required massive planning, not only in the supply of the necessary parchment, but in the accumulation of texts to copy: a figure of at least two dozen manuscripts has been suggested. A further factor to be considered is that the scriptorium which produced this anthology was producing another, almost but not quite duplicate, at the same time – the Simeon manuscript in the British Library, well over half of which is now lost.

The illumination, in a variety of hands which itself demonstrates the long-term nature of the Vernon's writing-campaign, consists of frequent decorated initials and border-extensions – lavish, if the book's size is considered – and a few miniatures, especially in the Marian *Miracles*. An allusion to the treatment of a Carmelite friar in 1384 provides a *terminus* at least for the completion of the book, but a date further towards the end of the century seems more likely. A localization in Staffordshire and even more precisely at Lichfield does not seem to stand up firmly to modern scrutiny, but it is true that by the late sixteenth century the manuscript belonged to the Vernon family of Houndhill, Staffordshire. It was presented to the Bodleian, perhaps around 1677, by Colonel Edward Vernon of Trinity College, Oxford, whose inscription of gift proclaims, proudly, if irrelevantly, that he had been a dashing Cavalier officer.

created Doctor of Civil Law in August 1677 it is most likely that the degree was the University's way of honouring the donor, and this would give an approximate date for his gift. The volume concerned (Plate 109) could not easily be overlooked, since each of its 350 thick vellum leaves stands almost two foot high and is proportionately wide. Its sheer bulk makes it one of the heaviest single manuscripts in the Bodleian, and the more than 400 different items which it contains make it the largest single assemblage of Middle-English texts to have survived.

The other manuscript, written in Ireland some five centuries earlier, is a masterpiece of Celtic illumination by a scribe named Mac Regol, and is now called after its donor the 'Rushworth Gospels' (Plate 110). The first leaf, which would have contained a full-page painting of St Matthew writing his gospel, has been lost, which would be doubly unfortunate if, besides the missing 'portrait', it had also borne, as it might well have, some mediaeval inscription or pressmark which would indicate where the manuscript remained after it came over from Ireland and was given a complete interlinear gloss in Old English some time in the tenth century. As it is, there is from then on a total gap in its history until it appears in the possession of the historian John Rushworth about the year 1655, when notes of its glosses were taken by the great Anglo-Saxon scholar Junius (Plate 106). When and where Rushworth became its owner is not known. He had received his M.A. while secretary to Lord Fairfax at Oxford in 1649, and is remembered today for the eight volumes of his *Historical Collections*, describing the affairs of state from 1618 to 1648. He himself long took an active part in politics; he represented Berwick-upon-Tweed in five Parliaments, the last of these being that held at Oxford in March 1681. That was the occasion for one of the most dramatic incidents in the reign of Charles II, when the spotlight of history may be said to have focused for a moment on the peaceful complex of ancient buildings which is now termed the Old Library. The King, secure in the knowledge that by secret agreement with his cousin, Louis XIV of France, he was not dependent on Parliament to finance him, summoned it to meet at Oxford, thereby avoiding the pressures of the London mobs. As they had done in the Oxford sitting during the plague year of 1665, the Lords occupied the Geometry School (north of the Schools Tower on the first floor, and now a reading-room) and the Commons sat in the uncomfortable confinement of the Convocation House, below Selden End. On Monday 28 March the King was carried in a sedan chair from Christ Church, where he had been lodging, to the Lords, with his robes and crown concealed in another sedan chair which followed him. He summoned the Commons to join him there, and those of them who managed to stream across the Quadrangle and struggle up the corner stair of the Tower (Plate 49) will have witnessed the monarch step

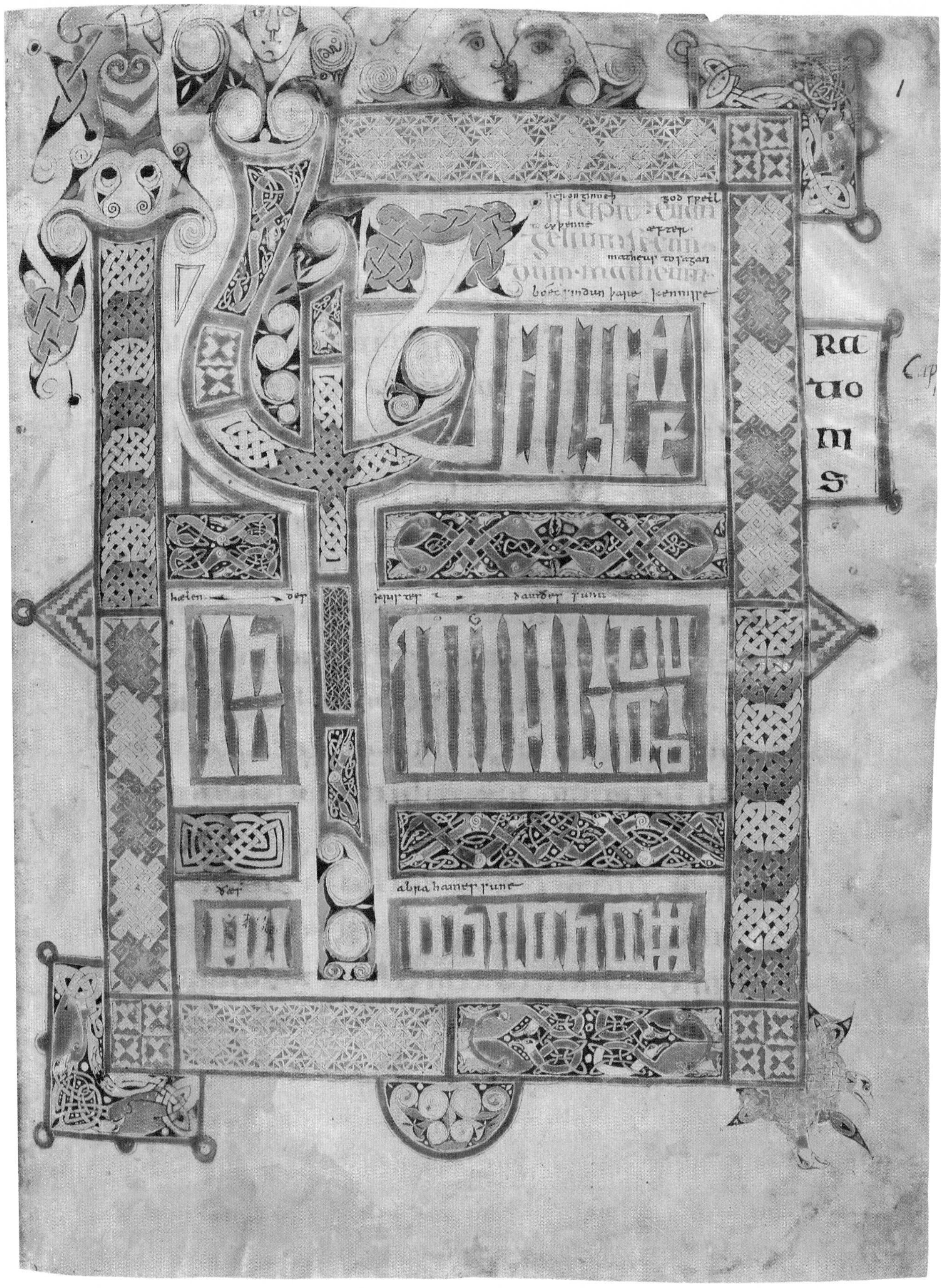

forth in his State robes and tell Parliament, to its general surprise and the utter dismay of the Whig opposition, that it was then and there dissolved. It has been suggested that it was during this Parliament at Oxford that Rushworth gave to the Bodleian his magnificent gift.

The striking of the Bodley Medal (Plate 87) in 1646 and the publication a year later of the autobiography of the Founder, were cited in Chapter IV as proof that in Oxford at least there were men who would not let his memory perish. Another such man was Dr John Morris, Regius Professor of Hebrew, who died in 1648. Under the terms of his will the sum of £5 was to be paid annually to the University for an M.A. of Christ Church, chosen by the Dean, to deliver a Latin speech in honour of Sir Thomas 'as a panegyrick and encouragement of the Hebrew studies', which had always been the field of the Founder's own particular pride and care. This Bodleian Oration, as it was later called, was to be given in the 'Schola Linguarum' (on the north side of the Schools Quadrangle) on 8 November, the day of the annual Visitation of the Library, in the presence of the Visitors – the Library's governing body, subsequently named Curators. Only after the death of Dr Morris's wife was the bequest to come into effect, and as she lived till the end of 1681 it was finally by a decree of Congregation in 1682 that the series of speeches was begun, which lasted till 1985, when Christ Church declined to appoint further orators.

The talented and ambitious young man whose name, Elias Ashmole, was soon afterwards to be linked to that of the University, as it has been ever since, came to Oxford during the Civil War. His appointment as Excise Collector for the Crown in Lichfield, his native city, was

110. **The 'Rushworth (or Mac Regol) Gospels'**
Though they lack the magical finesse of the Book of Kells, these richly decorated pages are of the same genre; the luxury Gospel book, decorated for ceremonial display with a richness unparalleled outside the Irish sphere of influence. During the sixth century, a mysterious period of gestation when Ireland was more or less cut off from the Continent, the Irish had developed a unique system of scripts and a wayward intellectual energy which was sufficient to spread Irish culture in the following centuries via Iona to England, to Northern Italy and to France and Germany.

The international character of Insular book arts often makes it difficult to localize particular manuscripts (the Book of Kells, the supreme symbol of Irish art, is claimed by some scholars to have been actually produced in Scotland or Northumbria), but the Rushworth manuscript ends with a Latin colophon which places it firmly on Irish home-ground: 'Macregol painted this Gospel book. Let the reader pray for Macreguil the scribe'. The Irish chronicles record the death in 822 of a bishop called Mac Riagoil ua Magleni, Abbot of Birr in Co. Offaly. The chronicles stress the Abbot's scribal prowess, and his name is sufficiently unusual to make his identifcation as the scribe of the Rushworth Gospels a near certainty. This places the manuscript as one of the latest in the series of luxury Gospel books, before the Norse invasions wrought havoc upon Celtic cultural centres in the ninth century. The colophon is also important in proving, despite the differences of spelling, that the scribe and the illuminator were one and the same person.

Although the interlace-work of Mac Regol's abstract decoration is overwhelmingly Celtic, his portraits of Mark, Luke and John at the beginning of their respective Gospels and his clear formal small text script show a backwash of influence from the Romanizing innovations of his Northumbrian brethren. A peculiarity of Mac Regol's palette is the absence of blue and purple; the thick texture of his green, pinkish-brown, orange and yellow colours gives an almost enamelled finish to his work. Here, the opening words of St Matthew's Gospel, 'Liber generationis ihu cri fili dauid fili abraham', are almost hidden in the pattern of Mac Regol's elaborate ornamentation.

By the second half of the tenth century, Mac Regol's Gospels had crossed the Irish Sea. The Latin words were translated into Old English in a gloss written over each line of text by Owun and Farmon, the latter a priest of 'Harewood' – the place has not been identified with certainty, perhaps it was the hamlet in Herefordshire near Ross-on-Wye. The gloss is closely related to the one which was added to the Lindisfarne Gospels by Aldred at Chester-le-Street near Durham, a few years before 970. Although the Anglo-Saxon glosses added in these two great Gospel manuscripts are awkward word-by-word renderings rather than literary translations, they are nevertheless continuous. The Books of Lindisfarne and Mac Regol are therefore the earliest surviving manuscripts to contain any form of English translation of the four Gospels.

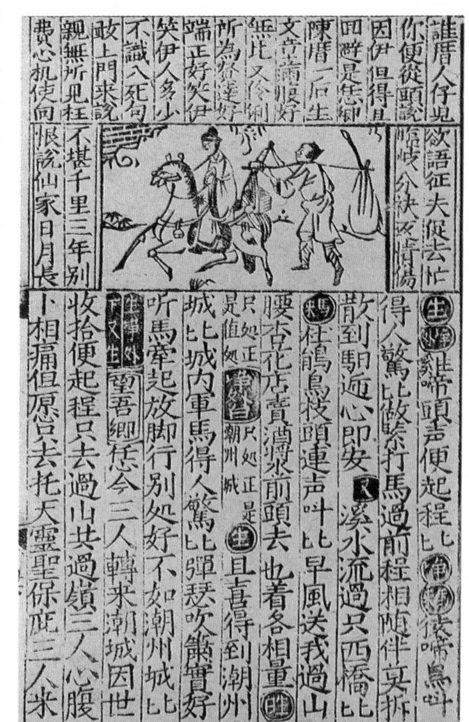

the beginning of a lifelong devotion to the institution and history of the monarchy. In Oxford he enrolled himself at Brasenose College and pursued those studies which led to his first book, published anonymously in 1650, an English translation of two alchemical works. He presented a copy to the Bodleian, and his personal copy bears an autograph Latin inscription punning on his surname 'Ash-mole' and claiming for his own versatility the title of 'Child of a hundred Arts'. His most important alchemical work followed two years later, a valuable annotated collection of verse texts by early English alchemists. It includes engraved facsimiles, the first ever published in England, of mediaeval illuminated pages. The development of his researches received great impetus when in 1649 after a long courtship he married as his second wife a wealthy widow, and was able to devote himself thenceforward entirely to the studies and friendships he most enjoyed and to start collecting, amongst other objects, the notable library of manuscripts and printed books which came, after his death in 1692, to rest in his Oxford Museum.

Just before the gift to him of the Tradescant collection, which was to lead him to the foundation of this museum, Ashmole, who among his many other interests was already esteemed by his contemporaries for his knowledge of numismatics, was asked by the then Librarian, Barlow, to make a catalogue of the Roman coins in the Bodleian, most of which were among the gifts of Archbishop Laud (Plate 68). He began the task in 1658 but eventually it took him eight years to finish. Its completion was held up by new commitments arising after the Restoration, when this ardent royalist swiftly became both Windsor Herald in the College of Arms and also Comptroller of the Excise, the latter a post which added significantly to his wealth. He was also asked in 1660 to catalogue the King's collection of coins and medals. The resulting catalogue of the royal collection is preserved among Ashmole's manuscripts in the Bodleian and includes a unique series of impressions taken by Ashmole in sealing-wax of coins and gems as they lay in the cabinet of King Charles II. Finally he was able to complete his Oxford catalogue in 1666, and a fair copy in three volumes written out by the author himself was presented by him to the Library in 1668. Later he told John Aubrey that this catalogue was 'what he most valued' among his accomplishments. The Library acknowledged the gift towards the end of that year, and during the next summer the University conferred on Ashmole the degree of Doctor of Medicine, its most suitable honour for a man whose interests ranged over so many fields including astrology, alchemy, botany and sympathetic magic.

The degree may also have been connected in some way with a rumour which had reached John Evelyn in 1670 that the University was contemplating the building of 'an elaboratory' and 'had beg'd the

111. A Chinese popular drama printed in 1566

Chinese books were among the Library's earliest acquisitions, and by the end of the seventeenth century the collections already contained over one hundred volumes, representing fifty separate works. They had been obtained by early travellers on voyages along the South China coast, and were produced in the province of Fukien, which was the main centre of commercial printing during the sixteenth century. When they arrived in Europe, they were broken up and distributed as curiosities, so that the fascicles of these works which are now treasured by several European libraries are often found to be parts of the same copy. The works are mostly popular literature, almanacs, textbooks, pharmacopoeia and reference books of a kind which were too cheap for inclusion in the libraries of the Chinese literati, and which are therefore rarer in China itself than in Japan and Europe.

The *Li ching chi* is a popular drama reprinted by the Yu family at Chien-yang in 1566, and is one of only two surviving copies, the other being at Tenri University Library in Japan. It is moreover the earliest extant text in a southern Chinese dialect. Each page is divided into three sections. The lowest is the text of the play, in which the various roles are indicated by the white characters in black frames. The middle section contains a picture illustrating an episode in the drama, with a descriptive couplet on each side. The top section, as is quite common in editions of this kind, contains the text of an entirely different work.

Reliques of old Tradescant, to furnish a Repositary'. The Tradescant collection of curiosities of all kinds had been built up by John Tradescant the Elder and had become one of the sights of London. It was added to by his son, a traveller, botanist and royal gardener like his father, and it was most probably the existence of a full-dress catalogue of it, written jointly in 1652 by Ashmole and his great friend the physician Dr Thomas Wharton, which prompted the younger Tradescant, who had no surviving male heir, to make over the collection to Ashmole by deed of gift in 1659. The catalogue, which was printed in 1656 at Ashmole's expense, is the earliest description published in England of the kind of 'cabinet of rarities' which collectors in several countries had begun to form in the sixteenth and early seventeenth centuries. It describes, with some attempt at classification, the very miscellaneous contents of the 'Ark', as it was called while in the Tradescant house at Lambeth. It did not, however, describe any of the books belonging to the Tradescant collection, not even the magnificent manuscript known as the 'Ashmole Bestiary' (Plate 113) which a traveller saw on display in the 'Ark' in 1638.

The Tradescant rarities formed the core of the collection which Ashmole presented to the University as soon as the delightful building erected to house them, on a site very close to both the ancient Library buildings and to the gleaming new Sheldonian Theatre, was ready. This was in 1683, and James, Duke of York, with his Duchess then opened it officially and watched some experiments performed in the Elaboratory on the lowest floor by Robert Plot, first Keeper of what is now the earliest still-continuing institutional museum to open its doors to the public.

Ashmole survived this moment of glory by another nine years, and at his death bequeathed to the University his own collection of manuscripts and printed books, which were kept in his Museum until transferred to the Bodleian in 1860. A bitter parallel can be observed between the fire in the Inner Temple which almost certainly burnt a significant portion of Selden's mediaeval manuscripts housed in his chambers there, so that they never reached the Bodleian, and a later fire, this time in the Middle Temple in 1679, which largely destroyed the immense collection of over nine thousand brass, silver and copper coins which Ashmole had spent thirty years in forming, and with it his medals and the rest of those other collections of his own making which led Anthony Wood to describe him as 'the greatest virtuoso and curioso' England had ever known. Among those lost parts of his collections, all of which he had intended should eventually be housed in the new Museum which he stipulated the University should build for them, were many printed books, together with volumes of notes, a series of seals (which reflects his preoccupation with heraldry) and his prints. On the testimony of Wood and other contemporaries who were shown it before the conflagration which destroyed it, his print collection included a very large number of engraved portraits of famous persons, with topographical prints and also engravings of great ceremonial occasions, a field in which Ashmole as Windsor Herald for fifteen years, and as historian of the Order of the Garter, had a professional interest. It would appear that this assemblage, had it survived, would have had no rival in England except that of Samuel Pepys, still happily preserved at Cambridge.

The library brought together by Ashmole himself forms a single sequence of numbered volumes obviously bought for their contents and not for show, being bound, for the most part, in unornamented brown calf bearing only Ashmole's arms in gilt. Unlike most of his contemporaries he did not build up any considerable number of religious books, though he did own certain mediaeval ones which have fine illuminations, for example the Bromholm Psalter, and so he has a claim to be one of the earliest collectors in England who would buy a manuscript for its miniatures rather than for the text. Yet he certainly believed in a profoundly ordered universe, and one which combined the hierarchic with the mysterious. Although an early member of the Royal Society, for him order in Creation was manifested alike in the celestial and terrestrial spheres, the former studied in astrology and the latter investigated by alchemy. He could be at once elaborately detailed in his documentation when researching numismatics or heraldry and yet alert to read everywhere hidden meanings, which were to be learnt by means of symbolism, magic or divination, the pathways to arcane knowledge. The two subjects astrology and alchemy were at the outset, and always remained, at the centre of the lives of himself and his closest circle of friends. Increasing wealth enabled him to acquire, often *en bloc*, the books and papers, indeed sometimes the entire libraries, of men who had been his predecessors in those studies, such as John Dee, Simon Forman and William Lilly. In all fields his manuscripts generally include important texts written as far back as the early Middle Ages, and almost all are of English provenance. Later on, under the influence of Dugdale, his interest in history intensified and he accumulated its raw materials both national, local and even colonial (Plate 114), so that his library was further enriched with chronicles, cartularies and original documents, including rolls, bearing especially on heraldry and genealogy, besides a quantity of Middle-English texts mostly poetical. As they lie on the shelves in their present apparently random order, the printed books (almost nine hundred in number) mingled among some one hundred and twenty manuscripts, they reflect most vividly the diversity as well as the range of his interests, and the multiplicity of sources from which they were assembled.

Besides this important accession of the library of Ashmole himself,

112. **Bishop Barlow's copy of the first book printed in Oxford, '1468'**
Two years after Caxton had set up his press in the precincts of Westminster Abbey, the new art of printing was brought to Oxford by Theodoric Rood, a German from Cologne. All we know about this first Oxford press derives from the books it produced, for there is no mention of it in surviving contemporary records – an extraordinary silence in the presence of an invention which was to affect profoundly all aspects of society, rather as if there were no records three-and-a-half centuries later of the introduction to Oxford of another technology which was to have equally revolutionary effects: the first motor car built by W.R. Morris at his Longwall garage in 1912. Seventeen books have been attributed to the press, six of them known only from fragments; only two books mention Theodoric Rood, only five give the place of printing, and only eight are dated. The first product of the press, *Expositio sancti Hieronymi in symbolum apostolorum* (really by Rufinus of Aquileia), is misdated by ten years, a roman ten having been omitted from the colophon date M.cccc.lxviii. Three references in local records probably denote the printer: as a goldsmith called 'Dydycke', and as a tenant 'Dyryke Dowcheman' and 'Dedyck Teutonicus' – the English clearly had difficulties with his name.

Recent scholarship suggests that he was invited to set up his press in Oxford by James Goldwell, Bishop of Norwich, in order, initially, to print the Rufinus text from a manuscript in the Bishop's possession. The use of an edition printed in Rome in 1468 to correct the manuscript may explain the error in the Oxford colophon. The first use of the imprint 'in alma universitate Oxon.' in 1481, in his fourth book (his first three had given Oxford alone as their place of printing), and his partnership with the University stationer Thomas Hunt in 1485, may mean that the

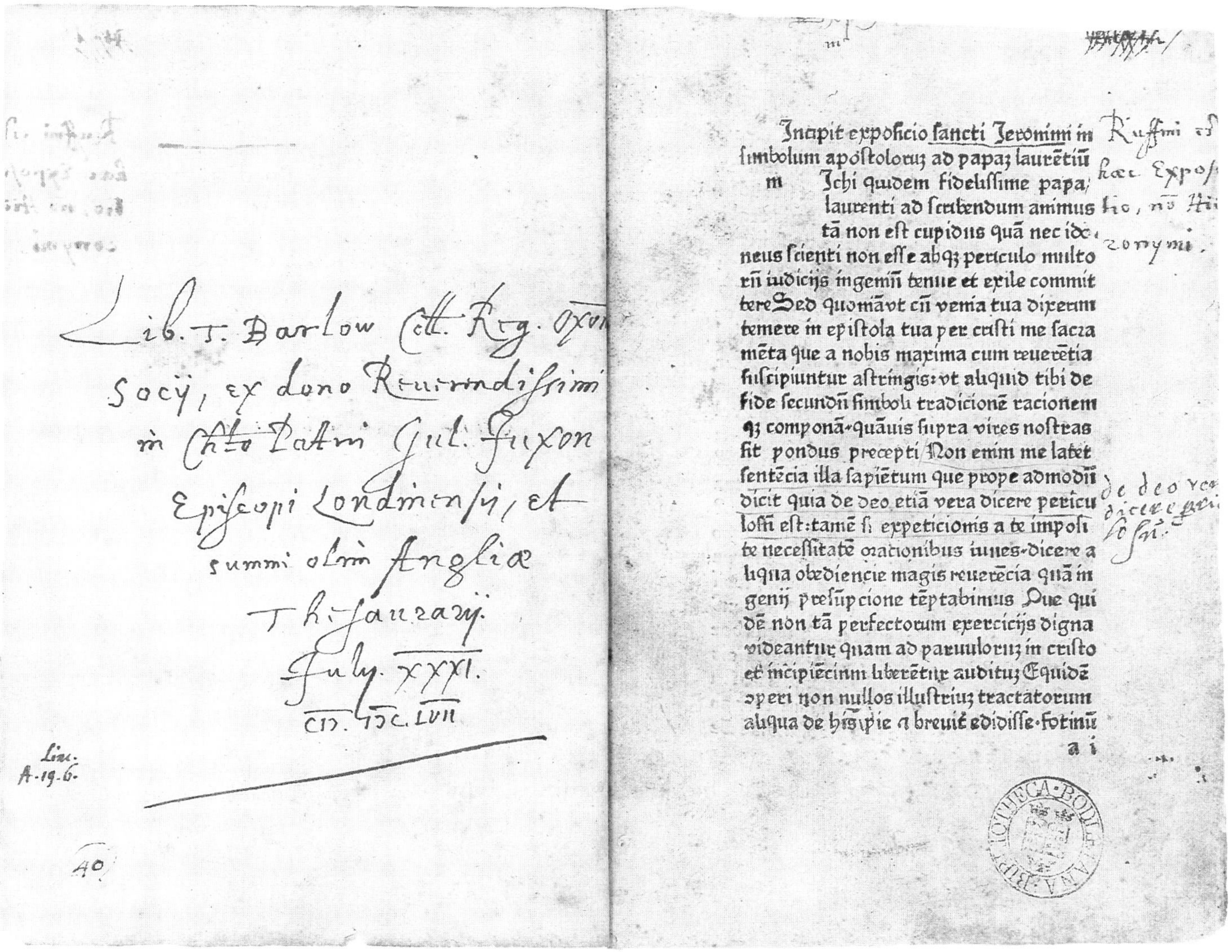

University took some sort of responsibility for Rood's press after Goldwell had ceased to be its sponsor. The press was certainly catering for the latest methods of teaching Latin with John Anwykyll's two grammars, written primarily for Magdalen College School, and an edition of Cicero's *Pro Milone* which was the first classical text printed in England. In 1487, Thomas Hunt issued the last book from the press, and for thirty years there was no more printing at Oxford.

Barlow's copy of the 'St Jerome', characteristically full of his learned marginalia, was given to him on 31 July 1657 by his friend William Juxon, who earlier that year had presented four oriental manuscripts to the Bodleian. As Bishop of London and Lord High Treasurer, Juxon had been an intimate counsellor to Charles I, and it was he who stood alone with the King on the scaffold on 30 January 1649, and to him was spoken the King's last word, 'Remember'. At the Restoration he was appointed Archbishop of Canterbury, and as such officiated at the new King's coronation.

113. The 'Ashmole Bestiary'
The mediaeval Latin bestiary developed during the twelfth century from the Latin version (fifth century) of the Greek *Physiologus*, a compilation in which fantastic descriptions of real and fabulous animals and birds were used to illustrate Christian allegories and teach moral lessons. In one form or another the pictures were known in Anglo-Saxon England; the illustrated bestiary was a characteristically English class of book, especially popular in the thirteenth century.

The Ashmole manuscript, from the early part of that century, is one of the most luxurious of all mediaeval bestiaries. Its chief glory is the quality of its raised and burnished gold. This is used as the background to set off the animal pictures. The effect is achieved by first painting onto the parchment a thick layer of a gesso-like composition, then applying gold-leaf, and finally burnishing with a stone or tooth. The technical achievement of producing large surfaces of glittering gold is itself considerable, and the craftsman goes on to impress patterns and even letters into the gold with a hard-point – not an uncommon technique in luxury manuscripts of this period, but carried out here with superb skill.

Stylistically the manuscript belongs to the transitional period (c. 1180–1220) between Romanesque and Early Gothic; the artist loves to arrange his animal shapes into the formal patterns of Romanesque, but his elongated figures are lively and expressive. In the picture shown a dog, which changes colour in the final scene, apprehends the murderer of his master. It seems likely that such a lavish and relatively secular book would have been a private commission for some high-ranking individual; but there is no evidence whatsoever to identify its mediaeval owner. The transition from the purely ecclesiastical ownership of books is mirrored in the changeover in the circumstances of production, from monastic scriptoria to lay workshops. The 'Ashmole Bestiary' was probably (but not certainly) produced by laymen; it belongs to a group of three which has been most recently attributed to a workshop in the North Midlands, perhaps Lincoln.

The manuscript was highly prized by its succession of sixteenth and seventeenth-century owners. It was seen in 1638 by the German visitor G.C. Stirn on display in the 'Ark', the museum of the elder John Tradescant at Lambeth, and passed with the rest of his and his son's 'rarities' into the hands of Elias Ashmole, who bequeathed both his own and the Tradescants' collections to his newly-founded museum in Oxford in 1692.

which is in fact the largest portion of his personal collections to have survived relatively intact (having been kept in his Lambeth house and not in the Middle Temple), the Curators of the Bodleian were offered in 1858 not only the books and coins which formed part of Ashmole's gift to his Museum but also the antiquities. The latter they declined, but with Ashmole's own library there also came those of other men which, ever since its opening, the new Museum had begun to attract and to house. According to the Bodleian practice, initiated for Selden's library, the five principal collections actually transferred to it in 1860 preserve their separate identities and are shelved and referenced under each donor's name. As so often then and since, collections such as these became focal points of interest in the writers concerned, and by subsequent Bodleian vigilance and the generosity of benefactors the Library has not infrequently managed to augment the original gifts with noteworthy additions, either by donation or purchase.

Earliest among the cluster of smaller collections which accompanied Ashmole's library when it arrived in the Bodleian was a part of the library of Dr Martin Lister, later physician to Queen Anne. His gift had been made in 1683 when he moved from York to London; it was followed by further printed books, manuscripts and papers, chiefly medical and scientific, bequeathed at his death in 1712. A second benefaction came to the Ashmolean by bequest of the 'grand old man' of English historical studies, Sir William Dugdale, who died in 1686. Dugdale, whose daughter Elizabeth married Ashmole after the death of his second wife, had first met his future son-in-law about the year 1655 and the younger man was much influenced in his own historical and heraldic studies by Dugdale's combination of a massive use of original records with a remarkable assiduity in getting great works of learning into print. As early in their friendship as 1656 an engraving was made of a prehistoric implement in Ashmole's possession, for inclusion in Dugdale's *Antiquities of Warwickshire*. The original axehead perished in the 1679 fire, so the engraving is not only a unique record of the breadth of antiquarian interests shared by the two men but also the earliest such representation of a flint implement in any English historical publication. The manuscripts bequeathed by Dugdale to the Museum consist almost entirely of transcripts from original sources (some of which have since been lost) and were for the most part written out by Sir William himself. A very different character was John Aubrey, a great friend who shared Ashmole's astrological and antiquarian interests. He is now chiefly remembered for his 'Brief Lives', a gossipy and haphazard but eminently quotable collection of materials, put together to help another member of the fraternity, Anthony Wood, with his *Athenae Oxonienses*. Aubrey had sent, by the hand of Wood, a valuable manuscript of Matthew of Westminster to the Bodleian in 1675 and to the Ashmolean he gave several manuscripts before his death in 1697.

Last among the collections of books and manuscripts placed in the Museum in the early years of its existence was that of Anthony Wood, historian and bibliographer. Born in 1632 of an Oxford city family, Wood took his M.A. from Merton College in 1655 but failed to get a fellowship there and never subsequently held any University appointment. He lived instead on a modest private income in the same house where he had been born, opposite the College gate in Merton Street, and there he died in 1695. The appearance in 1656 of Dugdale's seminal book *The Antiquities of Warwickshire*, followed by Wood's own discovery of Leland's manuscripts in the Bodleian, fired in him that 'insatiable desire of knowledge' which possessed him thenceforward and led him to devote himself to compiling the history of the University and City of Oxford. In later life, increasing deafness robbed him of the musical enjoyments which were his other consuming passion (Plate 120); typically, he left materials for a biographical dictionary of English musicians.

In 1690 the Library had bought from Wood for £30 twenty-five mediaeval manuscripts which now form a sub-group within the Wood collection. One quarter of these had belonged to his close friend and fellow-antiquarian Ralph Sheldon, a recusant squire who died in 1684. Wood had often visited him in his Warwickshire home, had catalogued his library and wrote a brief life of him. The rest of Wood's library, however, which came by bequest to the University in 1695, was for the most part of an entirely different character. The one hundred and twenty-six volumes which, in addition to original charters, form the manuscript part of Wood's collection, were described by Edward Lhuyd, then Keeper of the Ashmolean Museum, for Bernard's 1697 Catalogue. They comprise much, though not all, of the materials used by him in writing his three great works, *Historia et Antiquitates Universitatis Oxoniensis* of 1674, and *Athenae Oxonienses* and *Fasti*, both published in 1691. Besides an autograph copy of the real English text of the History, which the University Press, to Wood's exceeding annoyance, would not print until it had been translated (by another, and indifferent, hand) into Latin, to ensure it a wider overseas circulation, there are copies of his three printed works with his own annotations and corrections. Much of general interest for family, county and local monastic history is to be found in various manuscript volumes put together by Wood and certain of his antiquarian friends, notably Sheldon, which are preserved in his collection. But the history of the University and the Colleges had to be written, then as now, principally from their happy wealth of original archives, and it is the great mass of extracts, transcripts, lists and indexes made mainly by Wood himself from those originals which illustrates so fully the sources and methods of this untiring researcher who produced, on his own initiative, a body of historical writing about Oxford which will never wholly be superseded or replaced.

Irreplaceable, in a different sense of the word, were the losses which occurred before Wood's printed books were transferred to the Bodleian. Unique items, which included broadside ballads, were either lost or stolen, and some of these copies have been identified in the libraries of later book-collectors which have since found a permanent home elsewhere. Even so, Wood's nine hundred and seventy volumes of printed books form in themselves a collection that is unparalleled not only in the Bodleian but (in many of its elements) also in any other library. Neither his tastes nor his means made him a book-collector in the conventional sense; his contemporary Pepys, a much wealthier man who shared some of Wood's more unusual interests, in ballads and chapbooks for example, left behind him a very different kind of library. An extant manuscript catalogue of Wood's books, begun in 1681, is really a description of the contents of the study which he had had fitted out for him in the attic of his Merton Street house, as arranged by him for convenience of his own reference system. Thus organized, it formed the workshop of a scholar, and enabled him to carry through his enormous undertakings. His *Athenae Oxonienses* in particular, in which he described the lives of all Oxford writers from the University's shadowy beginnings up to his own lifetime, and listed their writings, was a feat of research which long antedates any other attempt to perform the same task for a similarly huge group of men. For this he used not only personal enquiries and information gathered from friends and correspondents, but also his own chosen printed sources, comparatively few of which were texts in book form. What could be consulted in the Oxford libraries around him Wood generally did not duplicate on his own shelves, unless for purposes of adding, as he did in his own copy of Andrew Maunsell's 1595 *Catalogue of English Printed Books*, manuscript annotations, indexes and cross-references to other parts of his collections. Instead, he gathered what libraries did not provide for him. His private sets of newspapers include many Civil War *Mercuries* and a run, complete from its start up to his own death, of what is probably the oldest continuous periodical in the world; begun as the *Oxford Gazette* while Court and Parliament were in Oxford in 1665 to escape the great London Plague, it is still being published today as the *London Gazette*. Materials hardly collected by others for use, if collected at all until very recently, include his eighty catalogues of English book auction sales, of which the earliest was not held till the year 1676. From these he dredged with painful toil many authors' names, titles and imprints of books which he had never seen. Equally typical of what he owned and studied are *Term Catalogues* and other publishers' and booksellers' catalogues and even prospectuses. His play-lists are still important for the study of English drama.

Spanning the years continuously from 1641 to 1695 is his large collection of almanacs, often several different ones for each year. What gives them lasting importance is that among them are thirty-nine volumes interleaved, which have his diaries written in them. These are the famous diaries, magnificently edited by Andrew Clark, which hold up a mirror to his life and times, even if a highly individual and sometimes a distorting one. Less intimate and personal but much wider in scope is his pamphlet collection. The scale of this cannot be appreciated without realizing that within his nine hundred and seventy volumes as now bound a very high proportion are collectaneous; in them are gathered many times that number of individual items on a variety of topics ranging from ship-money to witches and ghosts, arranged by subject and mainly in chronological order; for example, one group of nine consecutive volumes covering the Civil War contains almost five hundred different pamphlets, and another five volumes hold over five hundred broadsides.

Much of what gives the library which Wood left behind him its special and often unique flavour and importance is his concern with the printed word, even at its most trivial, as a source of historical reference. He collected, identified and annotated in his small, neat hand what other men (sometimes even the authors themselves) disowned or did not bother to keep. Printed matter of all kinds, especially of Oxford origin (Plate 119) was preserved, referenced and found its appropriate place in his collections; a handbill thrust at him by a huckster is duly located in time and place by the note 'Batholem. Faire 1688'. To such windfalls were added his more methodical assemblage of popular literature, so often fragile and vulnerable of its nature: chapbooks, ballads, carols, elegies, garlands, drolleries, satires and the like. Wood's garner of seventeenth-century ephemera takes up the genre which Robert Burton had initiated fifty years earlier and looks forward across the centuries to the future Bodleian glories of Douce, Johnson, Harding and Opie.

The name of Elias Ashmole, the founder of the Museum in which Wood's library was placed by the University, had appeared, along with those of Barlow and Dugdale among others, as a subscriber to the Anglo-Saxon/Latin/English dictionary published at Oxford in 1659 by William Somner, the book which laid the foundation-stone for the general revival of Anglo-Saxon scholarship, and began the gradual transfer of its centre of gravity from Cambridge to Oxford. A 'font' of Saxon letters, namely the type first used for printing this dictionary of Somner's, was supplied to the University in 1656 by Nicholas Nichols. His model was evidently the type cast at Amsterdam for Francis Junius (Plate 106), who edited the 'Caedmon Manuscript' (Plate 107) there in 1655. Appended to the Dictionary was the Old English grammar and glossary of Aelfric, Abbot of Eynsham, set up from a

114. **A Map of Virginia by Captain John Smith, 1612**

Captain John Smith was one of the men who sailed from England to establish the first permanent English settlement in North America. Landing was made in May 1607 on the river Powhatan, now called James River, and the town of Jamestown was built and named in honour of the British sovereign. During the next three years the area was systematically explored and surveyed, one of the aims of these explorations being to determine if there were a passage from here to the East India Sea. Much of the information gained was the result of expeditions by small parties of the English settlers; other knowledge was gained from the native Indians with whom Captain Smith bartered for food. He was himself captured in 1607 by the great Chief Powhatan, who is shown holding court on this occasion in the upper left-hand corner of the map. Manuscript drafts of the explorations, containing some of the most vivid and detailed descriptions of Virginia, were dispatched to England as they were made. Late in 1609 Captain Smith returned to England where he set to work on his map. The original manuscript has not survived, but it was no doubt used by William Hole when he engraved the copperplate for printing the map. This coloured copy of the map, which is in its first state, was included in the interesting manuscript narrative by William Strachey containing much about Sir Walter Raleigh and his successors, and ending with the settlement of the colony in 1607, entitled *The Firste Booke of the Firste Decade contayning the Historie of Travaile into Virginia-Britania.* (An uncoloured copy, published in 1612 in Smith's *A Map of Virginia. With a Description of the Country, the Commodities, People, Government and Religion*, belonged to Robert Burton, and came to the Bodleian with his bequest.) Being the first printed map of the area it is the first to name topographical features,

thus providing one of the best sources for Indian names and locations for pre-English Virginia. It became the basic prototype map for the Chesapeake Bay area until 1673, being copied by cartographers such as Blaeu, Mercator, Hondius, Montanus and Speed. The accuracy of the map is remarkable considering the lack of scientific instruments. The portrait in the upper right-hand corner is of the greatest of the Sasquesahanocks, and is almost certainly taken from an engraving by Theodore de Bry.

transcript (now in the Bodleian) made by Junius from an early manuscript shown him by the painter Rubens.

Junius himself, though born in Heidelberg and the son of a French Protestant refugee, had spent many years in England, where in 1621 he had entered the household of the great collector and patron Thomas Howard, Earl of Arundel, as his librarian. For thirty years, with the help of frequent visits to the Bodleian, Junius happily pursued what became his lifelong preoccupation with the study of the languages of Northern Europe, viewed from the somewhat novel standpoint of comparative philology. Amongst his other formidable linguistic accomplishments he made himself the leading Anglo-Saxon scholar of his generation, and his influence was paramount in founding and fostering the great Oxford School of Anglo-Saxon studies. By a deed of gift made three months before his death in 1678, Junius gave the

University his 'bookes, writings and printing utensils'. These last included Anglo-Saxon and Gothic types which he had caused to be struck in Holland for his own learned publications there. The possession of these special types helped still further to equip the resurgent University Press to play a foremost part in spreading throughout Europe the products of the new Oxford scholarship.

The gifts of Junius include the original manuscript of such unique early texts of the highest linguistic importance as the 'Caedmon Manuscript' in Old English (Plate 107) and the *Ormulum*, a Middle-English poem of homilies on the Gospels (bought at an auction in Holland), the Old High German group of glosses bound with the 'Murbach Hymnal' (Plate 108), and the tenth-century Latin Psalter, with interlinear translation in Old English, known as the 'Codex Vossianus', given to Junius by his nephew Isaac Vossius. There is also a large number of valuable transcripts in various Northern European languages made by Junius himself, some from manuscripts since lost or damaged. Among his printed books are many with his annotations and collations, and there is even a block-book *Biblia pauperum* and the rare early incunable edition of the laws of Frisia in the Frisian language (a second copy of which, once also owned by Junius, came to the Library with his friend Marshall's bequest).

Thomas Marshall had been yet another of those future Oxford worthies whom the Parliamentary Visitors displaced. A young B.A. of Lincoln College, he was expelled for absence. Having served in the Royalist army he had not waited for the Visitation but had already gone abroad and for six years he acted as chaplain to the Merchant Adventurers at Rotterdam. He accompanied them when they moved to Dort and it was there that he published his Latin 'Observations on two ancient Gothic and Anglo-Saxon versions of the Gospels'. The learning he displayed in that book led his old Oxford College to offer him, unsolicited, a fellowship in 1668. He took his D.D. a year later and in 1672 he became the College's Rector, which he remained until his death in 1685.

During his long stay in Holland he not only acquired a knowledge of Dutch and collected books and manuscripts in that language, but also must have had many opportunities to enjoy his friendship with Junius, who had been the inspiration of Marshall's own Anglo-Saxon studies. Junius was living in Holland during most of the years Marshall spent there, and returned to England after his friend had been elected Rector. Eventually Junius settled in Oxford to be near his former pupil and Marshall was one of the witnesses to Junius's deed of gift of his types to the University. Marshall's familiarity with Holland had already proved invaluable when Dr John Fell was negotiating to secure types and matrices from Amsterdam for the University Press, and he undertook several missions there on Fell's behalf.

115. An Arabic translation of the fables of Bidpai

Kalila wa-Dimna in its various versions was one of the most popular books in the literature of the Islamic world. It was originally a Sanskrit work composed about the year 300 and only later attributed to the sage Bidpai. The Arabic translation was done from the Pahlavi (Middle Persian) by Ibn al-Muqaffa', a Zoroastrian convert to Islam, who died c. 757. The book takes the form of animal fables in which the animals behave as human beings; Kalila and Dimna are two jackals in the first story. It was intended as a manual of rules of conduct for princes, and the moral of the story illustrated by this painting, 'The hare and the king of the elephants at the well', from a Mamluk manuscript dated 1354 and probably produced in Syria, is that a small clever person can overcome a stronger opponent by using his intelligence. The learned hare Fayruz is effecting his plan to rid the neighbourhood of a herd of elephants. The scribe, who gives his name in the colophon of the manuscript, is known only from this work; unfortunately, no mention is made of the illustrator. The manuscript contains seventy-seven paintings. Seven illustrated copies of these fables are known to have been produced in Egypt or Syria in the Mamluk period, and of these the Bodleian and Paris manuscripts are considered to be the best.

The translator wrote an original preface to the fables and made some additions of his own. His edition was a stylistic work of art which was influential in the formation of Arabic prose literature. The widespread popularity of the work may be gauged from the fact that the Arabic version became the basis for further translations into some forty other languages.

Like so many of Oxford's learned men at this period he displayed an astonishing breadth of scholarship. He was known as an orientalist and his library shows that he was conversant not only with Hebrew and Syriac but also Arabic, Coptic and Armenian. Yet it was also under his leadership and with the stimulating example of his mentor that Lincoln College came to be the original centre for the rising group of Oxford 'Saxonists' which was to produce as its principal ornament the former Lincoln tutor George Hickes, the greatest of all Anglo-Saxon scholars. Yet it was also the same learned Dr Marshall who published in 1679 a little booklet which, at Fell's suggestion, he had written to explain the Church Catechism. It sold for twopence and had a great success, being many times reprinted during the following century and a half, and was also translated into Welsh.

Under the terms of his will the Bodleian took from his library his manuscripts and its choice out of his printed books. The wide variety of his linguistic interests is shown by the presence in his books of languages which were certainly rare at that period in the libraries of Englishmen such as Frisian, Irish and Romanian. Manuscripts brought into the Library by his gift include a precious ninth-century Latin text of Philo's *Onomasticon* on Hebrew names; this copy can be traced through the libraries of three Benedictine abbeys: Soissons, Malmesbury and St Augustine's, Canterbury. His long sojourn in Holland had enabled Marshall to acquire a score of manuscripts written in that

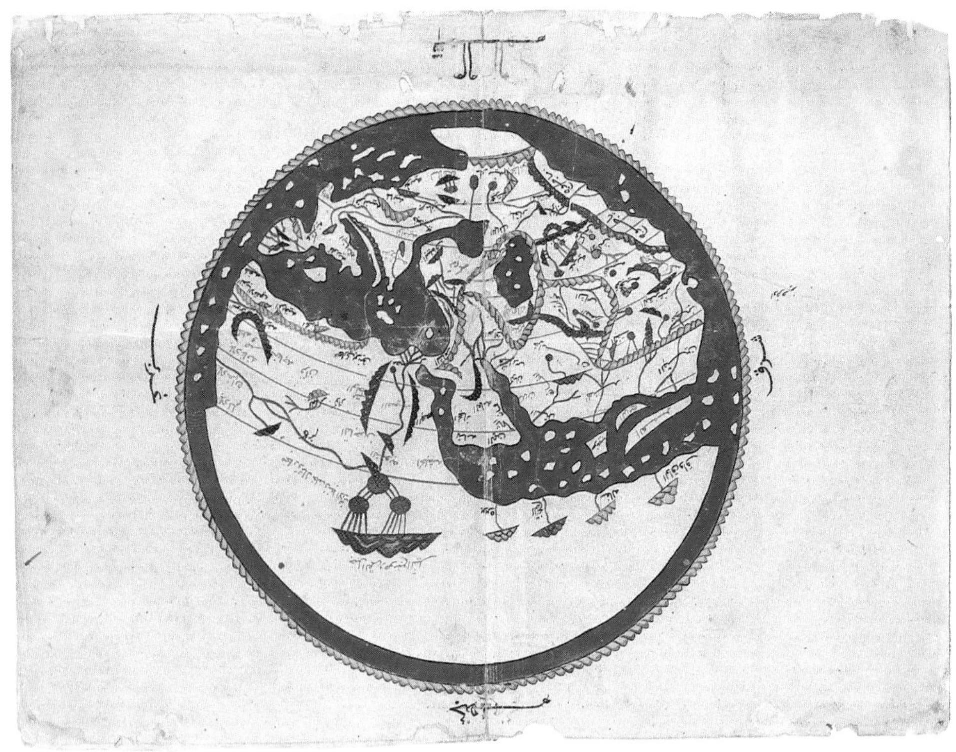

116. **An Arabic world map of the mid-twelfth century**
This map of the whole globe is taken from the geographer Idrisi's description of the known world. As in most Arabic maps, south was at the top, but the reproduction of it here has been inverted to make its three land masses, Europe, Asia, and North Africa (featuring the sources of the Nile) more recognizable to modern eyes.

The Norman King Roger II of Sicily encouraged learning and science of all kinds. At Palermo he collected tales of distant lands from travellers who came to his court from all parts of the world. This led him to the idea of incorporating this material into a description of the world, with a map. For this task the King commissioned Idrisi, a learned Arab prince, born in Morocco, who after travelling extensively had settled at his court, to compile a book containing all the available information on the topography of the known world. Agents were dispatched to various countries to collect data, and the text and map were completed at Palermo in 1154 after fifteen years' work. The map was engraved on a silver table and was the largest and most detailed twelfth-century map of the countries

country in the Middle Ages, most of them in Dutch, a language not hitherto much represented among the Bodleian's collections, though the earliest known written evidence for it is there (Plate 24).

In 1691 died at the age of eighty-four Thomas Barlow, Bishop of Lincoln, the only one of Bodley's Librarians (so far) to leave his library chair and eventually find a seat on the bench of bishops. By his will he left to the Library over which he had presided his manuscripts, since bound in fifty-four volumes, and his very extensive collection of printed books, with the proviso that his own old College of Queen's should have whatever of his books were found to duplicate copies already in the Bodleian. It took two years to complete the transfer of his library, not from Lincoln (it is not certain that Barlow ever even visited his own episcopal city) nor yet from the palace at Buckden near Huntingdon where he actually resided, but from nearby Queen's College, where his library had evidently been kept since his resignation as Provost there. The substantial residue which went to the College greatly enriched its holdings, and led to the building of its own noble new library between 1691 and 1695.

Barlow's manuscripts (of which there were seventy-eight listed in Bernard's *Catalogue* of 1697 – the list presumably having been made while they were still at Queen's, for only fifty-five actually came to the Bodleian) are fairly miscellaneous, ranging from an early fifteenth-century *Canterbury Tales* to Henry Savage's autograph, dated 1661, of *Ballio-fergus*, his history of Balliol College; from a finely illuminated English Psalter of the early fourteenth century to some of the of the Old World. The map consists of seven climate zones each divided into ten sections, making seventy parts in all. The names of 2,064 towns which were then flourishing are shown; many of these are only villages today but most of them are still identifiable. Mountain chains are drawn as snake-like diagrams and rivers and lakes are shown. A small circular zonal map of the world with curved parallels, together with text in Arabic script describing the features of places and details of routes and distances between various points, complete the work, which is called *Kitab Rujar* – the *Book of Roger*. Compared with Western mediaeval monastic maps this Arabic map shows considerable advances in design and geographical content, since it was compiled from new, contemporary material.

Of the seven surviving copies of this work, two are in the Bodleian. One text, less complete, brought from Egypt by Thomas Greaves, the Deputy Professor of Arabic, was bought with other oriental manuscripts from his library in 1678. Then in 1692 came this copy, written in Cairo in 1533, and acquired from Syria by the great orientalist Edward Pococke.

theological and antiquarian collections made by Archbishop Ussher and his secretaries. The printed books received by the Library represent a more coherent scholar's collection, reflecting Barlow's 'prodigious reading' in the religious and intellectual controversies of the time. They are particularly rich in English books: most notably the first book printed in Oxford (Plate 112), but more extensively the large collection of material from the time of the Civil War and Interregnum, when a tide of publishing activity swept across the country on an unprecedented scale, producing a mass of literature which was considered by contemporaries too ephemeral to be acquired by a great academic library, but which by the end of the century was already being seen as the historical witness of that great upheaval in English life and society. Political, theological, philosophical, these tracts for the times were often cautiously anonymous, and it is thanks to Barlow's unrivalled familiarity with them that so many of their authors have been identified on his testimony; even when in doubt he annotated the titlepage of a work by a former pupil and Vice-Chancellor thus: 'I suppose (I am not sure) Dr John Owen is the Author of this Discourse'.

The size of the collection, which was identified by the shelfmark *Linc.* from Barlow's episcopal title, necessitated the provision of additional shelving, and in 1693 wooden galleries were built above the book-presses along the sides of Duke Humfrey's Library. They rested on timbers driven into the walls, and their fronts were suspended from the roof by metal straps. Barlow's books in quarto and smaller formats were placed in the south gallery in 1696, having been sorted and arranged by the Janitor, Emmanuel Pritchard; the folios, of which there were not many, were intercalated into the existing holdings. (The Library's smaller format law books were removed to the north gallery.) At present there are some ten thousand titles in the *Linc.* collection, but a significant proportion never belonged to Bishop Barlow. The south gallery was evidently known by the *Linc.* affix, and when Barlow's books were found not to fill all the shelving the Library's officers could not resist the lure of empty space and other accessions were housed there throughout the eighteenth century and into the nineteenth. This gallery, with its great weight of books bearing directly onto the south wall of Duke Humfrey, rapidly accelerated its tendency to lean from the true, and by 1700 its top was found to be seven-and-a-half inches from the perpendicular, and the vault of the Divinity School to be badly cracked. No small sense of urgency prompted the Vice-Chancellor to send the Savilian Professor of Astronomy, David Gregory, post haste to London to consult an earlier incumbent of that chair, Sir Christopher Wren (Plate 118). He immediately advised, but his suggestions were deemed unacceptable by the University mason, Thomas Robinson, who proposed alternative remedies. Wren in turn, not surprisingly, refused to alter his counsel which, after a form of arbitration which occupied many months, was accepted: additional buttresses were built to support the south wall, the standing book presses in Duke Humfrey were trussed up to both walls, the cracks in the Divinity School vault were filled with lead, oyster-shells and wooden wedges. Some one hundred and seventy-five years later the wall was again bulging into Exeter College garden, and the floor of Duke Humfrey was found to be resting on the Divinity School vault; among other measures taken to relieve the problem was the removal, at last, of the two galleries in 1877, when Barlow's books were taken to one of the Library's lower rooms.

The erection of the galleries and the accession of Barlow's bequest resulted in major book moves in the Library, which Hyde conducted with astonishing disregard for the usability of the collections by failing to annotate the catalogue or shelflists with the altered locations. But Hyde, who had been Librarian for some thirty years, was not happy in his post, and for many years had held the reins rather loosely, even apparently condoning the lending of books. His dissatisfactions began with the vast expenditure of effort over his *Catalogue*. Soon after its publication Sir Joseph Williamson, Secretary of State, for whom Hyde provided translations of diplomatic documents received from the Levant, urged him to proceed with a sorely needed new catalogue of manuscripts; Hyde's reaction was determined: 'it would be a work of some years if I should attempt to do ye whole thing myself; & also an hard task for me who have been so lately tired with nine years hard labour in making & publishing ye Catalogue of Printed Bookes, whereby my health is impaired'. He would be prepared to 'oversee & manage' others' work, and would himself catalogue 'ye Eastern Bookes' but he had 'no reason to be very forward in pulling business upon myself . . . having been so slenderly rewarded for nine years labour already, & am only fed here with empty & fruitless promises of making my small place better'. Another cause of keenly felt distress, expressed in his letter of resignation in 1701, was his not being allowed to spend on books what little money the Library had: he had regularly put forward to his Curators lists of books he considered should be bought, only to be 'chid and reproved by the Vice-Chancellor for offering to put them to so much charge in buying books. These things at last discouraged me from medling in it'.

Although Hyde found the daily drudgery of maintaining the Library increasingly irksome, his interest in things oriental grew ever stronger. It was under his direction that the first sinological work was done on the Bodleian's Chinese collections. Sir Thomas Bodley had acquired a book in this language as early as 1604 (Plate 34) and by the end of the century over one hundred volumes in Chinese were in the Library, many of them examples of the popular literature of China

117. **A presentation inscription by Samuel Pepys**
Although the great diarist was a Cambridge man, graduating from Magdalene College, where his splendid library is still preserved entire, he enjoyed many contacts with Oxford, especially after his retirement from public life in 1689, which gave him more leisure to pursue his tastes as connoisseur, book-collector and friend of learning. He had paid a visit to Oxford in 1668; the city he then saw was just as Loggan was to record it seven years later, and in his *Diary* Pepys described it as 'a very sweet place' and again as a 'mighty fine place and well set and cheap entertainment'. Later in his life he numbered among his friends and correspondents several distinguished senior members of the University, including the great mathematician Dr John Wallis, whose portrait Pepys at his own expense commissioned Kneller to paint, so that he might present it to be hung in the Bodleian Picture Gallery. Another close friend was Dr Arthur Charlett, Master of University College from 1692, who was a fellow book-collector for whom Pepys designed the well-known bookplate used in Charlett's own collection of books. It was half a century after the diarist's death that the Bodleian became a leading repository of Pepysian materials. This was principally thanks to a characteristic rescue operation by the great collector Richard Rawlinson, who enriched the Library with the official correspondence of Pepys as Secretary of the Admiralty. Rawlinson had saved it from ignominious destruction at the hands of perfume-sellers. With the twenty-five volumes of these papers he also bequeathed a shorthand diary describing Pepys's mission to Tangier and various ancient naval records which Pepys had collected with the aim of compiling a work on naval history which he never actually wrote. Around the same period other

Dec. 28. 93.
From ye Author
for the Publick Library in
Oxford:

Pepys material came to the Bodleian among the manuscripts bequeathed by Thomas Carte and by George Ballard.

The only book published by Pepys in his lifetime was his *Memoires relating to the State of the Royal Navy of England*, 1690, a workmanlike account of the reformation and restoration of the British navy, to which this capable and devoted civil servant had given most of his working life. Pepys presented a copy of these *Memoires* to the Bodleian, modestly bound in mottled calf with gilt tooling, having an autograph presentation inscription prefixed and also a copy of his own nautical bookplate pasted onto the final leaf – a quiet assertion of his authorship of this anonymous book.

(Plate 111). In 1687 Hyde worked with a Chinese scholar on the accumulated riches. Shen Fu-tsung, who had arrived in Europe some years earlier with a returning French missionary, was the first person in Oxford able to understand these volumes, and from him Hyde learnt much. The presence of a Chinese was evidently a rarity, for when James II was entertained by a banquet in Selden End that year he quizzed the Librarian about him, 'a little blinking fellow', and about Chinese philosophy and religion.

Hyde's distinction as an orientalist was acknowledged in 1691 when he succeeded Edward Pococke as Laudian Professor of Arabic, and in the following year the University bought thirty-nine manuscripts, mostly Persian and Arabic, but containing a couple of Chinese vocabularies, from Hyde's private collection. The practice of the University buying collections from its own funds for the Library, which began with the Hatton manuscripts, reached previously undreamt heights in 1692 and 1693 with the purchase of two notable oriental collections, Pococke and Huntington, the accession of which must surely have greatly appeased the disgruntled Librarian.

Edward Pococke, Oxford born and, like Fell and Wood, educated at Thame School before becoming an Oxford undergraduate, first showed his scholarly acuity by his discovery in the Bodleian of four missing epistles of the Syrian New Testament which he edited and, with Vossius's encouragement, published in Leiden in 1630. Already he had been appointed Chaplain to the Levant Company at Aleppo, where he became fluent in Arabic and studied Hebrew, Samaritan, Syriac and Ethiopic. His friendly relations with scholarly Jews and Muslims enabled him to collect with a confidence and assurance uncommon in this field at that time. Laud commissioned Pococke to acquire oriental manuscripts and offered to appoint him first holder of the Professorship in Arabic which bore the Archbishop's name, when he came back to Oxford in 1636. The following year, at Laud's insistence, he returned to the Near East with his friend John Greaves (whose brother Thomas deputed for Pococke in the latter's absence), making Aleppo his base for three years, and continuing to collect and study with eminent native scholars, notably Jacob Romano. In 1648 he was elected Regius Professor of Hebrew, and on an appeal, supported by Selden, to the Parliamentary Visitors, he managed to keep both his professorships during the Interregnum.

On the publication in 1650 of *Specimen historiae Arabum*, a landmark in cultural studies, Pococke's reputation as the foremost Arabic scholar in Western Europe was established; the book was also remarkable in the history of printing, containing some of the earliest examples of Hebrew and Arabic printing from the University Press. When Pococke died in 1691 the University bought from his widow for £800 four hundred and twenty manuscripts, nearly three hundred of which were Arabic (Plates 115, 116), the rest Hebrew and Armenian.

Robert Huntington was of the next generation, and was encouraged in the study of oriental languages at Oxford by Pococke. In 1670 he followed the pattern set by the latter when elected Chaplain to the Levant Company at Aleppo. There he remained for ten years, travelling extensively and collecting assiduously. He corresponded with other orientalists such as Pococke, Hyde, Edward Bernard, Fell and Narcissus Marsh. These two last commissioned him to buy for them, and during a visit to Egypt he displayed to the full 'that industry which he made use of in tracing the dark steps of manuscripts', searching out rare Coptic books on behalf of another correspondent, Thomas Marshall; many of these 'proxy' purchases came to the Library via such collectors. Like Pococke, Huntington was a keen botanist, sending seeds and dried plants from the Near Eastern countries to the University's 'Physick-garden'. He returned to his Fellowship at Merton College in 1681, but was disappointed in not gaining a University position; instead he became Provost of Trinity College, Dublin, on the recommendation of Fell and Marsh. He left Ireland after nine years, returning thither to be consecrated Bishop of Raphoe in July 1701, but died only a few weeks later. On three occasions Huntington presented a total of thirty-five oriental manuscripts to the Library; in 1693 the University bought over six hundred more for the princely sum of £1,118 18s 8d (paid in two instalments), easily the largest sum expended in this manner to date (though it was only just over a third of the £3,000 which the University had apparently considered spending on the library of Isaac Vossius some three years earlier).

Such major accessions only made more pressing the need for the printed catalogue of manuscripts which Williamson had urged Hyde to set about in 1675. Despite Hyde's reluctance to accede, preparations for such a catalogue were clearly being made soon after this date. It was finally published in 1698 as the *Catalogi librorum manuscriptorum Angliae et Hiberniae*, the titlepage being inexplicably dated 1697. The broad lines of its genesis and development can be traced in the Contents list prefixed. This shows how it began as a project to print a listing of all the manuscripts in the Bodleian – something of which the need had long been felt. Such a listing was in fact already to be found in a surviving manuscript transcribed in the hand of the Janitor, Pritchard, and dated 1686. This embraced all the various manuscript collections and acquisitions which had come into the Library since its re-foundation. It was this catalogue, much of it abbreviated from the detailed descriptions made over a long period by Gerard Langbaine, which in 1692 one of the most highly respected of Oxford scholars, Dr Edward Bernard, the successor to Christopher Wren as Savilian Professor of Astronomy, recommended to the Curators should be

118. **The monogram of Sir Christopher Wren**
Wren held the Savilian Professorship of Astronomy from 1661 till his resignation from it in 1673. It was probably then, on giving up his academic post to devote himself entirely to architecture, that he presented to the library of the Savilian Professors a number of printed books. The donor's initials tooled on their spines distinguish books given by Wren from presentation copies received from other professors, notably John Wallis, the Professor of Geometry.

printed. But some revision was evidently required and eventually it was Bernard himself, who was in poor health but anxious to see the catalogue in print before he died, who accepted the invitation to be its editor. As an astronomer and critic with a European reputation his name added weight to the undertaking, though his death in 1696 prevented him seeing the publication of what has come to be generally known as Bernard's *Catalogue*.

Meanwhile a group of younger scholars, who shared his ambitions for it, had become involved in the revision of Pritchard's catalogue and in preparing for print lists of the accessions which had arrived in the Bodleian since 1686. Among these young men were three who afterwards made great names for themselves in the world of learning, and who all became bishops. The eldest, who was still only thirty-two at this time, was White Kennett, who rewrote the inadequate earlier description of the Dodsworth manuscripts. The next was Edmund Gibson, who at the age of twenty-three undertook the cataloguing of the Dugdale and Aubrey collections. Already, be it noted, the project had begun to expand, for those were not at that time part of the Bodleian's collections, being housed in the Ashmolean Museum. The youngest of the three, and Gibson's close friend, was Thomas Tanner, then aged only eighteen. He was a protégé of the Master of University College, Dr Arthur Charlett, whose powerful backing gave continual impetus to the whole enterprise. Tanner, who was responsible for the Junius and several other collections, eventually left among his enduring monuments his *Bibliotheca Britannica*, a vast encyclopedia on British writers (which could not have been compiled without the prior existence of Bernard's *Catalogue*), and the library with which he enriched the Bodleian after his death in 1725.

The work of these and other young men such as Edward Lhuyd, the new Keeper of the Ashmolean, made it possible to include those other collections which were housed there, notably Anthony Wood's, and also the manuscripts in the library of the Savilian Professors which, though kept in the Tower of the Five Orders (Plate 49), did not become part of the Bodleian till 1884. The influence of Langbaine, who had also toiled over the catalogues of most of the college libraries, and the fact that the eager young scholars were, of course, college men, explains how easily the second part of volume one of Bernard's *Catalogue* came to comprise the listings of the Oxford college manuscripts. An obvious sequel was to include Cambridge libraries. Only four lists from the latter were actually sent in, so for the rest the entries published by Thomas James in his *Ecloga* in 1600, just before he took office as Bodley's first Librarian, were used instead. Following repeated requests printed in the London *Mercuries* for further contributory lists for inclusion, a second volume was added which covered certain cathedral and other institutional libraries, and many which belonged to private collectors, such as Pepys, Evelyn, Sir Hans Sloane and Bishop John Moore; a final section in the second volume described several collections in Ireland, among them that of Archbishop Marsh, whose oriental manuscripts were subsequently bequeathed to the Bodleian. Inevitably in a large co-operative project the standards were not uniform throughout. Yet the benefit to this day of being able to consult in one published work a 'state of the holdings' of so large a proportion (the *Catalogue* estimates it, at thirty thousand, as about half the possible number) of the manuscripts possessed in Britain almost three centuries ago, is beyond calculation. The *Catalogue* fully justifies the hopes expressed by its editors that it might bring glory to Oxford and advantage to many users elsewhere.

In fact, ever since its publication, it has served to put countless students on the track of manuscripts of their chosen authors, and it lies behind many of the great advances made in English historical and legal studies during the following centuries. But this function as a guide to sources could not have come about without its author index. At the end of the seventeenth century very few printed catalogues either of institutional or private libraries, aside from those based on an alphabetical arrangement (where none was needed), had been provided with such an index, though Thomas James had made one for his 1605 Bodleian *Catalogue*, which listed the books in their shelf order. Edmund Gibson, besides prefixing to the 1697 *Catalogue* a life of Sir Thomas Bodley and a history of the Library, also wrote the anonymous introductory epistle (originally addressed to Dr Charlett). In it he reveals much about how it came into being, and describes the maker of the author index as Humfrey Wanley, 'a young man not only studious himself but also ready at all times to forward the efforts of other students'.

Studious the young man certainly was; a draper's apprentice in his native city of Coventry, he made time to teach himself Old English by copying out Somner's *Dictionary*. He was taken up by the learned Bishop of Worcester and routed to Oxford. There, as later in life, he was fortunate in his friends; it was probably thanks to Dr Charlett, who gave him lodgings in the Master's House at University College, that he was appointed an extra assistant at the Bodleian a year after his matriculation. His studiousness did not, however, extend to the normal academic curriculum, and as a result he never graduated. Instead, he was continually searching beyond Oxford for further materials for his Anglo-Saxon studies. A letter written in 1695 by Samuel Pepys in the name of himself and his friend Charlett asks Dr Thomas Smith, the Keeper of the Cottonian Manuscripts (then still privately owned) to allow this promising young Bodleian assistant to see the famous collection. Smith in turn became Wanley's mentor, but in 1697 he advised him to carry out his research 'in the Publick Library

119. **Two Oxford fly-sheets from Anthony Wood's library**

In one special regard Wood was a collector whom historians, notably the modern breed of social historians, have cause to bless. Continuously resident in Oxford throughout his adult life, Wood practised the all-too-uncommon habit of preserving the daily ephemera of town and gown life, and of annotating many of the pieces he preserved with dates and circumstantial details, written in his eminently neat and readable handwriting, notes which pin these butterfly specimens precisely to their place on the web of history. These two plates are taken from nearly adjacent items in one volume of broadsides from the library which was bequeathed by Wood in 1695 to the recently-founded Ashmolean Museum, and transferred to the Bodleian in 1860.

Obviously, immediately it came to hand, Wood wrote his note at the foot of the manifesto issued by the two enterprising stage-coach proprietors. He explains how and why the Vice-Chancellor, riding his high horse of University privilege ignored, had forbidden those under his jurisdiction to use the proposed new facility, which would have halved the two days then currently taken for the journey. About a fortnight later, it would seem, Wood became possessed of this copy of an actual printed leaf reiterating the Vice-Chancellor's immediate prohibition against the proposed 'Flying Coach'. But for Wood's omnivorous curiosity this small incident of University life might have escaped even passing mention; here it has been, in a literal sense, documented for us.

where you are fixed . . . without seeking for materials abroad'. Wanley, however, was never discouraged by the good advice of older friends from his self-appointed task of examining and describing Anglo-Saxon writings of every kind, wherever he could find them. Under the inspiring influence of another friend, Dr George Hickes, Wanley's growing mastery of Anglo-Saxon learning and Old English palaeography was to lead some years later to his most important publication, a catalogue of Anglo-Saxon manuscripts, which he contributed to Hicke's *Thesaurus* of ancient northern languages. Hickes, with the materials for that magisterial compilation taking shape under his hands, complained to Charlett in 1700 of his discouragement at hearing that the Bodleian Curators 'have denyed Mr Wanley leave to take the Catalogue of the Saxon Manuscripts in the Cotton Library'. In the event the tug-of-war between Wanley's private researches and his Library duties became too much for him, and after 1700 he was no longer employed by the Bodleian.

Yet the five years he spent in its service were not without value both to him and to the Library. Experience of working in the greatest library in England stood him in good stead when he became librarian to the first and second Earls of Oxford and took so large a part in the formation of their splendid Harleian library. Hickes, whose judgment no lesser scholar was in a position to query, recommended him to Robert Harley in 1701 as already having 'the best skill in ancient hands and manuscripts of any man not only of this, but, I believe, of any former age'. The Library, for its part, had been able to employ in quite varied and extensive ways the exceptional talents of its young assistant. Besides his author index to Bernard's *Catalogue*, to which he prefixed an unsigned foreword (unwittingly echoing that of Hyde in his 1674 *Catalogue* of printed books, in explaining the difficulty of identifying authors when multiple attributions, or none, confronted him), he also contributed at least four of the constituent catalogues included therein. Even before his employment at the Bodleian these catalogues had earned Charlett's warmest praises. Again, Wanley's acumen and percipience had been shown when the Library commissioned him to report on Bernard's printed books. He knew, perhaps from direct contact with Bernard himself, the strength of the collection in a field which had received hitherto little attention in the Bodleian. His choice had been highly thought of, but Hyde made a list of other desiderata, and Wanley's comments on these revealed his very low opinion of the Librarian's abilities and of his knowledge of the contents of the Library of which he had charge. Similar views hostile to Hyde were expressed in two memoranda drawn up by Wanley in 1697 in response to an invitation to members of the staff by the Curators to submit suggestions 'for the better regulating any present disorders'. Wanley toned down and shortened his first draft, but the recommen-

OXFORD
One day Stage-Coach.

THeſe are to give Notice to all Perſons that have occaſion to go to *Oxford* by Coach; Let them repair to the *Greyhound* in *Holborn*, where they may be furniſhed with a good Coach and able Horſes, which ſets forth every Monday, Wedneſday, and Friday for *Oxford*, performing the Stage in one day; and ſets forth from the *Mitre* in *Oxford* for *London*, every Tueſday, Thurſday, and Saturday; performed if God permit, By

Widow STONEHILL.
JOHN FOSSET.

The Stage begins Munday next, being the 17th inſtant *April*, and ſets forth preciſely at Six in the Morning.

This coach was silenced by ye vicechanc: order stuck up on evry corner in Oxon Apr: 15. 1671. because it was set up without his leave.

By Order from
Mr Vice-Chancellour.

THeſe are to give notice that whereas *Thomas Dye* and *John Foſſet* hath without Licence from Mee, and in contempt of the *Chancellor*, *Maſters* and *Scholars* of this *Univerſity* (to whom the Ordering and Governing of all Carriers of what kind ſoever Tradeing to or with the *Univerſity* and *City* of *Oxford* doth of Right belong) preſumed to ſet up a Flying Coach to travaile from hence to *London*: Theſe are to require all Scholars, Priviledged Perſons and Members of this *Univerſity*, not to Travaile in the ſaid Flying-Coach ſet up by *Thomas Dye* and *John Foſſet*, nor to ſend Letters or any Goods whatſoever by the Flying Coach aforeſaid.

PETER MEWS

Vice-Chancel:

Oxford *April* 27. 1671.

dations he actually submitted show a remarkable mixture of shrewd analysis of what had in fact been going wrong in Hyde's administration, and how to remedy the situation, together with suggestions for future practices which, however desirable they might be, were quite impractical given the smallness of the Library's staff. Wanley's opinion of Hyde was not wholly disinterested. He saw there would be no change for the better while Hyde remained and for a time he hoped to succeed him. Hyde himself had grown so weary of his Library post, to which he had recently added the duties of Laudian Professor of Arabic and Regius Professor of Hebrew (which made him one of his own Curators), that he was ready to give up the Librarianship in Wanley's favour. But Wanley's lack of a degree precluded him from this office, and his ambitions appear to have looked elsewhere for their fulfilment.

The collection, on part of which Wanley had been instructed to report, had been left by Bernard at his death in 1696 to his wife, with the wish that the Bodleian would buy it, as in fact was largely done. A selection of his printed books was bought in 1697 from his widow for £140, and in the following year most of the manuscripts which had been listed under Bernard's own name in the 1697 Catalogue, including printed books with manuscript collations, were bought for a further £200. These purchases brought into the Bodleian not only

120. *A Choice Collection of Catches* from Anthony Wood's library
Although primarily engaged in his laborious studies of the history of both the City and the University of Oxford, some of Anthony Wood's time was spent in less exacting pursuits; afternoons were often passed in visiting bookshops, and evenings in common-rooms, taverns or coffee-houses, enjoying conversation, cards or music. By the beginning of 1656 Wood writes that he 'had genuine skill in musick, and frequented the weekly meetings of musitians in the house of William Ellis', where the singing, by unaccompanied voices, of rounds and catches would have occurred much as depicted in the vignettes on this engraved titlepage to a *Choice Collection* of 1652 from Wood's library. The music was often set round the page to enable one of the parts to be read from the other side of the table, the part sung by the standing figures in the pictures. This particular volume is one of the earliest publications of John Playford, who was the father of English music-publishing. Compositions by a score of musicians, among them William and Henry Lawes, Thomas Holmes and Edmund Nelham were included by the editor, John Hilton. He himself, though chiefly remembered as a church musician, was responsible for no fewer than twelve of the canons and thirty of all the other pieces. This is the first edition of the collection, which proved to be very popular, being reprinted many times in various forms. A macabre note is struck in Wood's manuscript account of Hilton's obsequies: 'He died in the time of Oliver, & was buried in the Great Cloyster of Westminster, at wch time the singing at burials being silenced, as popish, the Fraternity of musitians who intended to sing him to his grave sang the Anthem in the House over the corps before it went to the church, & kept time on his coffin.'

books representing Bernard's oriental studies, in such customary fields as Hebrew, Arabic, Coptic and Persian, but even examples of languages as remote at that time as Siamese and Sinhalese. But of greater value still was the contribution made by Bernard's library in the field of classical scholarship.

In 1682 Bernard had travelled to Leiden to attend the auction of the library of Nicholas Heinsius. Nicholas, who had been a reader in the Bodleian forty years earlier, was a classical editor and book-collector of international repute and the son of the no less celebrated Daniel Heinsius, he who had exchanged gifts with the young Selden and had once been the pupil of Scaliger. It was from the Heinsius sale that Bernard had carried off the largest part of those prizes which give his collection its special flavour and importance. In addition to mediaeval codices of the authors of antiquity, such as two tenth-century manuscripts of Virgil, Bernard had also acquired more than fifty classical editions from the early years of printing. Not infrequently they afford texts derived from much older manuscripts and these are present in copies made even more valuable by annotations and collations added by great scholars who had formerly owned them.

The acquisition of much of the library of Edward Bernard and the publication of his 1697 *Catalogue* were the last important events before Hyde's long Librarianship of over thirty-four years came to its end a few months into the new century. By then it was just over one hundred years since Sir Thomas Bodley had made his historic offer and had set about equipping Oxford with a library worthy of the renown its ancient University had once enjoyed. During that first century his vision had in large measure been realized. Starting without any preceding nucleus inherited from the past except the beautiful shell of the mediaeval library building, three generations of men, pre-eminently those who themselves were or had been members of the University (though helped also by countless other benefactors inspired by the launch of what Francis Bacon had termed Bodley's new 'ark to save learning') had between them added a major new library to the academic map of Europe. A feature of its collections which was otherwise still rare in the libraries of Western Europe at that time was the extent, in both breadth and depth, of its oriental holdings. As its stock had continued to expand by gift and purchase, its two extensive printed *Catalogues* would now be available to make its accumulated riches known to an ever-widening public of learned men. The Library had survived both political and domestic upheavals and was gradually becoming an institution of such recognized importance that in future it could not be ignored or allowed to run down, and by its existence it continued to invite new benefactors to place their treasures in its care.

Index

Plate numbers are in brackets